Clare Boothe Luce

A BIOGRAPHY

by Stephen Shadegg

LESLIE FREWIN of LONDON

© *Stephen Shadegg, 1970 and 1973*

First published in Great Britain in 1973

by Leslie Frewin Publishers Limited
Five Goodwin's Court
Saint Martin's Lane
London WC2N 4LL, England

This book is printed Photolitho by
Biddles Ltd., Guildford, Surrey
and bound by R. J. Acford Limited
Industrial Estate, Chichester, Sussex, England

ISBN 0 85632 017 X

Contents

[Illustrations follow page 126]

Introduction

To attempt to tell the life story of a living person is a hazardous under-taking. When the subject is a notable personage—the possessor of such special talents as to have achieved recognition in a variety of fields—the task becomes even more complicated. Clare Boothe Brokaw Luce is a much better than average writer. She is also an experienced editor, a competent, sometimes caustic critic. It would be hopelessly naïve to ex-pect Mrs. Luce to agree with or approve the portrait of her life and times presented in this book.

It is possible to construct a biography in the form of an historical document, overburdened with footnotes, loaded with attributable quotes, and bound with the tight twine of careful chronology. This is not that kind of an effort.

The vignettes and profiles which have been written about Mrs. Luce suffer greatly from their concentration on one single aspect of her re-markable life and careers. The abundance of available material would support at least four lively books—Mrs. Luce in Letters, Congress-woman Luce, Ambassador Luce, and Mrs. Henry R. Luce, Empress to the Emperor of *Time-Life*. It seems safe to predict all of those books will be written when Clare Boothe Luce is no longer living.

In these pages the reader will find a simple reflection of Mrs. Luce as she sees herself and as others see her. The inevitable contradictions evidence the controversy which has surrounded her life and her work.

The writer makes no pretense that this is a critical biography in the commonly accepted meaning, nor is it intended to be a worshipful account of Mrs. Luce and her accomplishments. Admittedly, it is impossible to know her and to know of her achievements and not admire her. She commands respect and provokes strong emotional reactions.

Mrs. Luce's enemies and critics have called her an ambitious phony, a conniving beauty, a designing, determined climber without compassion or consideration for others. Her friends see her as a lonely, brilliant figure—warm, loyal, trusting—one who has marched through life the perpetual target of her less talented, envious competitors.

The beauty of Mrs. Luce's youth was more than a fairness of face and figure, although many of her contemporaries in the early twenties were content with the external evidence. Had she been a plain Jane with thick glasses, the beauty of her mind might have been more universally appreciated. But the packaging was too perfect. Women resented the fair skin, the even features, the shimmering blond hair, and cold eyes lit with an inner fire. Men were dismayed when the "dumb blonde" challenged their intellect and plainly indicated she preferred conversation to caresses.

Mrs. Luce's intuitive reasoning has led to tormentingly correct conclusions, but her mental processes are extremely logical, reinforced with a vast fund of acquired information. She grew up with an understanding of the world's selfishness—until her conversion to the Roman Catholic Church she lived with the conviction that all men are unredeemably evil.

If Mrs. Luce in her lifetime had done nothing more than invent the various roles she has played, it would be a record to intrigue the observer. The standards of performance she set for herself required her to do more. She has had to live the parts—to deliver a convincing performance before audiences generally skeptical. It is quite understandable that under the circumstances Mrs. Luce has overdramatized both the tragedies and the triumphs of her life.

If the normalcy of middle-class American life is dull, plodding, uninspired and at times stifling, the upper and lower limits are characterized by abnormalities. Excess of power, wealth, position—or poverty, misery and ignorance—contribute to an exaggerated style of speech, action and thought which when viewed from the middle ground is mistakenly assumed to be something less than genuine.

As a member of the subculture of the very rich and powerful, editor-journalist Clare Brokaw exposed the pretentious frivolities of her own class, provoking most justly their wrath and indignation against her. As playwright Clare Boothe, she laid bare the feline proclivities of her sex, and the men who "knew it all along" were made to feel uneasy, the women betrayed.

Congresswoman Luce, representing largely a working-class constituency, opposed the working man's hero President Franklin D. Roosevelt and at the same time refused to be a mouthpiece for wealth and privilege.

The controversy which has surrounded Mrs. Luce most of her life is a reflection of the inner conflicts which have driven her to excel in so many fields.

Mrs. Luce has been most generous in making available to this writer her papers, published and unpublished, and her personal recollections of the events and personalities reported and described in this book, which was commenced long before the death of Henry Robinson Luce.

Henry Luce was one of the giants of our time. The stature of his wife and widow is no less impressive. They were a remarkable couple—each contributing to the more than thirty years of happy married life they enjoyed.

The Luces dealt with ideas, rendered judgments—sometimes harsh, infrequently erroneous. They were both generous contributors to those enduring understandings which have enriched our society and our national life. They were exciting, vital human beings toward whom the world and their contemporaries could never maintain an attitude of indifference.

Everyone who has been privileged to come into contact with Mrs. Luce—friend or foe—is quick to confess that she is one of the most challenging, brilliant, intriguing, vexing, inconsistent, charitable, complex women of this century—and that, hopefully, is what this book is all about.

1

Childhood

The Reverend J. W. T. Boothe, Doctor of Divinity, believed God's will should govern the lives of men. When the Baptist Church of Holyoke, Massachusetts, called him north some ten years after the end of the Civil War, he left the Maryland of his birth and moved with his wife Sarah and three small children to take up the Lord's work in a strange city among alien people.

Pastor Boothe was a fundamentalist. He regarded card playing, alcoholic beverages, dancing and most public entertainment contrary to the commands of his Master. Perhaps he preached the gospel of reconciliation to the congregations who came to worship, but when his oldest son, Will, at the age of forty, divorced his first wife and then married an eighteen-year-old chorus girl, he neither forgave his son nor reconciled himself to the new wife.

The Reverend Dr. Boothe combined an adamant Baptist morality with a soft Southern charm. His ministry lasted almost half a century. He was called to larger churches, first in Scarborough and later in Port Chester, New York. Sarah bore him six daughters and four sons. Preacher Boothe's family owned a small, well-established piano-manufacturing company in Philadelphia. The steady extra income from this business enabled Sarah and her husband to give their children a better-than-average education. Dr. Boothe would have been delighted had all or any of his sons felt a call to the ministry. None did. When young William Franklin showed a marked talent for the violin, his father sent him to the best instructors available.

In the spring of 1896 Will Boothe went to Philadelphia to work in the piano plant. Three months later he wrote to his father, who was then filling the pulpit in Scarborough, New York, to say that he was married, that the piano business didn't suit him, and that he planned to seek a career in music.

During the next four years the Boothes heard very little from their son. He and his wife never went home for a visit. His infrequent letters told of a succession of jobs in theater orchestras. In the spring of 1901 he wrote them to say he had been divorced for more than a year, that he was in love and would soon be married to a girl who was dancing and singing in the chorus in the theater where he was playing. Her name, he wrote, was Anna Clara Snyder.

Anna Clara was the youngest of three children born in America to German immigrants, William and Louisa Snyder. William had come to America to escape conscription in the German Army about 1862 and settled in Hoboken, New Jersey, where there was a large colony of fellow refugees. Industrious and ambitious, he gradually acquired enough capital to enter the livery-stable business. William married a neighbor-immigrant's daughter who bore him two sons and one daughter. Their first boy, Charles, died of tuberculosis; the second, Arthur, of spinal meningitis.

When his daughter was eighteen, she left home to work in New York, first as a salesgirl in a department store, later singing and dancing with the chorus in a New York theater. When Anna Snyder went on the stage, she Anglicized her name and henceforth was known as Ann Clare. Ann Snyder was strikingly beautiful, with long chestnut-colored hair. Her admirers described her eyes as violet. She had a fair singing voice and a good figure. No doubt she was ambitious for a career, but like most girls her age, when the choice came, she preferred love and marriage.

A violinist in the theater orchestra, William Franklin Boothe, stocky and well built, with even features and a fine thick turn-of-the-century mustache, promised both. Ann Snyder fell in love with him. When they eloped, it was a tragedy to both their families. William and Louisa Snyder, devout Roman Catholics, believed that despite the civil ceremony performed after the divorce, their daughter was living in sin.

In Port Chester, Dr. Boothe and his wife Sarah were equally dismayed. Will's behavior was contrary to the beliefs on which their lives had been built. To the Baptist Boothes, divorce was as unforgivable as it was to the Catholic Snyders. Worse perhaps, in their eyes, than divorce was that he had taken a papist chorus girl for his second wife. To them, the theater was a place where only the vulgar came to witness sinful goings on.

The bride and groom set up housekeeping in a family hotel in New York City. Their first baby, a boy, was born on March 10, 1902. They named him David Franklin.

At that time, New York's Riverside Drive, where Will, Ann and their baby had moved, was a good address. But there was very little class and no luxury at all in the flat where Ann Clare, their second child, was born on April 10, 1903. Will Boothe's income was uncertain; his job took him away from home almost every night. Soon after her marriage to Will Boothe, Ann had to learn to scrimp and save. At twenty-one her rainbow of romance had turned into a routine of cooking and washing and tending babies.

Clare's earliest years were spent in a Bohemian atmosphere. Ann and Will Boothe's friends were musicians, actors, writers—a convivial lot, gay and moody, hopefully confident one moment, deeply depressed the next. Life in such circles is never prosaic or dull.

Apparently the Boothes didn't live in any one place long enough to enter their children in public school. But Will Boothe taught his children to read at an early age. He encouraged them to explore literature and was always bringing books home, usually secondhand, found at a bargain table. Clare read books of history, biography, fiction more suitable to adults than to children. She remembers that her father started her on Gibbon's *Decline and Fall* before she was nine years old. On those evenings when Will Boothe wasn't working he read to his children until they fell asleep.

Will Boothe did not neglect his daughter Clare, but their relationship was not as warm as that between father and son. Both Ann and Will Boothe revolted against their parents' religions when their parents renounced their marriage for religious reasons. The Boothe children were brought up unchurched and grew to adulthood both believing their parents were atheists.

Clare had few childhood playmates other than her brother David. Forced to rely on her own resources and the pleasures she could find in books, Clare still speaks of these years with a sadness tinged with bitterness. When the weather was bad and she had to stay indoors, and she was tired of reading, she played cards or other games with David. When they wearied of the usual games, Clare invented new ones.

In the fall of 1911 Will Boothe took his family on the road. He had a new job as a concert violinist with a traveling symphony orchestra. The tour ended in Nashville, Tennessee, when the promoters went broke. There a local patron of the arts helped Clare's father get established in a soft-drink bottling business while he was trying to compose for the violin. The venture prospered sufficiently so that, for a year or so, Clare was able to attend the primary classes in the fashionable Ward Belmont School in Nashville.

Mrs. Boothe was apparently delighted with the new order in her life. For the first time they had a steady income, her husband was working days instead of nights, and the business prospered. But Will Boothe for the second time rejected a career in commerce to return to what he called "my fiddle." He sold the little bottling plant for a small sum and moved his family to Chicago, where he had been offered a place in the orchestra of the grand-opera company in that city. Years later, Mrs. Boothe told her children the soft drink bottled by their father was Coca-Cola, and that if he had stayed in Nashville, the family would certainly have become very rich. Clare has never been able to verify this. She remembers the names of the drinks bottled by her father as Celeryade and George Washington Coffee.

Clare, who was nine years old at the time, recalls the Chicago period as one of the happiest in her childhood. The family lived in a comfortable flat, her mother and father entertained on a modest scale, Will Boothe enjoyed a steady income as "first fiddle," and Clare went for a brief time to the Chicago Latin School, where she had a chance to make friends with children of her own age.

It ended abruptly when Will Boothe left his family to go off with another woman. Mrs. Boothe told David and Clare their father was dead. This, doubtless, seemed the best explanation to give to them. They were old enough to know their father had not been ill and to wonder why there was no funeral service. They couldn't understand why Ann Boothe exhibited more anger than grief.

Mrs. Boothe's bitterness toward her husband was expressed in many ways. (Her distaste for music was certainly one of them.) She never mentioned Will Boothe's name, nor did she let her children discuss him. She proudly refused to accept help from the Boothe family—or perhaps none was offered.

Mrs. Boothe took her children home to Hoboken. Grandfather Snyder did the best he could for his daughter. He made his grandchildren welcome, but the automobile was rapidly replacing the horse and his once prosperous livery business had fallen on bad days.

When Ann Snyder married Will Boothe, she had been young, beautiful and naïve. After ten years of marriage and two children, she retained her beauty, but she was considerably more sophisticated, and very disillusioned about men and life. She contacted some of Will's old friends, and through them made new connections in the world of theater and entertainment. Clare was especially aware of her mother's charms and remembers that her mother had many beaus. She didn't like any of them. When Mrs. Boothe went out to parties and dinners, it seemed to Clare her mother was being disloyal to her dead father's memory. During this period Mrs. Boothe worked at various small and low-paid jobs, including waitress in a luncheonette. In the summer, the children were usually sent to live with Mrs. Boothe's friends in the country, sometimes for a few weeks, sometimes for the whole summer. One summer Clare went to Wisconsin to stay with an old friend of her Grandmother Snyder who ran a summer boardinghouse. She doesn't remember the name of the town or the name of the family that took her in, but it was near a logging camp on the Turtle Lakes. The friendly timbermen taught Clare and brother David to shoot a rifle and to logroll in their bare feet.

Grandfather Snyder died in the fall of 1912. Mrs. Boothe moved with her children and a widow friend to a dingy flat on Columbus Avenue in New York City. It was at this time that Mrs. Boothe took it into her head that her pretty, little curly-haired blond daughter should become a child actress. She managed an interview with David Belasco, who hired Clare as an understudy to Mary Pickford in the play he was about to produce, *The Good Little Devil*. Little Miss Pickford never missed a performance. On the other hand, little Miss Boothe never missed a pay check.

When the Belasco production closed, Mrs. Boothe got Clare a part as understudy to the child star in the Ernest Truex comedy *The Dummy*. Clare did a half-dozen performances when the child star was ill or absent. She had very few lines since the part called for her to spend most of her time on stage tied to a chair with a gag over her mouth. "Just as well," Clare commented years later, "I was a born nonactress."

When *The Dummy* finished its run, Mrs. Boothe took her budding little actress to the old Biograph Studios for a screen test. Again the results were something less than startling, but Marie Doro, an early Biograph star, did encourage the director to give the curly-headed child a walk-on part in the film *Over the Hill to the Poorhouse*.

In the fall of 1913 Mrs. Boothe announced she was sending David to a military school in Wisconsin and taking Clare to Paris for a year abroad. Will Boothe, who by then had opened a music school in Los Angeles, was sending his divorced wife a small but regular allowance; one of Mrs. Boothe's friends, a Wall Street broker, guided her to "a good thing in the market," all of which helped a little. Also Ann Boothe came into a small sum of money when Grandfather Snyder died, and she used this capital to gamble in the market—a gamble that seems to have paid off.

In any event, Mrs. Boothe had been told one could live comfortably abroad for half of what it cost in the United States.

Clare and her mother spent two months in London and then moved on to Paris and found lodgings in a small pension on the Rue Balzac. Clare studied the language. When she wasn't with her tutor she played in the Tuileries garden or went sightseeing in Paris. Mrs. Boothe didn't know much about art, but she knew that a knowledge of it was part of a good education, and she traipsed her small daughter through every museum and cathedral in Paris.

When war threatened in 1914, along with hundreds of frightened tourists, Mrs. Boothe and Clare came home on a packed, blacked-out liner across an ocean where U-boats were already prowling.

The next twelve months were miserable. They moved into one

room in a family hotel. The money Mrs. Boothe had saved for the year in Paris was soon gone. She got a job as a saleswoman in Tecla's selling imitation pearls. David's tuition at the military school had been paid for in advance but something now had to be done to give Clare an education.

Mrs. Boothe's energy, determination, and possibly her talent for finding helpful and generous friends brought results. By the fall of 1915 she had a new job as a saleswoman for costume jewelry and was able to keep David in military school for another year and to enroll Clare at the Cathedral School of St. Mary in Garden City, Long Island.

It may seem strange that a woman of Mrs. Boothe's background and circumstances would be so adamantly opposed to the free public schools, but she was ambitious for her children. Perhaps she believed the boarding schools offered the best alternative; possibly her ex-husband's superior background gave her a false sense of pride. The school selected was an Episcopal parochial preparatory institution. It had a good reputation for scholarship and an admissions policy which favored the daughters of clergymen.

When Clare entered St. Mary's she was twelve years old and twenty pounds overweight. Her eyes were an unusual shade of cerulean blue. Her face was full and her chin was firm. She had never, up to that time, lived away from her mother in the winter. She was scared and homesick. In some ways she was far more mature than most twelve-year-olds, but the hand-to-mouth existence of her earlier years made her feel defensive and insecure among her classmates.

Miss Miriam A. Bytel, the headmistress, was a stern, humorless scholar. She knew of Clare's lack of any continuous formal instruction, yet after giving her a written test, she placed her new student in the eighth grade. This tells a great deal about the ability Clare had to absorb learning from her lonely book reading, and her year in France.

The school records show that Clare was admitted on a scholarship basis, which was granted to children of church-connected parents. When the other girls asked her where her father had preached, Clare jumped to the conclusion that her mother had told a whopper about her father's profession to avoid paying full tuition fees. Actually, she was accepted as the granddaughter of the highly respected Dr. John William Boothe. Her mother, as usual, didn't bother to explain the true situation, probably because she didn't want Clare to feel beholden in any way to her father's family.

Clare was assigned to quarters on the top floor which the students called Paradise Alley because once, when the school was first beginning, it was the area that housed the original chapel.

About her quarters Clare says, "My bed stood where the old altar had been. There were two very crummy-looking stucco praying angels on the wall. I thought they were rather pretty and I used to say my prayers trying to look and feel as pious as those angels. One night a girl from the room next door popped in and caught me imitating the angels' pose. She burst into laughter and called me 'Angel Face.' I was stuck with the nickname for years."

Clare was thankful the girls had to wear uniforms. She knew that however low the tuition, it put a strain on her mother's financial ability. She had seen the dresses and coats and hats and shoes in the other girls' closets. Her own wardrobe was too skimpy to stand any comparison. The uniforms made comparison unnecessary.

Most of her classmates came from above-average-income homes where luxuries Clare had never experienced were regarded as necessities. She determined that no one should know the truth of her own home situation and pity her.

The curriculum was traditional. English, history and literature were the important subjects, with penmanship, spelling and arithmetic far down the scale. Clare could speak and write French. She was familiar with books most of the upper-class girls had never heard of. Without ever having been taught the basic rules of grammar, she excelled in English composition. Her knowledge of history and literature had not been confined to textbook examples. She did not do well at spelling. Her spelling was frequently phonetic. Clare practiced hard on penmanship, forming her letters very carefully, though sometimes the words crowded together, revealing haste and impatience.

Clare, with the other girls, got into trouble with her schoolmistresses. She was severely punished for one prank—snapping butter balls from her napkin to stick on the dining-room ceiling. The object was to have the melting butter drip on the head of a teacher. When it did,

Clare went without butter for a month. Clare did not like the noncompetitive physical setting-up exercises on the playground. At that time she was still a fat little girl. But she played backstop on the school hockey team with such determination that some of the girls were offended by her roughness.

When the other students talked of weekends at home and holiday adventures, Clare became silent. She knew her lack of formal education was a handicap, so on weekends she dug into books, saying she couldn't bother to become involved in the frivolous parties boarding-school girls go in for on weekends. She even avoided the afternoon bull sessions the other girls enjoyed. She stayed in her room, reading. Or, if the weather was fair, she climbed her "secret tree" in the school's old apple orchard and read there. As a result of her aloofness, most of her classmates thought her stuck-up. In the annual of that year she was described as "the most conceited girl in the class."

Clare missed her mother, but she missed David even more. She chafed under the rules and regulations, and she yearned for her early years, spent with exciting adults. The children at St. Mary's seemed awfully young. She also worried about her mother, who was now frequently ill and living alone in a single room in the old Belmont Hotel on Columbus Avenue, with no one to take care of her except a big, red-faced Irish woman who lived in the room next door. Mrs. Boothe seemed to be obsessed with the fear of dying of tuberculosis, as her older brother had died in his twenties. The slightest cold would drive her to bed.

It was taken for granted that all the girls at St. Mary's, and particularly the scholarship students, would follow the course of instruction required for confirmation in the Episcopal Church. Daily morning prayer was read in chapel. At the end of that first year Clare was confirmed by the Bishop of Long Island in the Episcopal cathedral at Garden City. Academically she was at the head of her class—one of two in the entire student body to make the honor roll.

Her teachers applauded her appearance of poise and self-confidence, although Clare was beset with emotions of shyness in the presence of strangers. In addition to her concern for her mother's health and financial situation, there was another reason for her sense of insecurity

—her weight. She cried when one of her classmates called her "Angel Face Tubby." She also suffered from that sense of awkwardness which so often accompanies the approach of puberty.

Clare did make two friends at St. Mary's—Elizabeth "Buffy" Cobb and a somewhat older girl Helen Atwater, who was later to become Mrs. Philip K. Wrigley. But Buffy was the friend she really adored. Buffy was the daughter of the famous humorist Irvin S. Cobb; she was also an eighth grader at St. Mary's. Like Clare, Buffy was a pudgy little girl, but here the resemblance ended. The raven-haired daughter of Irvin Cobb had everything: a wonderful home and family, a father eminent and respected, money, clothes, and numerous teen-age boy friends. She was voluble, outgoing and immensely popular with her fellow students. This warm friendship lasted for more than forty years. Buffy died of cancer in 1959. Clare spent many days sitting beside the hospital bed of her oldest and dearest friend.

Clare was invited to spend her first boarding-school Thanksgiving holiday with the Cobbs. And Buffy's father, with his big hands and his potbelly, apparently recognized something special in the little friend his daughter had brought home for a visit. When he tried to tailor his conversation to what he thought was the twelve-year-old level, he was surprised to discover that Clare was quite at home in the idea world of adults. Clare called him "Daddy Cobb" and his wife "Moie"—Buffy's own contraction of "mother." All the Cobbs, now dead, exchanged opinions and ideas and visits with the little Boothe family to the end.

The Cobbs were so taken with twelve-year-old Clare that they invited Mrs. Boothe to come for a visit. Irvin Cobb has described Clare's mother as a charming, beautiful and resourceful woman. He enjoyed Mrs. Boothe's sense of humor and admired her determination to advance the education of her children, whatever the sacrifices to her.

In 1915 thirty-nine-year-old Irvin S. Cobb was one of the great figures of journalism. He had been editor of the Paducah *Daily News,* columnist on the Louisville *Evening Post,* and was now firmly established as a member of that almost legendary group recruited by George Horace Lorimer to work for *The Saturday Evening Post.*

The old *Post* was probably the best-read magazine in America at the time. Certainly its writers were the best paid. The humor was wholesome, the fiction buoyant, the editorial policy conservative, and the by-lines provided a "Who's Who" of successful craftsmen—Booth Tarkington, Harry Leon Wilson, Clarence Budington Kelland, P. G. Wodehouse and George Randolph Chester, among others.

At the Cobbs' Clare met such luminaries as Flo Ziegfeld and Fanny Brice, Grantland Rice, and George H. Doran, who later on merged his publishing company with the house of Frank Nelson Doubleday, Kathleen Norris, and Richard Harding Davis, then at the peak of his fame as a war correspondent, and the then reigning figure in journalism, Mr. George Horace Lorimer. Her acquaintance with literary celebrities seems to have predated by years her marriages.

In 1916, when Clare returned to St. Mary's to commence the fall term, she discovered that her one friend wasn't coming back to school. Buffy Cobb had failed to recover satisfactorily from an intestinal infection, and her family was sending her to Florida for the winter. Clare was still invited to spend weekends at the Cobbs' home, but St. Mary's without Buffy wasn't the same. At school she was moody and more aloof from her classmates than ever. She brooded over the cruelties of a fate that had taken her beloved Buffy away, just as they had become bosom friends. She hated her second year at St. Mary's. Nevertheless, she finished the term with the second-highest grades of any student in all the classes.

On April 6, 1917, the United States officially declared war on Germany. In the fall of that year Clare entered the Castle School at Tarrytown-on-the-Hudson as a tenth grader, a move which indicates some small improvement in Mrs. Boothe's financial situation. Clare does not know quite how her mother managed. The market had risen rapidly, responding to an expanding wartime economy, and at that time her mother had a well-to-do admirer called Percy Frowert of Philadelphia. Mrs. Boothe had hinted to her children that she might marry him. The Frowert children, all about the same ages as Clare and David, were good friends, and Clare remembers many happy hours spent with them. The marriage did not take place, though for what reason Clare does not know. The Frowert daughter, now Mrs. Dorothy LaMarche, and Clare are still good friends.

Miss Cassity Mason, headmistress of the Castle School, catered to children from middle-income families. Born in Florence, Alabama, the child of a prominent actor, "Cassy" Mason worked and taught in several American colleges and in Europe. In 1891 she was named principal of the St. James Hall Diocese School of the Episcopal Church of West Tennessee. She moved from there to Brookhall Seminary in Pennsylvania and founded the Castle in 1895. Clare admired the iron-willed mistress. Her affection for the Castle and for "Cassy" endured long after she left Tarrytown.

At St. Mary's Clare had never quite been accepted as one of "the group." At Miss Mason's it was different. For the first time in her life she had nice clothes to wear. She began to shed a little weight and gradually lost her feeling of awkwardness. Living in the shadow of her mother's great beauty, Clare thought of herself as an ugly duckling. Her features were stronger than her mother's, resembling more her father's. The growing realization that she was not unattractive gave her new confidence. And she was proud of her long, blond, curly hair. Buffy Cobb, who had returned to St. Mary's, came over to visit her one weekend. When she said to Clare, "Honey, you're really pretty," Clare threw her arms about her friend. If Buffy said it, it might be true.

In December of that year Mrs. Boothe moved from the Belmont Hotel in New York to Old Sound Beach, Connecticut, a very small town on the outskirts of Greenwich. There she bought a somewhat dilapidated six-room house, giving Clare and David, for the first time in their lives, a home of their own. Clare lived in Sound Beach until her marriage six years later, and her mother lived there until her death, twenty-one years later.

At the end of the first school year, Miss Mason offered Clare a chance to skip a grade and graduate a year early. In literature, language and history Clare was already doing college-level work. Her fluency in French had been increased by her studies at Garden City. She still wasn't very good at math, but Miss Mason's girls were not expected to become bookkeepers or accountants. Clare had very little instruction in biology, chemistry or physics, but she did have an understanding of their application, which seemed to be more than adequate in Miss Mason's eyes.

Clare accepted the offer. Skipping a year to become a senior meant more work, but it also offered a challenge. Clare became editor of the school newspaper, *The Drawbridge*. Scholastically, she was at the head of her class and she was easily the school's best swimmer. After the move to Old Sound Beach, she spent most of the summer vacations in the water. She was a good enough swimmer to win a tryout for the American Olympic team when she was seventeen years old.

Her best friend at the Castle, Dorothy Burns, who, like Buffy Cobb, remained close to Clare in later life, remembers that nothing was ever allowed to interfere with Clare's studies. "When the other girls were reading a racy, contraband account of their favorite movie star, Clare would have a volume of Racine or Molière. She wasn't stuffy about it. She just didn't have time for trash. She even read while she brushed her hair or when she bathed, propping a book on the faucet of the tub. She took longer baths than any girl I have ever known before or since."

The Castle girls helped the war effort by rolling bandages for the Red Cross, and amusingly enough, doing military drills and parading in formation. Miss Mason was nothing if not a feminist. Clare even thought she was in love with a boy named Lloyd Miller, who had enlisted in the Army Air Corps and reportedly was killed in a dogfight over France. When Miller showed up much later on and began to tell Clare of a girl he hoped to marry, Clare suddenly found him a bore and noted in her diary that "all is over."

In 1918, when David Boothe was sixteen, he falsified his age and joined the U.S. Marine Corps for a three-year tour of duty. Mrs. Boothe was distraught, but Clare was very proud of her brother. When he went overseas she wrote him daily letters. Her graduation thesis which was in French was titled *"Qui sème le vent, recolte la tempête."* It was a girlish essay on the wickedness of the Kaiser's minions in starting the war.

During the summer of 1918 Clare worked as a volunteer for the Sound Beach Red Cross. She also walked briskly the three-mile shoreline around Tood's Point every morning in an effort to lose more weight. She wrote and directed a children's play, cast with the neighborhood kids. One performance was given in the recreation hall of the Congregational Church. The local newspaper tells that the proceeds, totaling $62.50, were donated to the Red Cross.

In her final year at the Castle Clare wrote a great many articles and poems for *The Drawbridge*. She also produced, along with the other contributors, some cartoons and drawings. At Castle she also met her first multimillionaire—the most authentic one of all, John D. Rockefeller. The Rockefeller Tarrytown estates adjoined the school grounds. Mr. Rockefeller, who was fond of Miss Mason and enjoyed talking with the girls, would sometimes drop in for lunch in the school dining room. All the girls wondered how such a diffident, quiet little old man could have become the mightiest industrialist in America.

When the war was over, Miss Mason resumed the practice of taking senior students to New York on regular excursions. They went in for lunch, visited museums and took in matinees. Clare saw most of the best plays on Broadway that season. She was also taken to the Metropolitan Opera House, but like her mother, she had little interest in music.

Clare was graduated from the Castle School in June 1919 at the head of her class. At sixteen years and two months she was the youngest girl ever to complete the Castle's traditional requirements. In the annual, beneath her picture, there appears this prediction, upon which the entire senior class voted: "Famous author and illustrator."

The graduation ceremony at Castle was a great event for Clare, except for the absence of David. A Mrs. McBath, an old friend of her mother, came up from New York. Adele Schmeider, who had lived in Hoboken and New York, and was a member of that gay crowd Clare remembered as friends of her father, came with a gift, and there was a dinner party in a downtown restaurant.

Clare was glad to be out of school. She enjoyed having her mother to herself again, but now, for the first time, she began to go out with boys, who were beginning to notice her. Mrs. Boothe was still working, now as a saleswoman in Black Starr and Frost, jewelers.

One Friday afternoon in late August Clare went into New York to visit a girl friend and see a play. She climbed a long flight of stairs to reach the New Haven station at Old Sound Beach carrying a satchel which contained, among other things, the book she was currently reading. She bought her ticket, boarded the train and settled down with her book for the hour's ride into the city. She found herself seated next to a middle-aged man in a brown suit.

Presently she had an uncomfortable feeling that the gentleman sitting beside her was observing her much too closely. When she glanced up, he was indeed staring at her. There was, she thought, something vaguely familiar about the man's appearance, but she couldn't place him. She was not frightened. She knew she looked older than sixteen, and a few men as well as boys had already tried to flirt with her.

She tried to concentrate on the book, and at the same time to remember where she had seen the man. He was clean-shaven, with thick gray hair, and she thought him quite handsome for an older man.

As the train entered the tunnel approaching Grand Central Station the stranger suddenly asked "Is your name, by any chance, Clare Boothe?" She said it was. Then the man asked if her mother was still as beautiful as ever, and was she well?

The question convinced Clare she had been right in thinking they had met somewhere before. She replied that her mother was well and, indeed, as beautiful as ever.

The stranger also asked about her brother David.

Clare answered that he was still in the Marine Corps and was now en route to Nicaragua. Finally she mustered enough courage to ask the man where they had met and how he knew her mother and her brother.

The stranger smiled. "Why, child, I am your father. We haven't seen each other for a long, long time, but your mother sent me a snapshot of you and David a few years ago."

Clare immediately knew the stranger was telling the truth. And the reason he had seemed so familiar was because of his extraordinary resemblance to David. She was too shocked and confused to say anything more, and too taken aback to ask him where he lived or what he was doing. She didn't tell him her mother had said he was dead ten years before, or how much she had missed him. They left the train together. He walked down the platform with her and they parted at the exit. That was the last time Clare ever saw her father.

Ann and Will Boothe did not seem to be the kind of parents who confided in their children.

Clare didn't go to the play or to see her friend. She took the next train back to Old Sound Beach and confronted her mother. Mrs. Boothe confessed that she had concealed from her children that their father was living. But she had done so out of love for them. Then she told Clare that Will Boothe had fallen in love with another woman and gone off with her. The other woman, she said, was Mary Garden, the famous opera singer. Miss Garden was living in Chicago at the time Will Boothe had played in the orchestra. There is no doubt he knew Miss Garden, for Clare remembers carrying a great bouquet of red roses, in behalf of her father, to Miss Garden in her apartment at the Blackstone Hotel. The violinist may well have been infatuated with the great star. But by naming Miss Garden as "the other woman" Mrs. Boothe may simply have been trying to make her husband's desertion a little more understandable to her children than it would have been if she had said her rival was a quite ordinary woman.

Clare doesn't know when her parents were divorced. Mrs. Boothe probably sued for a divorce on grounds of desertion some time after she moved from Chicago to New York. As usual, her mother didn't give her children the sorrowful details of her life. And since she had told them their father was dead, she also had to conceal from them the fact that he had continued for many years to send her small sums of money to help pay for his children's education.

Clare never found out what Will Boothe was doing in Connecticut. Perhaps he had come from California to see his aging parents. She doesn't even know when her paternal grandparents died. She did hear from her father indirectly many years later when she had become Mrs. Brokaw and he was dying of pernicious anemia in California. Because of his illness, his music school had to close, and he wrote his daughter and asked for money. She continued to send her father money until he died.

Clare wrote her brother David about the meeting. Both children were unhappy that their mother had deceived them for so many years. But would they have been happier if their mother had told them the truth? In any event, Mrs. Boothe thought not.

In the fall of 1919 Clare Boothe left her mother's house in Old Sound Beach and rented a room in a cheap New York boardinghouse. Her reasons for running away are not quite clear. She left her mother a note but she didn't say where she was going. Perhaps the emotional shock of discovering that her father was still alive had something to do with it. At the time, she was profoundly unhappy over Mrs. Boothe's revelation, and no doubt equally unhappy that her father, having met her, left so casually. About her running away, she says, "Mother and I didn't quarrel. I had graduated from school, and I just thought it was time to earn my own living." Her brother David had struck out on his own when he was only sixteen, and at the Castle Miss Mason had repeatedly told her girls, "You can do anything a man can do, and probably do it better."

In New York City Clare found a job at Dennison's paper shop on lower Fifth Avenue, making nut cups and favors for the Christmas trade. Her salary was eighteen dollars a week, and she hated the dreary monotony of the work, but she stuck it out for almost three months until an angry appendix sent her home and into the Greenwich hospital for surgery.

Less than two months later Mrs. Boothe was admitted to the same hospital with symptoms similar to those which had caused Clare's return home. The surgeons discovered a ruptured appendix. Dr. Albert Austin, head of the hospital's internal medicine department, was called into consultation. Before the development of wonder drugs a simple appendectomy was considered a major operation. When the appendix had ruptured the prognosis was always gloomy.

Dr. Austin saved Mrs. Boothe's life, and in her convalescent period they fell in love. When she went home he sent his own housekeeper over to look after her and to make sure she rested sufficiently. He also came by every morning and evening to check on the condition of his patient. Mrs. Boothe must have recognized the doctor was displaying something more than a professional interest in her welfare. When he finally proposed, she promptly accepted him.

Dr. Albert Elmer Austin, a forty-two-year-old bachelor, was a solid New Englander. He had been born in Massachusetts and had been graduated from Amherst, where he later taught Latin. He then studied at the Jefferson Medical College in Philadelphia. He entered practice in Greenwich, served for a time during World War I as Regimental Surgeon in the 214th Engineers, then returned to his Greenwich practice until 1938. In 1938 he was elected to Congress as the Representative from Fairfield County, Connecticut.

Greenwich was just becoming recognized as the bedroom city for fashionable New Yorkers. Dr. Austin was chief of staff of the hospital, president of the Greenwich Bank and Trust Company, Grand Master of the Greenwich chapter of the Masonic Lodge, and an altogether highly respected community figure. Thirty-eight-year-old Ann Clare Boothe was still a very beautiful woman. Dr. Austin was charmed by her lively sense of humor and her sophistication.

Clare and David were delighted with their new father. Dr. Austin took David duck shooting on Long Island Sound and eventually helped his stepson join the Masons. And he gave Latin lessons to Clare.

Mrs. Boothe and Dr. Austin were married in the same Congregational Church in Greenwich where Clare herself was married to Henry Luce years later. Dr. Austin moved his new family into a comfortable old four-bedroom, two-story New England house, then took his bride to Florida for a honeymoon.

For Clare and David, the change produced by this marriage was almost too great to comprehend. Dr. Austin was not only comfortably well off and an important figure in the Greenwich community, he was a gentle and outgoing character. Clare called him "Cicero," but David called him "Doc." They were too old to feel comfortable calling him "Father." After all the uncertainties and insecurities of their childhood, they reveled in the new acceptance, at many levels, which had come to them with their mother's marriage. Above all, their mother was happier, more radiant than they had ever seen her. There was little doubt that she was loved and was in love, and for the first time in her life not worried about tomorrow. What could be better?

Clare, whose experience in the paper factory had convinced her she never wanted to be at the mercy of the unskilled-labor market again, enrolled in a business school at Bridgeport to study typing and shorthand. Meanwhile, she locked herself in her room and began writing short stories. These were furtively mailed to the magazines of the day. In every case, they netted more or less prompt rejection slips. She also wrote quantities of poetry, specializing in the fashion of the times, or sonnets. She wrote a sequence of eight sonnets to Woodrow Wilson. Some of the poetry was published in the local Connecticut papers.

Mrs. Austin didn't like the idea of Clare's working in an office, but she seems to have been disinterested in her daughter's literary ambitions. Mrs. Austin hoped that her daughter would go into the theater. She persuaded Clare to enroll in the Clare Tree Major School of the Drama of New York City soon after she finished her business course.

Miss Major, a devotee of Stanislavski, was a pioneer in what has come to be called the "laboratory method" of acting. Clare, herself, had no real interest in acting. She certainly wasn't star material. Toward the end of her first term, she was assigned to do a pantomimic improvisation around the words "You are a cave man, you must go out and kill a wild animal as dinner for your mate and offspring." The other students and the invited audience howled with glee at the spectacle of a pink-cheeked, delicate blond seventeen-year-old shuffling around the stage in an absurd imitation of a hairy-chested prehistoric cave man.

The laughter got to Clare. She stopped in the middle of what she was doing and announced in an icy voice, "This is ridiculous." She didn't think that even Sarah Bernhardt could give a convincing imitation of a cave man. In any case, it was her final appearance as an aspiring professional actress. She quit the school. But the theater had also got to her. When she returned to Old Sound Beach, she sat down and read every play Bernard Shaw, Galsworthy, Wedekind, Wilde, and other theatrical giants of the times had written. A framed photograph of George Bernard Shaw replaced that of poet John Drinkwater on her bureau. She wrote a half dozen one-act plays.

At the midsummer meeting of the Connecticut State Medical Society in 1920, Dr. Austin was chosen to go to Germany to investigate the reported new techniques in plastic surgery, developed to treat the maimed victims of World War I. It was a prestigious assignment. Mrs. Austin, who was enjoying her new situation of relative affluence, invited her old friend Adele Schmeider to accompany them as a companion for her teen-age daughter. David, who had volunteered in 1918 for the Marine Corps—a three- or four-year stint in those days—was in Santo Domingo. The party sailed for Bremerhaven on November 19.

In 1913, when Ann Boothe and her ten-year-old daughter went abroad, they had gone second class, their departure unnoticed. This time there were pictures in the New York papers of Clare and her mother as they embarked. They had new wardrobes and first-class shipboard accommodations. Clare started a scrapbook of newspaper clippings.

The Austins stayed for a short time in modest quarters on the Kurfürstendamm in Berlin. But this was the beginning of the period of inflation which ultimately destroyed the German Republic and paved the way for Adolf Hitler's Third Reich, and the Austins had the advantage of this inflation. They moved to the Adlon Hotel. It was the most splendid place Clare or the Austins had ever stayed, living like royalty on very few dollars a day in U.S. currency.

While the doctor pursued his medical inquiries in Berlin, Clare and Mrs. Schmeider went to the movies and to the theater. Clare remembers vividly her excitement over the plays being produced in Max Reinhardt's Schauspielhaus. They also took tourist trips. In Vienna, where they stayed for a week or so, Clare took riding lessons at the famous Tattersal School. She had taught herself to stay on the back of a horse during those childhood summers when she had been farmed out with friends of her mother. Now her instructors were Austrian ex-Army officers. She learned to ride an English saddle and take jumps four and five feet high.

When the season changed they went south to the Riviera. Clare won a local hotel beauty contest competing against the daughters of the tourists from England, France and the United States. For the first time in her life she became aware of her physical attractiveness. Her face was full but no longer fat, framed in long honey-blond hair which emphasized the delicate blue of her eyes. She was nearly five feet six inches tall, and those long walks around the point in Greenwich and the summers of swimming had firmed her legs and thighs.

Having Mrs. Schmeider along gave Clare a chance to do things on her own because it wasn't necessary to fulfill any obligations as a companion to her mother. She studied German, visited museums and cathedrals, and went to dinner and to dances with young American tourists and German boys she met through her stepfather's associates in Berlin.

A young Englishman and would-be poet named Vernon Blunt, who had spent the previous summer in Greenwich, had promised Clare to introduce her to his writing friends if she ever came to London. In March Clare left her mother, Mrs. Schmeider and Dr. Austin in Venice and traveled to England to stay with an English couple the

Austins had met on shipboard. The first place young Blunt took her was to a party at the Guards' Club, of which he was a member. There he introduced her to a tall, tweedy, handsome war hero named Major Julian Simpson. By the time the party was over, Clare was in love with the young major. It wasn't just a physical attraction. Julian Simpson was gay and witty and worldly. He had gone to Oxford, dropped the names of talented and titled people, and talked of having a career in British politics.

They met on the twenty-seventh of March, two weeks before Clare was to celebrate her eighteenth birthday. In four days she was due to sail for home. Julian and Vernon and a Bloomsbury friend or two took her to breakfast, lunch and dinner, to the theater and to the music halls. In the afternoons they "did" the tourist sights. Julian didn't quite propose, but what he did tell her was that as soon as he could settle his affairs, he would come to America to visit her.

In the schoolgirl diary she kept at St. Mary's, Clare had written on her sixteenth birthday that it was her lifetime ambition to become fluent in four languages, marry a publisher, have three children, and write something that would be remembered. Julian wasn't a publisher, but she must have thought a Member of Parliament was just as good.

When it came time to leave London, Julian drove her to Liverpool in a Rolls-Royce sedan. The trip took about four hours. Without making any definite commitments, they planned a future together. Clare spoke of her literary aspirations and her love for poetry. Julian, it seemed, loved poetry too. To prove it he recited Francis Thompson's entire "The Hound of Heaven." Clare was glad she had been confirmed an Episcopalian, and began to dream of being married in the High Church of England.

If the Austins had chosen to return from Europe on some ship other than the *Olympic,* Clare might have traveled a different path in life. But on that trip the passenger list included some very notable people who were destined to play important roles in Clare's future. They were Mrs. O. H. P. Belmont, one of the *grande dames* of New York society, Elsa Maxwell, society's most famous party giver, Max Reinhardt, the Berlin theatrical producer, and the socialite James Stewart Cushmans. For an ambitious girl, the voyage offered rare opportunities. Before the *Olympic* docked in New York, all of these people had begun to include Clare in their future plans.

Mrs. Belmont, who was born Alva E. Smith in Mobile, Alabama, first married William K. Vanderbilt. After her daughter by this marriage became the bride of the Duke of Marlborough, Alva divorced Vanderbilt to marry Oliver Hazard Perry Belmont. He died in 1908, leaving millions to his widow. Mrs. Belmont was not just a dowager duchess of New York society; she was also a lady with a "cause"—one which had triumphed when the voters of America approved the Nineteenth Amendment in 1920 giving the women the vote. The formidable Alva Belmont was not content to stop there. She moved to consolidate women's gains by organizing the Women's National Party. There were, she argued, more women than men in America, and if the women would vote as a bloc, the country would benefit.

The young girl from Old Sound Beach was flattered by Mrs. Belmont's attention, even if she didn't see herself in the role of leadership in the suffragette movement. She thought the old lady was charming, full of ideas and information, unlike anyone she had ever encountered before in her life. She was also impressed by Mrs. Belmont's money and her social prominence. Mrs. Belmont in turn was attracted by Clare's beauty, her clarity of mind, her vitality and her incipient feminism. Few students of Miss Cassity Mason's Castle on the Hudson escaped without becoming infected with the headmistress's belief that women were the intellectual equals and, plainly, of course, the moral superiors of men. This was an idea to which the belligerently feminist Mrs. Belmont wholeheartedly subscribed.

Mrs. Belmont saw in this young girl a possible replacement for Inez Mulholland, whose death earlier that year had robbed the suffragette movement of its most talented and beautiful crusader. A very practical politician, Mrs. Belmont realized that youth and beauty and a modicum of brains produced results. Younger than Miss Mulholland, and unknown, Miss Boothe nevertheless possessed the beauty and charm to capture the headlines.

Alva voiced these thoughts to her shipboard traveling companion, Miss Elsa Maxwell. "Mark my words," she said, "the world is going to notice that girl whether she joins up with us or not." To this Elsa Maxwell replied, according to her memoirs, "I'll have her to one of my parties. Whatever happens, then, she'll get a rich husband."

At seventy Mrs. Belmont had learned to be subtle when pursuing her desires. She wisely concluded that while Clare might be enlisted to serve the "cause," she couldn't be purchased with money alone. So she talked about the reforms which a full participation of women in a truly compassionate government could accomplish, stressing the need for better schools, medical care and housing for the poor, and the need to protect the workingman from his own ignorant excesses.

Clare didn't spend all of her time on that voyage talking about women's rights. She also talked about the theater. The second day out she found herself seated in a deck chair close to two gentlemen busily engaged in complimenting the weather in German. Clare couldn't see anything beautiful about the weather, and she said so in the same language. One of the men was Max Reinhardt, whose productions Clare had seen in Berlin that winter. His companion was Dr. Rudolph Kommer, the director's assistant and good friend.

Reinhardt was en route to New York to complete arrangements for the production of a spectacular morality play, *The Miracle*. Otto Kahn, the New York millionaire, had agreed to underwrite the venture, and Morris Gest had been engaged to manage the production. A second reason for his trip was to find a suitable blond virgin to play the role of the nun in *The Miracle*. The search for an "unknown" was, of course, a publicity angle—which was later used by Selznick in his search for a Scarlett O'Hara.

Before the *Olympic* was halfway across the Atlantic, Reinhardt declared that he might as well go back to Berlin. Dr. Kommer could handle his business affairs in New York. So far as finding a girl to play the part in *The Miracle,* he had found her on shipboard.

Clare accepted this declaration with a large grain of salt. It didn't seem reasonable that a man of Reinhardt's standing in the theater would offer her such a tremendous part on such short acquaintance, and in view of the fact that she had no experience as an actress.

When Clare raised this point with the director, he responded by saying, "There are no lines in the part of the nun. All you need do, my child, is look beautiful and ethereal. Finding an 'unknown' is part of our publicity plan."

Clare didn't tell him of her limited experience as a child actress or her failure as a pantomimist when she studied at Clare Tree Major's. She kept the door open.

The most influential emissaries of fate on that journey were the elderly Mr. and Mrs. James Cushman. Mr. Cushman was a socially prominent philanthropist whose particular hobby at the time was a chain of Allerton Houses, temporary homes in the big cities for young men and women. He was also a profoundly religious man, with a taste for poetry.

Clare says the Cushmans turned a very benign eye on her, possibly because they were themselves a childless couple, possibly because she was now able to quote a few lines from "The Hound of Heaven."

When the *Olympic* docked in New York there were reporters demanding interviews. The more serious ones wanted to talk to Dr. Austin about his experience in the hospitals, and to Dr. Bucky about his new medical invention, the fluoroscope. The Greenwich papers carried pictures of Dr. and Mrs. Austin returning home with their daughter. The New York papers carried only pictures of Clare. Clare's picture had been in the Riviera papers when she had won the beauty contest. The New York captions read: "Beauty of the Riviera. The people visiting the Riviera in France recently voted Miss Clare Boothe of Greenwich, Connecticut, as their most beautiful companion." Pretty girls even in 1921 sold more papers than scientific discoveries, no matter how startling.

The *Evening Telegram* reported that Clare said she had received offers of marriage when abroad, but also went on to say, "Miss Boothe modestly, though resolutely, said 'Europeans do not appeal to me.'" (She didn't consider an Englishman a European.) The rotogravure section of the same newspaper carried a picture of Clare against a background of shipboard ironwork with her legs exposed in the usual cheesecake pose demanded by the reporters. Skirts being long in those days, her knees were barely visible.

Clare, certain she would soon be marrying Julian, didn't even bother to give Max Reinhardt or Dr. Kommer her Connecticut address. Two weeks passed before a somewhat exasperated Dr. Kommer finally located her Old Sound Beach telephone number. He demanded that she come at once to discuss the part in *The Miracle.*

She did go to New York, where Kommer introduced her to Otto Kahn, Morris Gest, David Belasco, and other figures involved in producing *The Miracle.* Kommer told the press he had chosen Clare to play the part of the nun.

Meanwhile, Mrs. Belmont invited Clare to visit her for a weekend at Sands Point, Long Island, to discuss the Women's National Party. Later, they went to Washington together to visit the national headquarters, whose determined and dedicated head was Miss Alice Paul.

For a girl just turned eighteen (she had celebrated her birthday on shipboard) it was all pretty heady stuff. But Clare didn't want to become an actress or lead women to political power. She wanted to marry Julian Simpson. When Julian's letter arrived addressed to the Austins and asking permission to visit them in Greenwich, it seemed to Clare that a happy and romantic future lay in store for her.

Julian Simpson arrived on the fourteenth of June. Clare watched from the window as the taxi drew up in front of the Austins' house, then she ran down the walk to greet him.

From the moment of his arrival at the modest two-story house in the little Connecticut town, Julian appeared extremely preoccupied and a little aloof. Forty-eight hours later he was on the train back to New York, en route to London, owing, he said, to the "pressure of personal affairs." He would write later. When Clare didn't hear from him, she wrote to Vernon Blunt to inquire about the nature of Julian's affairs. Young Mr. Blunt answered bluntly that Mr. Simpson's "affair" was to find an American heiress. He confessed that as a joke he had told Julian that the Austins were a wealthy American family. It was, he said, a rather rotten joke on Julian, but it was a joke that had bounced on him, too. Julian had borrowed the money from Vernon to pay his passage and he would "never get it back from the rotter."

Clare wrote Julian a long letter. She said she knew about the joke, but she still loved him. Julian's reply was cold and final. He was deeply in debt, had no job, and was in no position to marry a poor American girl, and that was that. Clare never heard from him again.

2

Marriage

As a little girl, Clare had learned from her mother to keep her own counsel, to hide her feelings, and to accommodate herself in a pleasant manner to the desires and ideas of adults. During those two years at the Castle her defensive shell had cracked somewhat, and a more natural, less inhibited girl emerged. The fierce competitive nature which had made Clare such a serious student at St. Mary's became less evident. More confident of her own situation, she was less shy and secretive. But like most girls of her age, she was emotional, sentimental and romantic.

Even after Julian told her that he had been interested only in what he believed was her financial position, Clare had written a long schoolgirlish letter, pleading with him to marry her and to let her help him make his way in life. While the memory of his reply was plainly embarrassing to her, Clare discusses this disillusioning experience now without rancor. Nevertheless, it must have taught her early not to let her emotions with men take complete possession of her.

It was certainly Clare's disappointing romance which caused her to plunge into politics and the theater. She wrote Mrs. Belmont to say she would, after all, like to do something in the women's movement. Alva was delighted. They went to Seneca Falls, New York, together to celebrate the seventy-fifth anniversary of the Women's Rights Conference. Clare put on a leather helmet and goggles and went up with a local commercial pilot in a World War Jenny to drop leaflets over

Schenectady announcing the event. Her picture was taken in costume and appeared in several newspapers.

At her mother's urging, Clare also wrote to Dr. Kommer and expressed a renewed interest in *The Miracle*. Dr. Kommer responded enthusiastically. When he returned to New York that fall Clare was invited to parties and openings and receptions. It was at this time that Clare first met George S. Kaufman, Moss Hart, and Marc Connelly, the young American playwright whose new comedy *Dulcy*, written with Kaufman, had been one of the great hits of the 1921 season.

Meanwhile, as Mrs. Belmont's assistant, Clare was on the pay roll as a secretary, but her duties didn't confine her to typing or shorthand, although these skills were very useful. She appeared in half a dozen Eastern cities carrying the banner of women's rights and worked in Miss Paul's W.N.P. headquarters. Mrs. Belmont had been correct in her shipboard estimate. The reporters and the photographers were all eager to give the new Inez Mulholland publicity, and the "cause" benefited. On one trip Clare went to Chicago and visited her old Castle schoolmates Dorothy Burns and Helen Atwater. Helen had married Philip Wrigley, the heir to the chewing-gum fortune.

Clare's assignment was to attract public attention, enlist new converts, and help destroy the notion that feminine activists had to be rich, chesty old matrons or disgruntled, plain spinsters—in short, to radiate youth and sex appeal.

She also kept in touch with the James Cushmans. They invited her to hear Harry Emerson Fosdick, who was then pastor of the Riverside Church, and regarded by many as the most dynamic young clergyman of the period, and she promptly accepted.

Clare's lifelong fascination with religion probably dates from her confirmation in the Episcopal Church. Or it may also be rooted in the mystery about her parent's religious affiliations. In any event, she was fond of the Cushmans and eager to hear the preacher whose sermons attempting to reconcile religion and science were being so widely acclaimed. On a Sunday early in June of 1922 she boarded the train in Greenwich. The Cushmans met her at Grand Central and they drove to church.

During the singing of the hymns, Miss Boothe became aware of a rather distinguished-looking older man beside her in the pew. When she glanced his way, she found him studying her profile. The man was George T. Brokaw, forty-three-year-old millionaire playboy bachelor whose much publicized pursuit of many eligible young ladies had provided many a meaty paragraph for the New York gossip columnists.

After the service, Mr. Brokaw asked the Cushmans to introduce him to Clare. The net of this was that the Cushmans invited them both to have lunch at the Cushman home on Fifth Avenue.

During the meal George Brokaw led the conversation. He was, Clare thought, quite good-looking and charming with a courtly manner. When it was time to leave, he volunteered to drive Clare to the station.

The next day Mr. Brokaw called Mrs. Austin, introduced himself on the telephone and asked permission to call on her daughter. Mrs. Austin was delighted. An avid reader of the "Cholly Knickerbocker" society columns, Mrs. Austin knew George was the bachelor son of the millionaire clothing merchant Isaac Vale Brokaw, and an authentic Social Register character. She told Mr. Brokaw her daughter had mentioned their lunch at the Cushmans' with pleasure and would, she thought, be delighted to see him again.

When Mrs. Austin told her husband about George, the doctor's reaction was reserved. He knew of Brokaw's playboy reputation. He refused to believe that George was serious about Clare, and he didn't want his stepdaughter's name added to the long list of girls who had provided Brokaw temporary amusement. He was afraid she might be overawed by Brokaw's wealth and social position. But when George drove out to Old Sound Beach in his luxurious yellow Locomobile, he made a good impression on both Mrs. Austin and the doctor. His attitude toward Clare was both tender and protective. He returned the next night and took them all to dinner at the Pickwick Arms Hotel in Greenwich. It was certainly plain that George was head over heels in love with Clare. Dr. Austin began to modify his earlier opinion. Two weeks later, George took Clare to his home at 1 East 79th Street to meet his mother.

Mrs. Elvira Gould Brokaw, then in her middle seventies, was preparing to move to Elberon, New Jersey, for the summer season. The big old house was being readied for her departure. The shades were drawn, the drapes down, and all the furniture and pictures were covered with dust protectors. Clare likens the visit to "going to a house where nobody lived."

They had tea in the dark, dismantled drawing room. Then Mrs. Brokaw, rather abruptly, asked Clare to stand near the window where the light was better. George signaled his hope that Clare would indulge the old lady.

Mrs. Brokaw followed her to the window, scrutinizing her face. Clare remembers being acutely embarrassed and feeling "like a butterfly on a pin, under a microscope." After a minute, old Mrs. Brokaw turned to her son and said, almost as if Clare were not present, "She's a good girl and a healthy girl. Dawdie, you marry her." ("Dawdie" was George's own baby pronunciation of his name.)

George Brokaw jumped out of his chair and hugged his mother. He kissed Clare for the first time and rushed her out of the house into his waiting car. "Cartier's," he told the chauffeur. There George introduced her to Jules Glaenzer, the head salesman. "We've come, Jules," he said, "to pick out an engagement ring."

At that moment Clare wasn't at all sure she was really going to marry George Brokaw, despite the fact that he took it absolutely for granted she would marry him once his mother had announced her approval. But when they left the store, she was wearing a seventeen-carat blue-white diamond solitaire. Riding home on the train to Greenwich, she twisted the ring on her finger until the stone was in the palm of her hand. The size of the ring and the promise of a secure future that it implied left her a little dizzy.

At home, she showed her mother the ring, but tried to explain her feelings. George hadn't really wooed her. She certainly wasn't in love with him, anyway not as she had been with Julian. She thought Mrs. Brokaw was a dear little old lady, but if George really wanted to marry her, why did he wait until his mother told him he could?

Mrs. Austin's advice was to get over Julian Simpson and marry George Brokaw. She would certainly fall in love with him afterward. There was no doubt that Mrs. Austin thought George Brokaw offered her daughter the best match she might ever make.

A day or so later George came out to Greenwich to talk to Dr.

and Mrs. Austin about an early wedding. He said he didn't want to appear morbid, but considering his mother's age there was good reason for haste. His mother was eager to see him married and have children before she died. But he didn't want the Austins to announce the engagement until all the wedding details had been settled.

Clare could have called a halt to the entire proceedings. She might have asked George for more time. She didn't.

It was plain that neither Dr. and Mrs. Austin, nor George himself, were particularly eager to explore Clare's true feelings. She describes the gathering in the living room of the Austin home: three middle-aged adults sat in a circle, deciding her future. George Brokaw was forty-three years old, Dr. Austin two years his senior, and Mrs. Austin three years younger than the man she wanted her daughter to marry.

George had a reason other than his mother's health for wanting to set an early date for the wedding and for keeping the engagement a secret. He knew his sister, Mrs. William McNair, and her husband and his two brothers, Irving and Howard, and their wives would oppose his marrying. They had for some years now come to regard him as a confirmed bachelor. Possibly they also expected their children would inherit George's share of the Brokaw millions. In any event, George suspected they would attempt to break the engagement.

Clare Boothe and George Brokaw were married in the Episcopal Church in Greenwich, Connecticut, on August 10, 1923—four months to the day after her twentieth birthday. "Cholly Knickerbocker," writing in the New York *American,* devoted half a dozen columns to what he described as "the most important social event of the season." It was quite an affair. Twenty-five hundred guests were invited. According to the newspaper accounts, most of those who were asked attended, with some notable exceptions: George's sister and her husband, Mr. and Mrs. William McNair, and his brothers and their wives, Mr. and Mrs. Howard and Irving Brokaw.

Brokaw had asked Howard to serve as best man, but at the last minute, a Princeton classmate, Merrill K. Waters, performed that office. The excuse the other Brokaws gave for not attending was that they were observing the mourning period for President Warren G. Harding, who had died in San Francisco eight days earlier. The Brokaws didn't know Warren G. Harding and had never been active in the Republican Party. No one was deceived; the Brokaw family had declared war on George's young bride.

Following the ceremony, Dr. and Mrs. Austin gave a reception in the ballroom of the Pickwick Arms Hotel in Greenwich. The newly-weds spent their wedding night at the Plaza Hotel, and the following morning they sailed for Europe aboad the liner *Majestic*.

As the honeymoon couple toured the Continent, Clare found that George was a tender and considerate as well as an indulgent husband. He spent money lavishly and gracefully. Hotel clerks, cabdrivers and shopkeepers all seemed to be dedicated to satisfying the young Mrs. Brokaw's slightest wish. Clare bought books in London, clothes and jewelry in Paris. George approved everything she did, encouraged her to do anything, or have anything she wanted. One of the things she wanted to do in Paris was to visit the museums and the cathedrals she had seen as a child. She discovered that George knew a great deal more than she did about painting and music and history.

After nearly four months abroad, they came home on the liner *Aquitania*. Just off the Nantucket light, the ship encountered uncommonly rough seas. Tables and chairs in the main salon were upset, and Clare was knocked to the floor. The press reported that she suffered two cracked ribs and some painful bruises. The ship finally docked two days before Thanksgiving, and they went home to Mother Elvira and the big, old French château at the corner of 79th and Fifth.

The young bride was due for some more hard knocks, rather more painful than broken ribs. George's mother was warm and kind to her—after all, it was she who had pushed for the marriage. But the rest of George's family made it quite clear that in their opinion she was a fortune hunter who had somehow trapped George. They set out coldly and efficiently to blackball her from New York society. Along with her wedding band, she had acquired some very bitter enemies. George's male friends rallied around. But the girls—who may once have hoped to sign charge slips at Cartier's as Mrs. George Brokaw—(and their mothers) sided with her new in-laws. They were extremely parsimonious with their invitations. If this social warfare got under Clare's skin, she didn't let anyone know it. The devoted George seemed more upset by this family animosity than she did. The newlyweds had a warm ally in old Mother Brokaw, and as for the rest of the family, George and Clare found ways to deal with them.

In the beginning, the great game of society, in which she had been precast as a loser, challenged Clare. It was a kind of challenge she had never encountered before. The name of the game, she soon discovered, was getting your name in a pleasant way in the society columns, being invited to the right places, seated with the right people. She was twenty years younger and thirty pounds lighter than most of her female adversaries. And for all her feminine charm, her mind worked like a man's. She discovered that the tycoons of business whose power and wealth intimidated many of their associates were easy for a pretty girl to attract. With their wives, most of them friends of the Irving and Howard Brokaws, things were much more difficult.

That first fall and winter Clare and George were invited as a matter of course to all the large social events. But when Clare and George entertained, it was usually at a small dinner party. George, who knew his Social Register as well as the rest of the family did, made up their guest lists with great care. He knew everybody—she didn't. If they invited friends of his in-laws, they were seated beside someone who was friendly to his new bride. It was a simple strategy: Surround your enemies and then win them over.

In December, Clare discovered that she was pregnant. The prospect of an heir pleased George immensely. (So far there were no males in the direct Brokaw line.)

For the summer of 1924 George leased the Benjamin Thaw estate, Beachmond, at Newport, and Clare, seven months along, continued to play the social game with Newport's finest. When her baby girl was born in August of 1924, she named George's brother Irving godfather and Mrs. James Steward Cushman one of the godmothers. Mother Brokaw forced Irving to accept the honor on pain of sending her to her grave if he refused. The Reverend Henry Sloane Coffin, pastor of the Madison Avenue Presbyterian Church, presided at the christening of Ann Clare Brokaw. It was the only time on record that all the Brokaw clan attended a function given by Clare.

Clare was happy. There had been moments when living in the home of George's mother had produced an uncomfortable tension. Now there was a subtle but, in Clare's view, very happy change in attitude. Ann became the center of household attention.

When the season ended at Newport, "Cholly Knickerbocker" declared Clare the winner in her contest with the other Brokaws. He wrote: "That loveliest of matrons, Mrs. George Tuttle Brokaw, can now sit back and fold her hands, happy in the knowledge that her first season at Newport was a howling success. And if the easy-to-gaze-upon Clare was of a vindictive turn of mind, she might laugh impolitely in the faces of certain of her in-laws, for Clare has triumphed in the really bitter social feud that has existed in the Brokaw clan ever since George decided he was weary of bachelor days and took Clare for his bride.

"Mrs. Brokaw descended upon Newport, and Newport capitulated to her charms. It is doubtful if any young matron in the past ten years has so completely swept the Bellview Avenettes off their . . . I almost said flat feet."

That fall George paid $250,000 for the Julius Fleischmann estate at Sands Point on Long Island. The house was famous as having been the American headquarters for the English polo team and the favorite hide-out of the Prince of Wales. Located on six acres of ground with a private beach on the Sound, it adjoined the estate of Mrs. O. H. P. Belmont, with whom Clare continued to keep in touch.

Clare began to look forward to and enjoy the affairs of society. George hired the Russian artist Savely Sorine to paint Clare in oil, and the New York *World* ran a reproduction in its rotogravure section. Clare, with her hair done in coronet braids, wore a long-sleeved blouse and demurely clutched a book to her breast to conceal her pregnancy. Her companions on the page, who had also been painted by Sorine, were Mrs. Henry Rogers, Princess Serge Obolensky and Mrs. Nelson Doubleday. Sorine was the rage as a society painter, but between the hair styling and the bright-red lips, which were somewhat overdone, he made Clare look much plumper and older than her years.

That year the New York society pages carried photographs of Clare at the horse show; dressed for riding in the park; modeling a new spring suit (the coat came down to her ankles) in front of a Park

Avenue restaurant with Mrs. Reginald V. Hiscoe; at the Beaux Arts
Ball as an Aztec princess covered with beads and feathers; bidding goodbye to Mrs. O. H. P. Belmont, who was sailing for Europe; in a short
ballerina gown which won her first prize at Major Fullerton Weaver's
fancy dress ball at the Park Lane Hotel; with a group of feminists planning a charity bazaar for the Association for the Aid of Crippled Children; arriving for a party at the Vanderbilts' with George (in spats,
morning clothes and a high silk hat); dressed for the pre-Lenten annual
masked ball at Philadelphia, where she took part in a pageant, "The
Birthday of Louis XIV"; with baby Ann on the beach; with husband
George, a scratch golfer, on the golf course; in the Golden Horseshoe
at the Metropolitan; and—she was beginning to win the game—arriving
at Southampton to visit the Irving Brokaws. Reynoldo Luza, a *Harper's
Bazaar* fashion artist, chose Ina Claire, Millicent Rogers Ramos, Mrs.
Felix Double and Clare Boothe Brokaw as outstanding representatives
of the chic and charm of American women, and the *New York City
Journal* ran their pictures with his.

Mrs. Austin and Clare's brother David took full advantage of the
credentials they acquired by being related to Mrs. George Tuttle Brokaw.

Mrs. Austin was included in most of the society parties. She was
about the same age as most of George's friends. Her own beauty and her
wit helped her win an easy acceptance. When Dr. Austin was too occupied with his medical practice—and this was most of the time—
Ann Austin was always an available extra woman. Clare enjoyed having
her mother share her luxurious new life.

George Brokaw helped David get a job with a brokerage company.
These were the days of the stock-market boom. David was charming,
handsome, quick to catch on. It was comparatively easy, he discovered,
to sell stock to George's many friends. The times—and the situation—
were made to order for a handsome young man who, in his own way,
was as attractive as his sister. Money was easy to make and easier to
spend. David took an apartment in New York and established his own
circle of friends, culled more from the younger ranks of brother-in-law
Brokaw's sponsorship than from his own business ability.

With a somewhat monotonous regularity, society writers described
the George T. Brokaws as an ideally married couple. To outsiders, it

might have seemed that way. But within a year, Clare was no longer happy. After a honeymoon period of sobriety, George returned to his old ways and was drinking heavily. Perhaps because many of the married women he had known in his bachelor days had cheated on their husbands, under the influence of alcohol he became jealous and suspicious of his male friends and more and more possessive. If Clare went shopping, George tagged along. While he maintained a law office, he didn't practice. He had nothing to do but be with Clare. Friends of that period say that he even accompanied his wife to the hairdresser's.

At home, apparently out of fear or respect for his mother, George kept his drinking within bounds. But when they went out to parties, he was likely to imbibe much too freely. There was always some man at a party, single or married, happy to flirt with young Mrs. Brokaw. Knowing that the one thing that closes doors fastest to a woman is a reputation for flirting with other women's men, she remained aloof. When her attitude became known, most of the wives were relieved, but the men found her cold. Nevertheless, George continued to be jealous.

The hostility between George and the rest of his family, generated by his marriage, had ended in somewhat of an armistice when Ann was christened. But when Mrs. Brokaw, Sr., died in June of 1925, the old enmities were revived by a real family feud over their father's will.

Under the terms of old Isaac Vale Brokaw's will, the house at 79th Street had been left to his wife Elvira so long as she lived. With her death, possession passed to George for his own lifetime, but held in trust for his children. Clare had never been happy living in the vast old house which required seventeen servants to maintain. In any event George announced he was going to tear the house down and erect a million-dollar apartment building on the site. He and Clare would have the two top floors, and she could decorate them as she wanted.

Old Isaac Brokaw had built three other, somewhat less palatial residences adjoining George's 79th Street location—two on Fifth Avenue and one on 79th Street. Again, he had given only lifetime interest in these establishments to his children, Irving, Howard and Mrs. William McNair. George's sister liked the apartment-house idea, and wanted to have the ground on which her own house had been built included in the project. Irving and Howard, however, objected to the building idea. They feared that a high-rise building next door would not only diminish the value of their own properties but cut all the light from their back rooms and gardens. They filed a lawsuit to stop George from building, maintaining that in view of his father's will he did not actually own the property.

The litigation dragged on for more than two years. Finally the court ruled that while George was free to enjoy the house during his lifetime, he could not, under the terms of his father's will, build an apartment house on the site.

Clare, who by this time didn't care much one way or the other, had to be content with remodeling the old house. Her relationship with Mrs. McNair remained pleasant, but the enmity of Irving and Howard and their wives was increased by the quarrel over George's attempt to erect a modern apartment building.

Long before the senior Mrs. Brokaw died, living with George had begun to be intolerable. When he was sober he was very pleasant and a good companion. But as time went on he was rarely sober. And under the influence of alcohol he vented his jealousies, sometimes inflicting physical as well as verbal abuse on Clare. In the last four years of their marriage she suffered four early miscarriages.

After his drinking bouts, George Brokaw was always conscience-stricken. He would vow to go on the wagon, order the servants to lock up the liquor, and beg his wife to forgive him. But he wouldn't consult a doctor. When she suggested that he should go somewhere and take a cure, George became sullen and morose.

Even during these periods of avowed abstinence, George continued to get liquor somewhere. Clare hid the keys to the liquor closet and threatened to discharge George's valet if he sneaked anything to her husband. Then one day she accidentally discovered the truth. She noticed in his library that one of the many silver cups George had won playing golf was placed dangerously close to the edge of the bookcase shelf. She reached to push it back. Something slopped over the brim. It was gin. All the trophies on the high shelves were filled with it.

About two years after Ann's birth, Clare confessed her difficulties with George to her mother-in-law. The old lady was silent for a long few minutes. She then said, quite simply, "I can't live long. Please don't leave Dawdie until I've gone." The fact that the old lady had made such a plea suggests that despite her son's efforts to conceal his habits, his mother was more or less aware of them. The old lady's death in 1925 freed Clare of that promise. But another reason Clare continued to put up with George's weakness was Mrs. Austin's violent opposition to the idea of divorce. She pointed again and again to George's generosity, to David as well as to Clare. She insisted that Clare should wait until she found someone she loved and wanted to marry. Possibly it was also in her mind that no man could live long who drank so heavily (which turned out to be the case), and that if he died, Clare would be left a very rich widow with her whole life ahead of her. It was just stubborn stupidity for Clare even to think about divorcing so devoted a husband.

Nor did George want his adored wife to leave him. Both George and her mother pointed out that Clare had no grounds for divorce in New York State, and George, at that point, refused to consent to a Reno divorce.

It was Mrs. Austin who finally resolved the dispute, although in a way she had not intended. Will Boothe was dying in California and Clare had been sending him money. When Mrs. Austin accidentally discovered this, she became tearful and angry. She accused her daughter of being an ungrateful child and reminded her of the long years when it had been necessary for her mother to live a penny-pinching existence in order to give her children an education. Clare replied that at this late date she certainly wasn't siding with her father against her mother, or defending anything her father had ever done. But it was George Brokaw's money she was sending, not Mrs. Austin's. And if her husband didn't mind, what business was it of Mrs. Austin's?

There was a cruelly emotional scene. The end of it was that Mrs. Austin demanded Clare promise she would not divorce George, and that she would stop sending money to Will Boothe. Clare declared that she would continue to send her father money, and furthermore, she was going to get a divorce—somehow. And if Mrs. Austin didn't like it, she could go back to Greenwich.

Mrs. Austin returned to Greenwich.

The only ground recognized by New York law for divorce was adultery. George had not been unfaithful so far as Clare knew, so she decided to go to Reno, where no one would ask any questions. In most of these cases the wife engaged a New York lawyer to meet with her husband's lawyer and agree to a division of property. Where there were children involved, the matter of maintenance and education had to be settled. If the husband was the transgressor and happened to be wealthy, he could expect to part with a very substantial portion of that wealth. The actual court orders would be entered in Reno at the time of the judgment, but the arrangements were made in advance.

Clare knew all these things. She had seen her friends go through the process. She did talk to a lawyer, but only to ask him if under the Nevada law she could get a divorce without having to tell the whole story of the physical violence she had suffered at the hands of her husband. There was no other man in Clare's life. She had no plans for the future. She just wanted out.

On the fifteenth day of April, five days after her twenty-sixth birthday, Clare and Ann boarded the train for Reno.

The best indication of Clare's true feelings about the city of Reno and her reason for being there are expressed in her essay "Where Bonds Are Broken," published in *Vanity Fair* in January 1931. She described Reno as a "typical Western desert town, small but prosperous, gray and dun colored main street, with a single Stop-and-Go sign, a courthouse, a three-story brick hotel, innumerable cheap cars, moving picture palaces, filling stations, corner drug stores, hair dressing parlors, a Five and Ten, hybrid churches, a dry goods emporium, Chinese and Italian restaurants, quick lunches, a post office, railway station and speakeasies."

Reno, she wrote, was a city of eighteen thousand, earning $3 million a year from visitors who are attracted by the quick and easy Nevada divorce laws. And these exiles referred to their temporary stopping place as "the city of broken vows, the mecca of lost ladies, and the marriage exchange."

Clare and Ann stayed in the "three-story brick hotel," the Riverside, fulfilling the six-week residence requirement. One aspect of this enforced separation from New York was particularly pleasing to Clare. It was her first opportunity to spend long, quiet days and evenings with her four-year-old daughter, uninterrupted by social duties or the brou-haha that her child's father, when intoxicated, created in the house. She read aloud to her daughter, took her horseback riding, hired cars for trips to Virginia City to see the site of the famous Comstock Lode, where they drank ginger ale in the Old Crystal Bar, and to Tahoe to admire the beauty of that deep-blue mountain lake. The water was too cold for swimming.

Most of Clare's fellow exiles who had come to wait it out beside the waters of the Truckee River, for what Walter Winchell called "renovating," talked about the new husbands they intended to get as soon as they shed their old ones. Those who didn't have plans—the discards—were driven to boast about how much it was going to cost their soon-to-be-ex to get rid of them. Some of her sisters-in-misery made themselves available to any man who would look their way. Clare wasn't interested.

There seems to have been no second husband waiting for her in the wings. This supposition is supported by the fact that more than six years elapsed before she finally remarried. Nevertheless, the gossip of "another man" persisted. According to the records of the Washoe County Court, the marriage between George Tuttle Brokaw and Clare Boothe Brokaw was officially dissolved on Monday, May 20, 1929. The terms of the property settlement, mutually agreed on by the parties, called for a settlement in the form of a trust fund for Mrs. Brokaw of $425,000 to revert to Ann at her death. In addition to this settlement, Ann's father agreed to pay for her education. It was common knowl-edge that Brokaw was worth at least $12 million. When it became known that Clare had "let him off the hook cheaply," many of her acquaintances and all her enemies immediately assumed that she either had someone else in mind to marry or that George had discovered some casual in-fidelity. To them, there was no other logical explanation. That George was an alcoholic seemed to the gossips irrelevant; and that millions do not always make life tolerable seemed just as illogical.

Few members of the sophisticated circle understood or even cared to understand the real situation. Sister-in-law Mrs. McNair seemed to be an exception. She continued to see Clare and remained, for years, friendly to her. Strangely enough, with the passing of the years, most of the children of Irving and Howard Brokaw also became friends of Clare.

Clare was only twenty-six years old. She had no wise family friend to advise her concerning her own interests. Also, she had quarreled with her mother's purely materialistic—or possibly unwisely maternalistic—viewpoint. It is more likely that Clare's willingness to accept what George offered was an expression of her own genuine unhappiness in the marriage.

When the ex-Mrs. Brokaw returned to New York, it soon became apparent that the role of the gay divorcee had little appeal for her. Thirty years later in one of those "what might have been" speculations, she confessed to a friend that her life might have been easier, if less eventful, had she followed the usual course and promptly married the first attractive eligible man who presented himself. According to the gossip columnists of the day, the list included Vincent Astor, Bill Paley, Jock Whitney—and almost anyone Clare was seen with once or twice in public. It also included young Randolph Churchill, whose celebrated father, it is said, urged Clare to marry Randolph. Sir Winston, the son of an American mother himself, seemed to think every British generation needed an infusion of American blood.

Twenty-six years old, with an assured after-taxes income of more than $25,000 a year, her only responsibility a five-year-old child, the ex-Mrs. Brokaw was no longer in the millionaire class, but she could do pretty much as she pleased. She rented a penthouse apartment at 444 East 52nd Street. Her next-door neighbors were Rosamond Pinchot and Bill Gaston. (Debutante Rosamond Pinchot was the unknown who in the end had been chosen by Reinhardt to play the nun in The Miracle.)

Clare also engaged a fashionable decorator to redo the interior. The result was one gratifying break with her immediate past. Her decor was light, airy and modern, providing an atmosphere of fragile, delicate femininity, in direct contrast to the gloomy nineteenth-century interior of the old house at the corner of 79th Street and Fifth Avenue.

When the stock market collapsed on October 29, 1929, Clare didn't suffer any great personal financial loss. But she was deeply affected by the mood of hopelessness and depression which gripped the nation. Her feeling is revealed in an article, "The Real Reason," that she wrote for *MaCall's* magazine in 1947, after her conversion to Catholicism:

In the crash and depression years that followed the boom, some of the men and women found that they had abandoned, in moments of bitter revulsion, their very holds on life itself. Men jumped out of windows because they had lost their last or their first million. Some who had kept their millions, lost their minds. Many took to drink, a few to psychoanalyst couches, obsessed with the notion that somehow (they did not know how or why) they were responsible for the bread-lines that had formed in Times Square.

During the depression years, four of my good friends, two of them beautiful and adored women, and two talented men, committed suicide. Nobody knew the real reason. Perhaps life itself had become an "ism" they were tired of.

This flurry of "death by design" was as hard for me as it was for many to understand. It was like the very first leaves that drop from a tree on a still, autumn day.

Whether it was the economic collapse or her personal discontent because she seemed to have no goal in life isn't clear. But she was unhappy. There was no struggle to earn money; indeed, she had all she needed, and far more than most in the Depression. While, because of her own underprivileged childhood, she could identify with those who were suffering in the Depression, she apparently did not feel herself required to undertake charitable work.

However that may be, and perhaps because it was the thing everyone was doing, Clare decided to put herself in the hands of an analyst. Perhaps a contributing factor to this decision can be found in her relationships with her ex-husband.

George Brokaw had remarried soon after his divorce. His second wife was the pretty Frances Seymour—two years younger than Clare. At the time of the divorce, Clare had agreed to share her daughter Ann with George on a six-month basis. She now sought complete custody of Ann. Her lawyer put the proposition to Brokaw, who refused flatly and said he would seek the same thing himself. The lawyers' dispute lasted two years. The second Mrs. Brokaw asked for a personal meeting with Clare. George, it seemed, was not well. He was in an institution. Soon after he died there of a heart attack. Frances Seymour Brokaw made her proposition: If Clare would assume all of the financial responsibilities of supporting Ann, she could have the child entirely. Clare accepted.

It was during this period that she went to see Dr. Dorian Feigenbaum. Born in Lemberg, Austria, and a graduate of the University of Vienna in 1914, Dr. Feigenbaum possessed impressive credentials. He was a teacher at the Institute of Neurology in the College of Physicians and Surgeons at Columbia and attending psychologist at the Neurological Institute in the City of New York.

Years later, Clare wrote, "Analysis is the disease for which it pretends to be the cure." But at the time, she apparently hoped Feigenbaum could help her. Concerning her analysis, she wrote in the article for *McCall's:*

I was sopping up Freud's own books. My analyst was considered one of the best in America and he had studied under the master in Vienna. I wanted to help him by taking whatever shortcuts might exist to a patient who had a knowledge of Freudian doctrine and was willing to accept it. His orthodoxy was unquestionable and his technique by the book, quite correct. He was remarkably self-effacing. He only made suggestions when I was having real difficulty interpreting my dreams or giving a coherent account of the flotsam and jetsam and trash that rose to the surface of my mind, when I indulged in the tireless babbling analysis encourages. I see now he made his suggestions at the very moments I was most susceptible. . . .

According to my analyst my persistent worries were rooted in infantile sexuality. . . .

Clare, who remembers paying for this advice at handsome rates, wanted very much to accept the doctor's diagnosis, but increasingly she came to doubt that all her problems would vanish if only she were willing to accept that her difficulties were rooted entirely in her infancy and unhappy childhood.

One afternoon, en route to Dr. Feigenbaum's office for another session on the couch, she stopped to admire a display of Christmas wood carvings in the windows of Rena Rosenthal's shop. What caught her attention was a collection of angelic figures assembled in a choir and orchestra.

Dr. Feigenbaum had been urging her to fight her inhibitions and to obey her impulses. She went inside to inquire the price. They were $12 each. There were twenty-six figures in all. To buy them all would cost her $312. She compromised with her impulse and decided to buy just one. A $12 impulse was reasonable. She announced her decision to the clerk.

"Which figure would madam like to have?"

Clare said it really didn't matter and told the girl to just pick one out of the window herself and wrap it up. When she was settled on the analyst's couch, she handed him the little parcel with the explanation that she had obeyed one twenty-sixth of her impulse in buying it.

Dr. Feigenbaum removed the wrappings, examined the figure, nodded his head with satisfaction, and said, "Soooo."

Clare remembers being slightly irritated by the doctor's noncommittal response—which was his usual one. Then the doctor dangled before her the figure the salesgirl had chosen. It was an angel, seated on the streamer of a star, playing a violin. As Clare recalls it, the dialogue which followed went something like this:

"Now, Mrs. Brokaw, what curving comet does this remind you of?"

Mrs. Brokaw, by this time, was steeped enough in Freudian analysis to know the proper answer. She said meanly, "It reminds me of the male organ, Doctor."

"So, and what does the violin remind you of?"

"A female figure, Doctor. The shape of a violin has always reminded people of the female body."

With obvious satisfaction, Dr. Feigenbaum (who incidentally was a better-than-average amateur violinist) announced his classic Freudian conclusion. "You see, my dear girl, you are longing for a penis like your father and brother, and you are revenging yourself on your mother for childhood rejections by drawing this bow—or knife—across her abdomen." Whereupon Clare told Feigenbaum he was psychoanalyzing the wrong person. She hadn't personally selected that particular figure, and if there were any merit at all in his conclusions, she suggested that he look up the salesgirl at Rena Rosenthal's and analyze her.

Despite Feigenbaum's gloomy warning that she would carry a psychic scar to her grave if she walked out before her analysis was complete, Clare left then and there and never went back.

Almost the very same day, as Clare remembers it, it came to her that what she really needed was a job. It was natural for her to think of the theater, but in that Depression year, even experienced well-known actresses were having trouble finding work. Moreover, despite her years of Fifth Avenue, Newport, and Palm Beach, Clare had never ceased to cherish her childhood ambition to be a writer. She reviewed possible entrees into the publishing world. Condé Nast, owner of *Vogue* and *Vanity Fair,* two of society's favorite magazines, was an old acquaintance. Condé was perhaps New York's most elegant party giver. At the next dinner party to which he invited her, she approached the publisher with a directness which must have been disarming and asked him for a job on one of his magazines.

Nast thought he knew the type: wealthy, unattached, idle society woman seeking glamorous employment between husbands. Years later, he said, "At the time I didn't think she was serious. I thought it was just one of those momentary exuberances, a sudden notion she'd soon forget. I told her I was leaving for Europe the next day . . . and suggested she go around and see Mrs. Chase. I was counting on Edna to get me off the hook. Clare was a very pretty girl, you know."

Clare went to see Edna Woolman Chase, editor of *Vogue.* The result was a polite, if kindly brush-off, ending with an invitation to come back in a month or so. If anything had changed, Mrs. Chase would see what could be done then.

Clare waited three weeks. She wanted the job, and she also wanted to prove to Condé Nast that he was wrong when he had told her, "My dear girl, I've had many like you come and ask for jobs but you won't stick it out. You won't have any capacity for work; you'll want to go off to Palm Beach, or Long Island, or to Paris. You'll be getting married."

When Clare went back to the offices of the Condé Nast publications in the new Graybar Building on 43rd Street, she found that Mrs. Chase had also gone to Europe. Walking away from Mrs. Chase's office, she noted through the open door another editorial office where there were six desks. Two of them were vacant. She popped into the office and asked about the empty desks. Someone told her that two caption writers had left to get married. Clare took off her coat and gloves and settled herself at one of the desks with the brief explanation that she was ready to go to work.

"They gave me," she says, "an assignment writing captions for one of the picture features in *Vogue*. I was scared to death that someone would find out I hadn't really been hired. The girl came around with pay envelopes at the end of the week, and she was puzzled that there was no envelope in her basket with my name on it. I explained that Mr. Nast and Mrs. Chase were in Europe, and that I hoped they would straighten out my salary when they returned."

Clare had been on the job three weeks when Condé Nast came back. The publisher asked to see her work. He promptly revised his first estimate and Clare Boothe Brokaw went on the pay roll at $35 a week.

Vogue was basically a fashion magazine devoted almost entirely to clothes, couturiers, coiffures, cosmetics and the doings of what are now called "The Beautiful People." The ex-Mrs. Brokaw had learned quite a lot in six years about all these things. But by the time she had been working on *Vogue* for three months, Clare decided that what she really wanted was a job on the staff of *Vanity Fair*. *Vanity Fair* was a delightful, sometimes satirical, sometimes whimsical magazine. It aimed its arrows at society's squares, saved its wreaths for artists, writers and musicians. The editorial staff of *Vanity Fair* occupied offices adjacent to *Vogue* in the Graybar Building.

Young Mrs. Brokaw was wise enough to realize the tactics which had landed her first job would be useless in getting her on *Vanity Fair*. She didn't even mention her ambition to Condé Nast. He had hardly gotten used to having her on *Vogue*.

3

Vanity Fair

Cleveland Amory, in an introduction to his anthology *Vanity Fair,* published by the Viking Press in 1960, describes the magazine this way:

There never was, nor in all probability ever will be again, a magazine like *Vanity Fair.* She was born in 1914 and she died in 1936, and unlike legendary gentlemen of the old school who were very good at wars but not very good between wars, the lady who was *Vanity Fair* was not very good at wars and depressions, but between them and the golden days of the twenties she was very good indeed. And today as we look back at her out of the shadowy sixties, she seems all in all and all at once behind her time, ahead of her time and yet unmistakably of her time.

In 1913 Condé Nast put out one issue of a publication he called *Dress and Vanity Fair.* He wasn't pleased with the results and he turned to Frank Crowninshield for advice. Crownie had been the publisher of *The Bookman* and the editor of *Metropolitan.* When Nast went to see him he was working as the art editor of *The Century.* Crownie revised the style and content, dropped the first two words of the title and created *Vanity Fair.*

Long before Clare came to work for *Vogue, Vanity Fair,* its contributors, its staff, and most especially Frank Crowninshield were legends in the publishing world. The list of writers who either contributed to *Vanity Fair* or worked for a time on the magazine includes such later greats of the literary world as Robert Benchley, Dorothy Parker, Robert Sherwood, Edna St. Vincent Millay, Elinor Wylie, P. G. Wodehouse, Max Beerbohm, Compton Mackenzie, André Gide and D. H. Lawrence.

A sixty-year-old perennial bachelor, Frank Crowninshield (he once commented that "married men make very poor husbands") was one of the most gallant and gentlemanly editors of the period. He had an eye for pretty girls, but no amount of sex or feminine charm alone could get a woman a job on *Vanity Fair,* and Clare knew it. Where the magazine was concerned, Crownie responded only to talent—he was absolutely master of the house he had created.

Clare had met Crownie at Condé's social parties. But as a member of the editorial staff of *Vogue,* she soon met Donald Freeman, who had been managing editor of *Vanity Fair* since 1924. Freeman was twenty-nine years old, short, overweight, and with an alarmingly receding hairline. A native New Yorker, he had edited the Columbia campus *Spectator,* studied journalism in Vienna and Paris, and then accepted a beginner's job on *Vanity Fair.* By 1929 his talent and his devotion to the magazine had earned him a position among New York's literati second only to the editor in chief's. Clare happily accepted Donald Freeman's invitations to lunch and dinner. All the while, she boned up on back issues of *Vanity Fair.* Donald soon found that the young *Vogue* caption writer could talk quite intelligently about his editorial problems. Whenever she had an idea that might be particularly appropriate for his magazine, she gave it to Donald Freeman. He found some of them quite good. On the other hand, he seems to have mistrusted his own literary reactions in the beginning. He had fallen in love with her.

Clare has very fond memories of Donald Freeman. He was, she says, a great and true friend. "He encouraged me at a critical time in my life to believe in myself, and my talents. I loved him for that, but not in the same way he loved me." She wasn't ready to marry anyone, and Freeman, who understood so much, seemed to understand that, too. Despite his affection, when Clare asked him to help her make the move from *Vogue* to *Vanity Fair,* his response was sternly professional. He could only ask Crowninshield to consider her for a position on the staff. After that, it would be up to her.

57

As Clare remembers that first interview, Crowninshield was at his most charming. But, in between his flowery compliments, he explained that a magazine lives on ideas. He would like to believe that Clare might be qualified to work on a magazine pointed more at the literati than at society with a capital S. But he needed proof. He told her to come back in a week bringing him a hundred suggestions suitable for publication in *Vanity Fair*. When she had done that, he said, they could talk again about the possibility of a job.

Clare spent frantic nights typing, editing, rejecting the ideas that flowed into her mind. The hours studying the old issues and her long conversations with Donald Freeman had been excellent preparation. Almost forty years later Clare was able to describe the happenings of the following Monday morning in detail.

Crowninshield, twiddling his bow tie with one hand and fiddling with his watch chain with the other, looked wearily at the stack of papers she put on his desk. He told her to come back in an hour. When she returned, he said with a twinkle, "Well, well, you have done a lot of work. Now, confess, who was the bright young man under your bed? Who thought up all these ideas for you?"

Clare was so angry she almost burst into tears. Crownie, seeing that his flippant words had been taken in earnest, told her to sit down and warned her that she must learn never to take him—or life, for that matter—too seriously.

Some of the suggestions Clare had written were expressed in a single paragraph. Others required a page or more. Crowninshield had read them all. Patting her manuscript, he said, "If Condé is willing to have you leave *Vogue,* there's a small desk back in the corner for you, Mrs. Brokaw."

Clare could hardly believe her good fortune. "You mean," she said, "all my ideas were good ones?"

Crowninshield shook his head. "No, my child. Some of them are perfectly dreadful. But two at least are excellent. And one good idea a week is about all a magazine should expect from a novice assistant editor."

Clare went to work on *Vanity Fair* early in 1930. The duties that went with the title made her an arranger of interviews for other writers, an assistant and notetaker for the great photographer Edward Steichen and other photographers, a proofreader, and assistant to everyone else on the staff. The only writing she was asked to do, in the beginning, were captions for pictures. She was on probation.

Then when the magazine undertook to publish the works of the French writer André Maurois, Clare volunteered to translate the manuscripts from French to English. Margaret Case Harriman, who was on the staff of *Vanity Fair* and Clare's senior at the time, reported it this way in "The Candor Kid"—a profile of Clare that she wrote many years later for *The New Yorker* magazine:

Although she [Clare] had spent a year in Paris when she was ten, her French was limited to schoolbook phrases. Nevertheless, she regarded Freeman blandly, "Certainly I know French," she said. She took the stories home at night and translated them with the aid of a French-English dictionary.

Be that as it may, Maurois became a regular contributor to *Vanity Fair,* and he and Madame Maurois became good friends of Clare when they came to New York. Certainly Maurois, who spoke good English, found her translations satisfactory. Crowninshield too was pleased with her work and Clare continued to translate André Maurois, Paul Morand, and other French authors as long as she stayed with the magazine.

Gradually Freeman gave her more important tasks to perform. She did the first reading on all unsolicited manuscripts, passing on to him those she thought merited his consideration. But she still wanted to write herself. When she asked Freeman's advice, he told her to write about the things she knew best. On the nights when they had dinner together, Freeman would frequently send Clare back to her apartment alone, telling her to sit at her writing table and work. Even if the words didn't flow at once, she was to sit at her desk until they did. "No good writer," he said, "can depend on flights of inspiration. If you are going to let anyone or anything distract you, you'll never be a writer."

Clare Boothe Brokaw doesn't remember what she tried to write first. She does know her critical judgment told her that her first efforts were not good enough. These first pieces went into the wastebasket. But she kept on trying.

From the beginning, satire seemed to be Clare's flair and fate—perhaps because it was also *Vanity Fair*'s. In April of 1930 in a little essay lampooning the inanity of conversation in the smart set, she wrote, ". . . the purpose of the conversational game [in high society] is to be able to talk freely and at length in a spritely and voluble manner throughout an entire dinner, or in more grueling instances through an entire weekend without by any chance or misapprehension saying anything which everyone present doesn't already know. . . ."

She signed the essay with the nom de plume "Julian Jerome" and mailed it to *Vanity Fair*. When it arrived, she handed it, with three other incoming manuscripts, to Donald Freeman for his consideration.

The managing editor didn't get around to reading the submissions until late in the day. At a few minutes past four in the afternoon, Freeman came into Clare's office with a handful of manuscripts. "I don't think these will do for us," he said, handing her the top three, "but this fellow Julian Jerome has got something. Find out who he is and get him down here. I would like to print more of his stuff."

The article, under the title "Talking Up and Thinking Down," appeared in the August 1930 issue.

In the August 1930 issue, Clare introduced a new feature. The magazine had long been famous for its "We Nominate for the Hall of Fame" pages, giving recognition to the leading luminaries of the arts, literature, sports, politics and finance. Clare's innovation was a similar department captioned "We Nominate for Oblivion." Clare, who had been helping to select the nominees for the "Hall of Fame," and writing the captions to go with their pictures, applied this same treatment to her nominations for oblivion. Of magazine publisher Bernarr McFadden she wrote:

. . . because he has made hygiene indecent, because his career has progressed logically from biceps exhibitionism to publishing the raciest stable of cheap magazines now on the newsstands . . . because he plays both ends against the middle by deploring pruriency and advocating beautiful nudity . . . because millions of shop girls are promised better things by assiduous reading of his true stories et al. and because he is the biggest good, clean laugh of the whole United States.

Another character she assigned to obscurity was United States Senator Reed Smoot of Utah.

. . . because he would rather have a child of his use opium than read *Lady Chatterley's Lover* . . . because he is *the better half* of the title of the Smoot-Hawley [1] tariff . . . the most imbecile political feedbag in economic history . . . because his chief qualifications for holding the position of Chairman of the Senate Finance Committee is that he is an apostle in the Mormon Church of Utah and doesn't have to count on his fingers.

United States Senator Smith W. Brookhart of Iowa received the same kind of lambasting. The Senator had said he felt it was his duty to inform on anyone who served alcohol at a social gathering. And of him Clare said:

. . . because he has demonstrated that a Congressman had no legal obligation to be a gentleman . . . because he has made political capital out of snitching on those of his hosts who serve alcohol, and because he is one of the most triumphantly little provincial bores in the U.S. Congress.

Vanity Fair's "Hall of Fame" was one of the magazine's most popular regular features. In the months preceding Clare's move from *Vogue* the selections for this honor had included, among others, Pablo Picasso, Louis Bromfield, Thomas Mann, Jed Harris, Max Reinhardt, Walter Gropius, S. M. Eisenstein and Ernest Hemingway. Beside the photograph of each candidate there was a paragraph of text validating the selection.

One of Clare's first assignments on *Vanity Fair* was to write the captions for this feature. (If she assigned people to oblivion, she also

---

[1] This bill, adopted in 1930, increased already high import duties levied to protect American industry, and is credited with injuring world-wide trade and hastening the Depression of 1932.

crowned them with praise.) The subjects for both columns were chosen at meetings of the entire editorial staff. After an apprenticeship of a few months, Clare was permitted to join this group. Among the "Hall of Fame" nominees in those months of her tenure were Lawrence Tibbett, the English journalist A. P. Herbert, Columbia's John Dewey, Knute Rockne, Ivan Pavlov and Henry Robinson Luce.

Clare had a great deal of difficulty finding anything to say about the publisher of *Time* and *Fortune*. He didn't go in for any sports, he didn't have any known hobbies, he wasn't either in café or Social Register society. She finally wrote:

. . . because he originated a news magazine idea . . . because at the age of thirty-two he is the successful editor and publisher of *Time* and *Fortune* magazines . . . because he was once a humble newspaper reporter on the Chicago *Daily News,* and lastly because he claims he has no other interest outside of his work, and that this work fills his waking hours.

Luce took exception to this paragraph. He thought it made him sound a dull fellow. He let Nast and Crowninshield know of his displeasure. Clare remembers this as being almost the only time when someone about whom she was trying to say something nice complained to the editors. She concluded that Mr. Luce, whom she had never met, must be a rather thin-skinned young man.

Until she went to work for Crowninshield, Mrs. Brokaw had been apolitical. Her only opinion of Presidents was that Harding was successful in just one thing—giving the Brokaws a public excuse for not being at her wedding. Soon all this was changed. Most of the people with whom Clare had daily contact expressed strong political convictions, and in that period of uncertainty the economic remedies advanced for curing the nation's malaise were the subject of violent political controversy.

The people Clare gathered about her in her penthouse apartment were for the most part leaders in the fields of endeavor *Vanity Fair* presented to its readers—actors, producers, artists, writers, and a sprinkling of topflight pundits. Ray Moley and John Franklin Carter, whose political columns appeared under the pen name Jay Franklin, became regular *Vanity Fair* contributors. Walter Lippmann was a sporadic contributor. In addition, there were Ernest Hemingway, whose novel *A Farewell to Arms* had been published a year earlier; Dorothy Thompson and Sinclair Lewis, who had won the Nobel Prize in 1930; young William Saroyan, who was striving to make his first sale to *Vanity Fair;* and playwrights Philip Barry, Maxwell Anderson, Morrie Ryskind and George S. Kaufman.

In those days, even artists and fiction writers had come to believe that art should carry a political message. The theater itself had just begun to comment on social problems, as John Wexley did that year with *The Last Mile,* in protest against capital punishment.

Grant Wood's famous painting *American Gothic,* published in *Vanity Fair,* was regarded as a satirical protest against the dull conformity of rural American life. Erich Remarque, whose *All Quiet on the Western Front* was an enormous best seller because it was an exposé of the futility of war, was applauded by *Vanity Fair.* The editors were outraged when James Joyce's *Ulysses* was seized in New York by the Bureau of Customs on the grounds that it was obscene.

Condé Nast, in common with most men of wealth, tended to blame the Hoover Administration for the Depression. At that time he believed the Republican Party was as bankrupt as the country. On the other hand, the Democrats under Woodrow Wilson had taken us into World War I, and their old-fashioned idea of free silver and States' rights would never lead the country out of the economic doldrums. Condé Nast himself instructed contributor Jay Franklin to write a piece for *Vanity Fair* calling for a third party, a new political organization, which would not be hamstrung by historic party traditions.

Franklin's article, called "Wanted: A New National Party," provoked a great deal of comment, and his proposals enlisted a number of prominent supporters. Mrs. Harrison Williams, a perennial nominee as one of the ten best-dressed women in America, contributed $50,000 to the formation of a new party. Young James Forrestal briefly added the prestige of his name as treasurer. Clare was chosen by Franklin, the new party's leader, to act as unofficial executive secretary without pay. The New National Party rented an office on a floor below Condé Nast Publications to serve as headquarters.

Liberal in philosophy, loaded with panaceas, its only permanent contribution to the political scene was, in the end, the slogan which Clare thinks she coined for the brochure written by Jay Franklin. This tract was a simplified version of the earlier *Vanity Fair* piece urging a third party. The slogan of the party was "A New Deal for America." (When some months later, Jay Franklin joined the Roosevelt Brain Trusters, he took the slogan with him, and it served Franklin D. Roosevelt well.)

The sponsors of this new movement made elaborate plans to raid the party conventions. In 1932 Mrs. Williams was sent to woo the Republicans when they met on June 14, and Clare was selected to go to Chicago later that month to convince Democrats at their convention.

Newspaperman Arthur Krock, who was then a member of the editorial board of *The New York Times* and one of the most influential commentators on the American scene, became Clare's friend and frequent companion. He took her to theater openings, parties and sporting events.

Krock says it was Clare who gave Jay Franklin his national reputation, that her interest in politics was a natural result of her work on *Vanity Fair*. He recalls that she approached politics from a literary point of view, and has observed that her association with Bernard Baruch, Herbert Bayard Swope, General Hugh Johnson, Jock Whitney and William Paley, far more than her acquaintance with that roundtable of the literati which met at the Algonquin under the leadership of Alexander Woollcott, opened her eyes to the political realities. He claims her beauty was, however, the entering wedge. "Most of us were delighted to discover that a girl who could read without moving her lips didn't have to look like Dorothy Parker."

Krock confesses that he duplicated Condé Nast's mistake of underestimating Clare Boothe Brokaw when she asked him to help her become a better writer. "I remember thinking this is a beautiful kid, and they all think they can do something in writing." Thirty-five years later, he said, "I was wrong. Condé Nast was wrong. Clare had the stuff."

If she was, as some have suggested, the sex symbol of the literati, it was a reputation and a position based solely on externals. Arthur Krock says she was very loyal as a friend, but never demonstrative, never warm with anyone. She was, he says, " 'La Belle Dame sans Merci.' " Arthur could see her as John Keats's ". . . lady in the meads, Full beautiful—a faery's child," beyond the reach of any knight at arms. It is more than likely that thrown as she was among men, and generally men of fame or wealth, she received some offers of marriage. Perhaps she was enjoying her life as an editor too much to remarry. Or perhaps she was fearful of repeating her earlier mistake—marrying unhappily. Clare says that she had determined after her divorce that if she went to the altar again, it would have to be with a man who could hold her interest for the rest of her life. At sixteen she had written in her diary that she wanted to marry a publisher. Perhaps she still did.

The young editor arranged and adjusted her social life to support her work, and the policy of the magazine. Certainly the stuff she was writing was flavored with the amused, detached, cynical attitude of *Vanity Fair*. Because wealth and society and the stock market as well as the arts were *Vanity Fair*'s satirical target, she wrote about these things. Her resentment over the years she considered wasted in the Brokaw milieu is still visible in the form of satirical pieces which she wrote for *Vanity Fair*.

Clare followed Donald Freeman's advice to write about what she knew best. In the September 1930 issue she offered her advice to "The Dear Divorced" subtitled "Being a little handbook full of vitriol and balm for the use of those who have agreed to disagree."

She described the proper conduct for those who want to pretend their parting was amicable and mutual in these words:

When you meet in public at a dinner or a dance, your attitude must be at once elaborately polite and delicately indifferent. You must remember not to cause your host any embarrassment. Immediately turn away and flirt earnestly with your neighbor, or better still, try to convey the impression that your neighbor is flirting with you. You must give vent to a great deal of rippling laughter, listen to your vis-à-vis with rapt attention, make a point of waving across the room at all your ex's best friends. Above all, you must always leave the party before your recent mate does, and go with the most attractive and dangerous person you can find. This will show that you are not trying to outstay him.

She followed this in the October issue with "Ananias Preferred." [1] The article, a satire on hypocrisy in high society, begins:

Of all the social virtues, the most useful and ornamental, the easiest to practice and the loveliest, is lying. In all its delicate shades and gradations, under all its guises, evasion, exaggeration, understatement, hypocrisy, fiction, romance, tact and diplomacy, it is the constant handmaiden to our thought and words. Without it [lying] governments would fall, social structures collapse, high finance, dinner parties, marriages and disarmament treaties be scrapped.

It [lying] is the stock in trade of diplomats, head waiters, authors, real estate agents, dressmakers, lovers, stockbrokers, politicians, and parents. Lying increases the creative faculties, expands the ego, lessens the friction of social contacts and cultivates the memory, for without a good memory, no man can hope to become an accomplished liar, which is why all successful prevaricators are invariably people of intelligence. One should learn early to lie and to let lie; the trouble arises when the average man who cherishes his own, resents his neighbor's mendacity.

Years later, "Ananias Preferred" got her into political trouble. When she was running for Congress in 1942, her opponent cited this bit of satire in an attempt to convince Connecticut voters that what Clare had written in *Vanity Fair* constituted irrefutable proof that in politics she would lack integrity and would practice dishonesty as a policy. Margaret Case Harriman had scolded her soundly in her *New Yorker* piece, "The Candor Kid," for being too outspoken, blunt and honest. She was now being scolded for being just the opposite.

As the wife of George Brokaw from 1923 to 1929, Clare's activi-

---

[1] The story of Ananias and his wife is told in the Book of Acts. These two had sold a piece of property. In order to escape paying the full tithes to God, they lied about the sum received and for this God struck both of them dead. The name Ananias has become synonymous with liar.

ties had been reported regularly in most of the society columns. In her new career she attracted a different kind of attention. She went to Hollywood on a *Vanity Fair* picture assignment and the New York *American* reported her driving H. G. Wells on a sight-seeing tour of Beverly Canyon. The article said it was the British author's first ride in a "flivver," and reported his comment: "A rattling nippy little bit rather."

She went to Greensboro, North Carolina, to visit her Castle schoolmate Ruth Balsam, and a local newspaper reported her description of the interiors of the Hollywood homes occupied by Joan Crawford and Lilyan Tashman, adding, "Her Greensboro friends are intrigued by the plain black band she wears on her third finger, insignia of her divorced state."

The New York *Daily Mirror* declared, "One of the more interesting of the romances of our town is that of Clare Boothe Brokaw, the former Mrs. George Brokaw, and Condé Nast of publishing fame. As soon as all the strings are detached, they will march up the aisle." This was about on a level with many of the other rumors about her private life. Condé Nast had been seeking a divorce for a number of years to marry a friend of Crowninshield. He married Miss Leslie Foster soon after the rumor appeared of his pending marriage to Clare.

Columnist O. O. McIntyre confided to his readers that playwright George S. Kaufman and Clare Boothe Brokaw had been a twosome at the theater the night before. Her name was also associated with Vincent Astor as well as with Bill Paley and Jock Whitney in between their own divorces.

In many of these reports there is a not too subtle suggestion that Clare was using her sex and beauty to attract men for the sake of publicity. If she did deliberately seek to be in the company of people of prominence and power, it must be conceded she was amazingly successful.

When she went to the 1932 Democratic Convention, she was a guest in the box assigned to the widow of President Woodrow Wilson, along with Condé Nast, John Bolling (Mrs. Wilson's brother), Admiral and Mrs. Cary T. Grayson, and General Hugh S. Johnson.

It was in Chicago, while she was attempting to recruit for the New National Party, that Clare was introduced to Bernard M. "Bernie"

Baruch, the American financier who had emerged as a national hero after his service on the War Industries Board and Purchasing Commission for the Allies in World War I and adviser to President Wilson at Versailles.

Baruch was a "statesman without portfolio." He was on a first-name basis with all of the great world leaders, well on his way to becoming a folk hero as the favorite, unofficial adviser to Presidents.

Bernie was sixty-one years old and more than thirty years married. Clare was twenty-nine and divorced. Baruch fell in love with her. He invited her to Hobcaw, his South Carolina plantation. His attentions and intentions were so obvious no one attempted to deny the romance.

Arthur Krock has said it was perfectly clear to anyone who knew anything at all about Bernie, and no one knew Baruch better than Krock, that he wanted very much to marry Clare. He also believes that Clare never wanted to marry Bernie but that she was deeply fond of the handsome, wise, old multimillionaire.

As the Depression deepened and the election of 1932 approached, the tone and the content of *Vanity Fair* began to match the deepening mood of the country. Walter Lippmann wrote more and more serious "think pieces" on world problems: Jay Franklin did an article titled "Wanted, a Dictator." And economist John Maynard Keynes challenged the old economic orthodoxies in the magazine's pages.

When the Democrats nominated Franklin D. Roosevelt for President on July 1, 1932, in Chicago, Clare had acquired enough knowledge of practical politics to quietly drop her efforts in behalf of a third party. She was impressed by Roosevelt's stirring and dramatic acceptance speech, in which he promised America a New Deal. Clare decided to support and vote for F.D.R. So did Mrs. Woodrow Wilson's whole party —all of whom had been for Al Smith.

She remembers that when she was riding back to the Loop that night with Admiral Cary Grayson and General Hugh "Old Ironpants" Johnson, the General growled that in his opinion the Democrats had nominated a son of a bitch. To this observation Admiral Grayson replied, "Yes, Hugh, but he's our son of a bitch now."

The General soon after joined the group that became known as Roosevelt's Brain Trusters. Clare believes through Johnson she may have made a contribution to the Roosevelt Administration, which she would rather forget.

At this period in her life René de Chambrun, a charming Frenchman who enjoyed honorary American citizenship because of his descent from Lafayette, and Charles Poletti, a young political aspirant to the governorship of New York State, were friendly rivals for Clare's attention. It was summertime. Clare had rented a house on Long Island so that Ann might enjoy the beach. On the grounds, no doubt, that there is safety in numbers, she kept her two pursuers within bounds by always inviting them together.

Amintore Fanfani, a young Italian economist, had written a book in which he outlined Mussolini's success and defended the economic policies of Fascism. Poletti gave the book to Clare. Italy was making a great economic comeback, and according to the author, it had been accomplished by the grand plans of "Il Duce." Clare quickly absorbed the principles of a planned economic society. One evening soon after Roosevelt's inauguration, she was dining with Hugh Johnson at Dinty Moore's restaurant in New York City. She gave him Fanfani's economic explanation of the success of Mussolini's corporate state.

Johnson was interested. They sent out for some paper and drew up an organizational plan to show how similar economic controls could be applied to the United States. These ideas were kicked up to Raymond Moley, leading member of the Roosevelt original Brain Trust, who recommended their adoption to the President. The National Recovery Act was passed in June of 1933, and Hugh Johnson was installed as Blue Eagle Czar to administer and control the nation's business and economic activities. Clare sometimes wonders if the Blue Eagle would ever have been born if that dinner-table conversation had not taken place. She says now "the fatal flaw in the plan was the element of coercion." Fanfani's book hadn't bothered to explain that to make the corporate state work, the Fascist Government had to employ the force of bayonets. Soon after the Blue Eagle came into being Clare was made the public representative on the Motion Picture Code Authority. Watching its workings with increasing alarm, she shortly afterward offered her resignation to Hugh Johnson. "It won't work," she said, "if America is to remain a free country."

As the tempo of that 1932 Presidential campaign increased, Clare's interest in politics was heightened, but the magazine remained her primary concern, and she added zest to its pages with two new departments—"The Impossible Interview" and "Who's Zoo." The former consisted of imaginary dialogues between such divergent celebrities as Greta Garbo and Calvin Coolidge, Theodore Roosevelt and Franklin D. Roosevelt, or John D. Rockefeller and Joseph Stalin. The text was illustrated with Covarrubias caricatures of the participants, and for the Stalin-Rockefeller confrontation Clare wrote the following dialogue:

John D.: I never thought that even I would live to see Russia turn into a commune. Dear, dear! All that iron and steel and oil crying out for intelligent exploitation. And nobody profiting a bit by it.

Stalin: The people profit.

John D.: The people? Oh, yes. Of course. They profit . . . afterwards.

Stalin: Afterwards?

John D.: After decent intervals of character-building deprivation, during which industrial leaders prepare lovely periods of progress and prosperity for them.

Stalin: Now that sounds like my five-year plan.

John D.: (delighted) It does? (Peering at him) Do you run this plan?

(Stalin nods)

John D.: Can the people still take it?

Stalin: Take it from me, they take it.

John D.: Well, well. (Drops a dime in Stalin's outstretched hand) Thank heaven, dear boy, you've restored my faith in human nature!

In "Who's Zoo" persons of prominence were pictured with animals whose faces resembled the adjacent human physiognomy. The captions were in doggerel verse, which was written mainly by John V. A. Weaver.

George Wickersham, at one time Attorney General of the United States, who is remembered for his association with Prohibition, was pictured with a walrus. The accompanying text went like this:

I am melancholy.
To tackle that prohibition gag

Was folly.
Saddest
Of all amphibians am I,
Who perish in the wet—
Yet die in the dry!

Herbert Hoover was pictured with the face of a bulldog:

Mr. Hoover is not worried.
Unlike his pet,
Whose brow is furried,
The tireless watchdog
Of our Nation,
He has a firm grip
On the sitchee-ation.

Alexander Woollcott with an owl:

Children, this grumpy,
Fearsome fowl
Is known as
Alex Woollcott Owl.
He swoops
From the shadows in a trice
And snaps up
Poor little writing-mice.
He might
Be married like me or you
If only he had to wit to woo.

Under her own by-line, editor Brokaw continued to satirize the high society which she had come to know.

The titles suggest how closely she continued to follow Freeman's advice to write about things she herself had experienced and milieus with which she was familiar. She wrote "The Dear Divorced," "Bachelors Do Not Marry," "Life Among the Snobs," "The Bliss Girl," "Ex-Wives' Tale," "Portrait of a Fashionable Painter," "Wall Street Ladies' Man," and a dozen more essays in similar vein.

Arthur Krock suggested Clare gather all her *Vanity Fair* essays and put them in a book, which she did under the title *Stuffed Shirts* in 1933. The collection was most popular with the very people it lampooned. A few individuals who had ornamented the world of George Brokaw identified themselves with the characters in *Stuffed Shirts* and complained bitterly that "Clare would write about her old friends in such a fashion." Another of her innovations when she was with *Vanity Fair* was the introduction of candid photographs to illustrate personality pieces.

At the time when most of the critics were picking on Jimmy Walker, the Mayor of New York, for his failure as an administrator and for the indiscretions of his underlings, Clare wrote an article that was more admiring than acid. She said:

The one conspicuously unimportant thing about James Joseph Walker, the Mayor of the City of New York, seems to be his political record; the one fact of importance the existence of his irresistible charm. During his six years as Manhattan's Chief Executive, the personal popularity of this "small little man" has grown in direct ratio to the shrinkage of his prestige. In fact his prestige has now shrunk to such a microscopic point and his popularity expanded to such splendid proportions, that he no longer belongs to the realm of politics, but to the realm of legend and literature.[1]

The election of Franklin D. Roosevelt in November of 1932 had a very beneficial psychological effect on the country. People believed that F.D.R. would lead the nation out of the wilderness of the Depression. Nation-wide radio networks, available for the first time in our history, had carried the candidate's voice into almost every American home. It may have been the magic of the President's words which inspired this new confidence, or it may have been only that the people believed because they wanted to believe.

[1] To add interest to the profile, Clare used eleven candid photographs in a marriage of pictures and text not used in *Vanity Fair* before. The reaction was favorable. A few years later the magazines *Life* and *Look* earned tremendous reader acceptance following and developing this same format.

Clare Brokaw certainly had no clear political philosophy of her own at the time. Like most Americans she just wanted action. She accepted the notion that the laissez-faire policies of the Republican Administration favoring big business were responsible for the country's economic collapse. She was personally acquainted with most of the Brain Trust Roosevelt had called in to help him, and she had a feeling of personal participation in the campaign and the outcome. But her personal enthusiasm for F.D.R. didn't grant him immunity in the pages of *Vanity Fair*.

When the new President was inaugurated, *Vanity Fair* published a satirical drawing by Miguel Covarrubias depicting the event. Her friend Bernie Baruch was offended because he thought he should have been placed in a more prominent position in the cartoon as one of the men most responsible for Roosevelt's victory. The President himself is pictured receiving a garland of wreaths from Chief Justice Hughes, while at his side Eleanor towers above him by a good four inches.

Of all the men who have played a role in Clare's life, Donald Freeman stands out. He gave her the confidence to believe in her own talent. He not only encouraged her to write, he corrected her mistakes and kept her at it many times when otherwise she might have given up. Freeman seemed to be the first man in her life who treated her as something more than a pretty girl. In the office Freeman's attitude was strictly professional, even harshly so. When Clare's writing or editing didn't come up to standard, Freeman told her so in front of her colleagues. But he would also express approval when her work pleased him. Her professional relationship with him was an excellent preparation for her marriage to Henry Luce. It is possible that Clare's affection for Freeman was in some ways deeper than her affection for either of the two men she married. On the twenty-ninth of September, 1932, Donald Freeman was seriously injured in an automobile accident. He died three days later. This was her first encounter with the death of someone she cared for deeply. But it failed to cause her to question her own lack of faith.

Years later, when she described this period of her life in *McCall's* magazine, Clare said:

After my first marriage I moved from the town of Greenwich where I had lived as a girl and where, as I say, the air was mildly infused with Christian feeling, if not thinking, to New York. From then on I breathed in deeply of the air of irreligion and materialism. For a long time I liked it. It had a tang to it—bitter and sharp and a little heady. It made the sense reel pleasantly. Nothing at all like mothballs. In fact, rather acid.

The New York of my youth was a fat, rich, glittering, exciting, glamorous place. We wanted so much of what we had, and we had so much of what we wanted. Why weren't we happy?

Within six months after she went to work for *Vanity Fair,* Crown-inshield had promoted her to associate editor, and there are those—Arthur Krock is one—who say Clare would have made it on her own without Donald Freeman's helpfulness. (Clare herself doesn't think so.) After Freeman's death, Crowninshield made Clare managing editor at a salary of $12,000 a year.

In the spring of 1933, Helen Brown Norden came to work for the magazine. Her first article, "When Lovely Ladies Stoop to Follies," was delightfully frivolous. Mrs. Norden had once been married to a Cuban and her article about that experience, "Latins Are Lousy Lovers," achieved great notoriety. In 1933 she was an attractive as well as clever girl. Clare liked her enormously. This was the beginning of a friendship which was later to have a profound influence on Clare.

The March 1933 issue of *Vanity Fair* sought to entertain its readers by dealing most irreverently with what some people considered almost sacred subjects.

As a candidate for oblivion Clare nominated "the Forgotten Man," the catch phrase that Roosevelt employed in winning the Presidency. She said:

Peacefully buried for over two decades in the works of Sociologist William Graham Sumner, he was hauled out in the last campaign and made to become a political henchman for the Democratic Party because he [the forgotten man] is a very indefinable sort of a personage to whom all sorts of grandiose things can be promised without subsequent embarrassment to the speaker, and because now that the oratory is over, we find that he really means nothing at all.

74

The magazine also published side-by-side pictures, one a composite of two dozen smiling faces of F.D.R. and the other a painting of Eleanor, complete with hair net and knitting needles standing before a radio microphone. The caption: "F.D.R. and Mrs. Roosevelt—the laughing cavalier and the national dean of women."

In the same issue there was a parody of the weekly newsmagazine published by Henry Robinson Luce, with this explanatory note: "Encouraged by the popularity of *Time,* the newsweekly magazine which caroms off the news of each week at a bright, supercilious tangent, the editors of *Vanity Fair* have requested Mr. Riddell in turn to skim the surface of current events and report them for our own readers in the glancing manner of Messrs. Luce and Hadden's flip young weekly."

The article was titled "Time and a Half: Our Own Newsweekly Magazine Glances Over and Off the News in *Time*'s Supercilious Manner." The page make-up was a copy of the *Time* format. Under the heading "Letters" there appears:

Correction
Sirs:

In your issue Jan. 19, at p. 9 col. 3, you state: "Among those present was pigeon-toed, knock-kneed, cross-eyed H. Tecumseh Schmalz, etc., etc."

Nearly omniscient *Time,* holding the mirror up to nature, neglected to mention that I also have one leg shorter than the other, suffer from a nervous twitch.

(signed) H. Tecumseh Schmalz
The Rookery
Metuchen, N.J.

The early style of *Time* and its excessive use of pejorative adjectives had not gone unnoticed by other publications, but *Vanity Fair* was one of the first to focus public attention on the once-labored and flip "Timestyle." If the magazine was favorable to an individual, he was described as virile, strong or husky. Conversely, if the writers weren't of a mind to applaud, he would be described as overweight, pudgy or aggressive. All the good guys were slender and mature, the bad guys fat and aging.

Under "National Affairs," subhead "The Presidency," subhead "Historic Conference," the *Vanity Fair* spoof said:

Bandy legged, asthmatic Mrs. Tessie Messersmith rolled up her sleeves, trudged through a room of the White House last week with mop and pail of soapy water. Object: to mop the floor. Behind closed doors she heard two men arguing excitedly, recognized voices of Herbert Clark ("Smiley") Hoover and Franklin Delano ("Old Potato," *Time,* Sept. 26, 1932) Roosevelt. Scrubwoman Messersmith set down pail, stopped at key-hole to listen. The door opening, she stepped back suddenly to avoid pudgy President-reject Hoover (*Time,* Nov. 8, 1932), jammed her left foot into the pail of water, clumped out of the room with the pail stuck on her foot. Boiled Mrs. Messersmith later: "I couldn't make out a word that was said."

In the summer of 1933 Walter Winchell reported that "Noel Busch and Clare Boothe Brokaw are fighting the humidity together." And Ed Sullivan noted "her presence at the Colony Club with the Herbert Bayard Swopes and Bernie Baruch."

Clare insists she never seriously considered marrying Baruch, but she does confess she was fascinated by his knowledge of the world. Under his sponsorship she gained admission to that small, select group surrounding F.D.R. She became, she says, "the lowly kitchen maid of the New Deal cabinet."

It was Baruch who brought about Clare's appointment as a member of the NRA committee to develop a "code" for the legitimate theater. Clare was identified as one of three representatives of the playgoing public. Others on the committee were actors, producers and playwrights.

For Clare this venture was disillusioning. She expressed her reaction in a satirical play, *O Pyramids!,* which was never produced. She didn't think it proper to attack the NRA so long as she served on the committee, but after she resigned and by the time she finished her play, the Blue Eagle, the symbol of the NRA, was a very sick bird indeed, and no producer was interested in what Mrs. Brokaw had to say about it. But it was during this involvement that she began to see that her early enthusiasm for a planned economy had been naïve.

Everyone had hoped the new President would somehow quickly lift the nation out if its economic doldrums, but the Depression dragged on through the spring and summer of 1933. *Vanity Fair* lost both circulation and advertising linage. The expensive slick-paper format and fine four-color printing had to be cut down. The editorial masthead, formerly presented on a full page, was reduced to three columns. The magazine grew thinner. In the end it could be described as emaciated. Crowninshield, Clare, and Helen Brown Norden, who had been promoted to an assistant editor, fought to maintain the quality of the editorial content.

Possibly because Clare foresaw the demise of *Vanity Fair* or possibly because writing *O Pyramids!* had aroused playwriting ambitions in her breast, Clare told Condé she wanted to resign, and she might have resigned in the fall of 1933 if Nast hadn't faced his editors with a new challenge. What he wanted was a new format for *Vanity Fair,* something which would suit the changing times. Clare and Helen Norden Brown were each to create a new formula. He ordered them to work independently, authorizing them to use the facilities of the art department, under Dr. M. F. Agha, in developing their ideas.

The articles Clare had done on Jimmy Walker and Al Smith, illustrated with candid photographs, had aroused an unusual amount of comment from readers. She decided to expand this by using news pictures that would tell the news with a minimum amount of accompanying text. There was, she recognized, an air of authenticity about pictures which defies disbelief, particularly if they were unposed and had some sequential relationship.

Clare wrote a prospectus for the project. M. F. Agha, *Vanity Fair's* art director, and a pair of *Vogue* photographers, Tom and Andy Bruehl, helped make up the dummy. Meanwhile, the old humor magazine *Life* had gone bankrupt in the Depression. When Clare learned the title could be purchased for about $17,000, she thought it would be a very appropriate one for a new magazine, and titled her prospectus "Changing Vanity Fair into a picture magazine called 'Life.'"

In order to have plenty of room for the photographs, Dr. Agha used a layout with the page size somewhat larger than *Vanity Fair's.* Clare studied hundreds of photographs of people involved in every sort of activity—sports, politics, crime, science—with just enough accent on society to maintain the snob appeal of *Vanity Fair,* and to hold on to that segment of circulation.

In midsummer 1933 Clare went to London in her capacity as managing editor of *Vanity Fair*. She wanted to talk to her foreign contributors, particularly John Maynard Keynes, and view the London Economic Conference. Bernie Baruch, who was staying at the same hotel, introduced Clare to Winston Churchill. She was pleased and flattered when Baruch telephoned two days later to say that Churchill had asked him to "invite that pretty Mrs. Brokaw down to the country for the weekend." It was the beginning of a mutual admiration which endured until Churchill's death.

When Clare returned, Condé Nast called an editorial conference to examine his editors' ideas for a change in the style and format of *Vanity Fair*.

Helen Norden Brown proposed a thick, racy magazine with sexy text, provocative drawings and sensational photographs. It was remarkably similar to the magazine *Esquire* which appeared some years later and became famous and profitable under the guidance of Arnold Gingrich.

Nast and Crowninshield had some kind things to say about the prospectus and dummy of Clare's projected picture magazine. But neither was willing to risk what circulation they had with the old *Vanity Fair*. The original dummies were put in the Nast files for further study. Their creators kept copies.

In February 1934 Clare resigned as managing editor. It was, by all accounts, a cordial separation. Nast and Crowninshield gave a luncheon in her honor and invited the staff and all the contributors who could come. Clare announced she was going abroad to write a weekly column for Paul Block and the Hearst newspaper syndicate, and also to work on a play.

During the last half of 1933 and in the first four issues in 1934 which Clare edited there were a number of articles critical of Roosevelt, or at least questioning some New Deal proposals. George Sokolsky, in what might be regarded as a challenge to TVA, wrote "Public Ownership No Solution." Jay Franklin described the end of the governmental honeymoon. And Heywood Broun discussed Roosevelt's "Revolution by Charm." In the March issue *Vanity Fair* painted a slightly comic mustache on the staid face of Henry Luce's new magazine, *Fortune*.

Two months after she left, *Vanity Fair* nominated Clare Boothe Brokaw to its "Hall of Fame."

Clare visited Mr. and Mrs. Winston Churchill in England and the Maurois' and Morands in France. She went to Berlin and Rome. In Germany she tried to talk to the man on the street and found that he was politely optimistic and remarkably uncritical. Despite the language barrier in Italy (Clare couldn't speak Italian at the time) she was impressed by a similar attitude on the part of Italians. She decided it was fear which kept them silent—fear of the state police, fear that if they objected to the regimentation, the economic benefits both Hitler and Mussolini had promised might not be forthcoming. It was, she concluded, a combination of carrot and stick, bayonets and sausage, stilettos and spaghetti.

The columns she wrote for Paul Block reflected these conclusions. Very soon, Block stopped printing them. He had expected the former managing editor of *Vanity Fair* to concentrate on the frothy comings and goings of the international social set or, anyway, on tourism. He was dismayed when his blond reporter turned in copy suggesting that evil days and evil men had taken command of the Old World's destiny. The Hearst papers were strongly isolationist. Block killed her columns and canned the columnist.

Before leaving for Europe Mrs. Brokaw sublet her apartment, turning the management of her affairs over to her brother David. When she came home, she took a small apartment at the Sherry-Netherland Hotel, and between New York parties and trips to Washington and South Carolina, she turned in earnest to playwriting. Somewhere Clare has picked up a reputation as an effortless writer. The truth is that writing has never come easy for her. She labors in longhand over each sentence and paragraph, writes and rewrites.

She showed the first draft of the play to Bernie Baruch and his nephew Donald, who was a theatrical producer in association with Malcolm Pearson and Al Woods. They agreed to finance its production. Clare was in a euphoric state of mind about the possibilities of being produced on Broadway when she went to publisher Thayer Hobson's for a dinner party. Her dinner partner was Henry Robinson Luce. It was the first time she had met him.

Whether Mr. Luce was still feeling resentful over the treatment he and his magazines had received in *Vanity Fair* or whether he preferred his dinner partner on his left is not known. But he said hardly a word to Clare Brokaw. Her natural enough conclusion was that the master of *Time* was a pretty rude character. Men were not ordinarily so indifferent to her as a dinner partner. If Luce had displayed even the slightest bit of interest, if he had asked her opinion of the situation in Europe, or about the problems of publishing a magazine, she would probably have forgotten both the party and the partner. But the complete brush-off was a new experience. A year later Elsa Maxwell invited Clare to a party at the Waldorf-Astoria to honor Cole Porter.

The Starlight Roof was crowded with celebrities. It was well past midnight when Clare spotted Harry Luce making his way across the ballroom floor carrying two glasses of champagne. The dancing had stopped, the lights were dimmed in preparation for some special entertainment. Clare suddenly decided to give him a taste of his own treatment. She maneuvered the editor-owner of *Time* into a tête-à-tête and then began to ask him one rude question after another—her ultimate intention being to cut him off in the middle of a sentence and leave him fuming as he had done her. Clare took his arm. "We'll have to sit down somewhere, won't we, Mr. Luce?" she said. "And isn't it nice you have champagne for both of us."

They found chairs and Clare asked her first provocative question. When the lights came on again, Luce made no move to leave her. When the guests went back on the dance floor, Mrs. Brokaw and Mr. Luce kept right on talking. Luce, who seldom went to parties, and when he did was always the first to leave, suddenly hauled out his watch. He announced it was one o'clock and asked Clare to go with him to the lobby of the Waldorf. He had something important to tell her.

Not knowing what to expect, she went down with him in the crowded elevator. He led her to a quiet corner of the lobby, pulled out his watch again and said, "I can't take more than five minutes. It wouldn't be good manners. I want to tell you that you are the great love of my life. And someday I am going to marry you."

Considering the fact that Luce was married, that this was the second time they had ever been together, Clare's astonishment was quite genuine.

He asked her where she lived, and brusquely said he would call on her at her apartment in the Sherry-Netherland Hotel at 3:30 on Thursday afternoon, adding he would have to leave at 4:00 to keep an appointment. Then he escorted her back upstairs.

As the day approached, Clare ran over in her mind all the reasons why she disliked Mr. Henry Robinson Luce. He was abrupt, he was rude, he had been completely without finesse, even in telling her he expected to marry her. Like George, he seemed to take her acquiescence for granted. It seemed to her there wasn't a hint of subtlety or spark of romance in the man.

She decided that when he came—she somehow did not doubt he would—she would send her maid to the door to dismiss Mr. Luce with the announcement that Mrs. Brokaw had gone to the country. Then she thought, no, she would have the maid take his card, keep him waiting outside the door, then send the maid back, saying her mistress couldn't receive him.

But when Luce arrived, Clare opened the door for him. "It was," she says, "curiosity," the sin of Eve. Luce was very businesslike, very direct. He announced it would be wise of both of them to take a year getting to know each other. At the end of that time, if Clare should decide she loved him, and if he continued to feel about her as he did at that moment, they would be married. He wanted her to think it over very carefully. Then he left to keep his four o'clock appointment.

After he had gone, the somewhat bewildered young woman surveyed the situation. Perhaps Harry Luce wanted just to have an affair with her for a year. She didn't know how she felt about him, but she did know that she didn't want to enter into a liaison with Henry Robinson Luce. But she realized that he was a very determined man. She felt, unexpectedly, very unsure of herself. She telephoned Buffy Cobb. Would Buffy go off on a long trip with her? Three days later Buffy and Clare sailed for Europe. She wrote Luce a pleasant little note of regret that she could not tell him goodbye. The maid was to deliver it after her departure.

4

Life and Luce

If Clare is a controversial character, Henry Robinson Luce was even more so. His enemies said he suffered from delusions of grandeur. Liberal politicians considered him a stuffy conservative. Conservatives found him unreliable at crucial moments. Taft partisans tell you that Luce was responsible for the defeat of their hero at the 1952 Republican convention in Chicago, and consequently responsible for the nomination of Dwight Eisenhower.

To his friends and intimate acquaintances he was always known as Harry. In public prints and in the magazine he is identified as Henry R. or Henry Robinson. A gaggle of former *Time-Life* editors have published their judgments of Luce. Ralph Ingersoll did it with a novel, *The Great Ones,* a thinly disguised and embittered caricature of Clare, Harry and *Time.* Thomas S. Matthews indulged his animosities in *Name and Address.* He laments his association with Luce in these words: ". . . and how can I exonerate myself from membership in this [*Time*] son-of-a-bitch club? I can't in fact. For six years I was the chairman and must take the responsibility (under Jove) for everything that appeared in *Time* in those six years." There were others—John Hersey, John Emmet Hughes, Theodore White—all of whom left in a huff because of differences with Luce.

Harry Luce's father, the Reverend Dr. Henry Winters Luce of Scranton, Pennsylvania, graduated from Yale in 1892. He married Miss Elizabeth Root, a distant relative of the great Elihu Root, and went to

China as a Presbyterian missionary. Harry was born April 3, 1898, in the mud-walled missionary compound at Tengchow, the first of four children. He was named after his father and Charles E. Robinson, the pastor of Scranton's Second Presbyterian Church, which sponsored the Luces' missionary undertaking.

The family came through the Boxer Rebellion, which started in 1900, without suffering any physical harm, but that violent episode expressing the native animosities toward foreigners echoed and re-echoed throughout the early years of young Luce's life. He learned to speak Chinese at the feet of an opium-smoking amah before he spoke English.

In 1905, when Harry was eight years old, the family returned to America on a furlough. Dr. Luce was attempting to raise money to endow a university in China. One of his contacts, Mrs. Cyrus H. Mc-Cormick, wealthy widow of the founder of the International Harvester Company, took the Luces under her protection and became their bene-factress.

Mrs. McCormick wanted young Harry to live with her as an adopted son. After giving the matter some prayerful consideration, Dr. Luce and his wife concluded it was the Lord's will that their family stay to-gether. They took their son back to China with them. Two years later, when he was ten, he went to the British-run boarding school in Chefoo. Austerity, prayers and penitence had been the program within the mis-sionary compound. At Chefoo the word was discipline. The headmaster, an Irishman named McCarthy, followed with a vengeance the patterns established at Eton and Harrow. The students were forbidden to have any contact with native Chinese, a rule which young Luce thought ex-cessively restrictive and somewhat stupid, since his mother and father were devoting their lives to the cause of converting the Chinese to Christianity.

The students were compelled to study long hours and were flogged enthusiastically for any infraction of the rules. In one of those rare moments when the adult Harry Luce discussed his childhood, he told this writer of his reaction to the requirement at Chefoo that the last boy in line for morning inspection before forms be flogged.

"I asked the headmaster about this one day," Luce said, "explaining to him that even if we were all on time there must necessarily be one boy who would be last in line. I got a flogging just for asking the question."

The school was very religious, very rough and very tough. Luce said he hated Chefoo and loved it at the same time. He was terribly homesick. When he didn't have a bloody nose, a skinned knee, or a red bottom, his face and hands were swollen with chilblains. After Chefoo, Luce found the getting of A's at Hotchkiss and Yale a relatively easy matter.

The dimension of the barriers erected in Luce's mind by his school experiences in China is revealed by the fact that he seldom discussed his boyhood, even with his wife. During the years they were married, *Time* and *Life* magazines published accounts of Thornton Wilder's achievements. Clare had purchased some of the writer's earlier works for *Vanity Fair*. Harry told his wife that he and Thornton Wilder were classmates at Yale but never mentioned that they had been roommates at Chefoo. She learned this fact from John Kobler's biography of Luce, published in 1968 by Doubleday.

Certainly that early environment—the asceticism of the missionary compound, the brutal discipline of Chefoo—contributed to the reticence and inhibitions which many of Luce's friends and colleagues noted in him. It is possible that his psychological reaction to the disciplines of Chefoo manifested itself in a speech impediment that overtook him early in his Chefoo days. The echoes of his stutter or stammer sometimes reappeared even in later life. As a boy he stammered so badly that Dr. Luce sent him to England to be enrolled under the headmaster at St. Albans for speech therapy. He made such rapid progress he was able to accept a scholarship at Hotchkiss, and at Yale was taken on the senior debating team.

It had always been understood that young Harry would go to Yale. Reverence for knowledge was held only less than for God in the Luce household.

When he arrived at Hotchkiss, his classmates promptly nicknamed him "Chink," and taunted him by saying that his birth in China disqualified him from ever becoming President of the United States. At the age of fourteen Harry Luce was slender, redheaded and a little above average in height. When arguments failed, he used his fists so effectively on some of the upper-form boys that the nickname "Chink" was soon dropped. No one ever used it in his presence again, and his eligibility for the White House was conceded. But Luce deplored violence and regarded his use of physical force as a confession of failure to achieve understanding.

He was graduated from Hotchkiss at the head of his class, and when he took his college board Greek exams, he scored the highest mark in the country. He was editor in chief of the Hotchkiss *Literary Monthly* and assistant managing editor of the weekly school newspaper, *The Record.* Briton Hadden was the editor. Many of Luce's schoolmates thought of him as a bookish square; to the fun lovers he was a wet blanket who seldom went to a party or dated a girl. (Like Clare, the reason had something to do with his lack of a social background.) With the athletic students he wasn't popular—he had no aptitude for sports.

Luce and Hadden were both standouts at Hotchkiss. Hadden made *The Record* a breezy reflection of student life, and Luce made the *Lit* the envy of other serious student publications. Hadden won the Senior Declamation award reciting "Casey at the Bat." Luce won the extemporaneous contest with a speech on "Things Learned Outside the Classroom."

At Yale young Luce became managing editor of the *Daily News* in his sophomore year and Brit Hadden was elected chairman. Normally these prestigious posts went to upperclassmen, but with America involved in World War I, Luce and Hadden stepped into the vacuum when the seniors and juniors went off to training camps. In 1918 both boys went to Camp Jackson, South Carolina, as part of Yale's ROTC unit. The war ended about the time they were due to ship overseas. It was during those months in South Carolina that Hadden and Luce, bemoaning the fact that most Americans were ignorant of what made the world tick—and this resulted in unwanted wars—decided to publish a periodical which would correct this deficiency. Upon their return to Yale, they proceeded to implement this ambition by making the *News* an organ for their thoughts. They expanded the coverage of world events, took sides on controversial questions, and published articles criticizing the conduct and questioning the competence of the nation's newspapers.

They both were graduated in the Class of 1920. Luce, with a Phi Beta Kappa key, was voted the "most brilliant" and Hadden the "most likely to succeed." Hadden persuaded Herbert Bayard Swope, editor of the New York *World,* to take him on as a reporter at $25 a week. Luce went to England for a year of postgraduate study at Oxford on a scholarship grant.

When Luce entered Yale his father gave him $500. Beyond this small starting amount, he earned every dollar of the cost of his education himself. He waited on tables, ran a student eating house, got himself a job as a tailor's agent, and sold his classmates their first uniforms; he became campus representative of a dry cleaner, and got a rather good salary as editor of the Yale *Daily News.* When he was graduated he had $4,000 in a savings, enough not only to finance his stay in England, but to take numerous bicycle trips on the Continent. On one of his trips to Rome, Luce was introduced to a dark-eyed, dark-haired American girl from Chicago. Her name was Lila Ross Hotz. Her father, a Yale man, Class of 1891, had died two years earlier. Her mother had remarried, and Lila was in Europe on a summer tour.

Henry Luce was shy, serious-minded, and conditioned from birth to practice economy. To compensate for the stammer which still embarrassed him at times, he had learned to speak slowly, deliberately, which often seemed pontifical to others. The slim Lila was quite different. She was voluble, impulsive and extravagant. Luce, who had little time for girls in college, fell in love. Lila may have guessed his feelings. He didn't tell her. It would have been out of character for Harry Luce to think of marriage until he had finished his studies and found a job. But when the year was up he went to Chicago.

Lila probably wasn't the only reason he headed for the big city on the shores of Lake Michigan. The economy was in the postwar doldrums. Mrs. McCormick was still alive. She had contributed $1,000 toward Luce's postgraduate year in Europe, and he hoped she would help him get a job.

Mrs. McCormick was willing. But when one of her plant managers told Luce that if he went to work for International Harvester, they would have to fire someone to make an opening for him, he remembered his journalistic dreams at Yale and found a spot on the old Chicago *Daily News* as leg man for Ben Hecht. His salary was $16 a week. He liked the assignment and he didn't mind the pay. He left when Walter Millis, a Yale classmate, offered him a job on the Baltimore *News* at a salary of $40 a week. Millis made a similar proposition to Briton Hadden, who promptly resigned from the New York *World* to join Luce and Millis in Baltimore.

"It was the best job I ever had in my life" is the way Luce described his days in Baltimore. "No responsibilities, no obligations, more money than I'd ever had before, and a chance to work with Brit."

The two new men on the *News* spent most of their energy planning for the day when they could quit working for someone else. The idea of *Time* was born in Baltimore. Luce contributed the name, after noting how frequently it was linked in advertising with mankind's common goals—time to save, time to retire, time to get well, time to travel, time to think. The two young men, both almost twenty-four years old, settled on format, frequency and content. They polished the phrases in their publisher's prospectus before giving any thought to the problem of how to finance the project. Much of what *Time* was to become is predicted in that original section of the outline titled "Editorial Bias."

There will be no editorial page in *Time*.

No article will be written to prove any special case.

But the editors recognize that complete neutrality on public questions and important news is probably as undesirable as it is impossible, and are therefore ready to acknowledge that certain prejudices may in varying measure predetermine their opinions on the news.

A catalogue of these prejudices would include such phrases as:—

1. A belief that the world is round and an admiration of the statesman's "view of the world."

2. A general distrust of the present tendency toward increasing interference by government.

3. A prejudice against the rising cost of government.

4. Faith in the things which money cannot buy.
5. A respect for the old, particularly in manners.
6. An interest in the new, particularly in ideas.

But this magazine is not founded to promulgate prejudices, liberal or conservative. "To keep men well-informed" . . . that, first and last, is the only axe this magazine has to grind. The magazine is one of news, not argument, and verges on the controversial only where it is necessary to point out what the news *means*.

Luce and Hadden resigned their jobs and left Baltimore in February 1922. They rented an office in a New York two-story brownstone at 141 East 17th Street. It took them eight months to raise enough money to launch *Time*. Their goal was $100,000 capital. When the sale of stock had produced $86,000, they decided to proceed.

Luce's passionate devotion to his alma mater endured until the day he died. This may have been the case partly because *Time,* the creation of Yale men, was originally financed by other Yalies. The first investor was Henry P. Davison, Yale '20, and the final $25,000 came from the Harkness family—William Hale, Class of '22, his sister Louise and his father's cousin Edward put up $5,000; Mrs. Harkness invested $20,000. (A single $50 unit of the original *Time* stock was worth more than $20,000 in 1968 and had paid dividends of more than $11,000.)

Luce and Hadden recruited their staff from among their acquaintances in college journalism. Many years later, when being on the staff of *Time* had become one of the coveted jobs in journalism, those who didn't make it paraphrased Pascal's statement about Jesus Christ, in reference to Luce and Hadden, saying, "If you were a Yale man, nothing else mattered; if you weren't a Yale man, nothing mattered."

One notable early exception was young *Time's* circulation manager, Roy E. Larsen, who had been business manager of the *Harvard Advocate.* Writer Manfred Gottfried, who ultimately became a managing editor, was a Yale man, as were eleven of the eighteen people listed on the publication's first masthead. Among these were Stephen Vincent Benét and Archibald MacLeish.

The first issue of *Time* was published March 3, 1923. Nine months later, on the twenty-second of December, Luce went back to Chicago to marry the girl he had met in Rome, Lila Hotz.

The wedding service was performed at four o'clock in the after-noon at the Fourth Presbyterian Church with the Reverend Dr. Henry Winters Luce and the Reverend John Timothy Stone reading the service. Lila's stepfather, Mr. Frederick T. Haskell of 1100 Lake Shore Drive, gave her in marriage. Harry's sister Elisabeth was one of the bridesmaids. Briton Hadden was an usher.

The Chicago *Tribune* society story announced "Mr. and Mrs. Luce will be at home after January 1, at 1160 Fifth Avenue, New York City." Harry was twenty-five years old. *Time* was gaining in circulation and reader popularity, but he could afford only one week for a honeymoon.

At the time of Luce's first meeting with Clare Boothe Brokaw she was thirty-one, he was thirty-six. Time Inc. was then worth at least $10 million. Briton Hadden had died on the twenty-seventh of February, 1929, and Harry had become the undisputed boss of Time Inc. The new magazine for business, *Fortune,* had begun to equal the success of *Time.* The two magazines were rapidly becoming a power in the publishing world. But the young lord of this empire was a man with few friends.

Hadden had been gay and whimsical. It is generally agreed that he was chiefly responsible for that innovation now known as "Time-style." Luce was serious, determined, some.staffers called him stubborn, and always ambitious to improve on the magazine's coverage and broaden its scope. He had been admitted to the circles of power because he was recognized as a new force. But his personality was not so wel-come. His frequent retreat into periods of silent introspection, his lack of cheerful small talk, his aversion to society with a capital S (which greatly pained Lila and her mother, who now widowed had come to live with them), his inability to communicate any kind of emotion, his lack of what passes for a sense of humor, tended to alienate his con-temporaries. They respected him greatly, but they said he was cold, that it was hard to know him.

Clare Brokaw's own first impression of Luce reflected the prevail-ing view that he was a complicated and not easily understood character. At her second encounter his abrupt declaration without any romantic prelude or even a single compliment left her mystified, if somewhat shaken. When she and Buffy Cobb sailed for Europe, Clare assumed that she had heard the last of Harry Luce—that his pride would prevent him from getting in touch with her again. She had underestimated both his passion—it was a *coup de foudre*—and his way of getting what he wanted. Three weeks later she answered the telephone in her Riviera villa. It was Luce calling. He was in Paris and he wanted to see her.

The courtship which followed was not a particularly romantic one. Harry Luce found it difficult to express his love in the conventional words of lovers. Like Clare, he always seemed on his guard, fearful lest someone might discover the soft, eager, not-at-all-cocksure human being behind his gruff exterior. But his devotion and determination were unmistakable. Intellectually he was the most interesting man Clare had ever encountered. She fell in love with him.

In the personal files of Harry and Clare Luce some have been puzzled by the many communications—cables, letters, notes or gifts—addressed both to Harry and to Clare bearing the same signature: Mike.

"Mike" was a subterfuge they agreed upon when they met in Europe. Lila had not yet agreed to a divorce. The sticking point seemed to be the financial settlement to be made on her. Discretion dictated that they should both sign their communications "Mike." For years after, when Luce sent Clare flowers or wrote to her when he or she was away, he used the same pseudonym.

Buffy Cobb highly approved of Harry Luce and his suit. She couldn't understand why Clare had been so reluctant to say yes. There were not many who truly understood the girl Arthur Krock had called " 'La Belle Dame sans Merci.' " One of them was Bernard Baruch. And when Clare and Buffy returned from Europe, she went immediately to tell him.

Baruch didn't want Clare to marry Henry Luce or any other man. But he especially objected to Luce because he said that he had a reputation for coldness and ruthlessness. The meeting ended on a highly emotional note with Clare insisting that she loved Luce and that her marriage to him would not in any way affect her affection for Baruch.

In Paris, Clare had told Luce that she did not want to see him again until the divorce was a *fait accompli*. Friends say that Luce settled $2 million on Lila and made ample provision for their two sons, Henry Luce III and Peter Paul, who were at that time ten and eight years old, respectively. In any event, Luce and his first wife remained friends until the day of his death.

Harry had accepted Clare's decision that they should not see each other during this period. Meanwhile, with divorce in the air, Luce's name was whispered about in connection with other girls. Apparently the few friends who knew the real situation maintained a discreet silence. After the divorce Clare returned to New York. But she put off marriage to Luce in order to devote herself to the rehearsals of her first full-length play, *Abide with Me,* scheduled for a Broadway opening the fall of 1935.

Luce turned with equal zeal to his business. He was deeply in love with Clare, but *Time* had been his first love. It would continue to claim his devotion and affection through all the years of their life together.

If Clare had ever entertained the notion that being Mrs. Henry Luce would bring her preferential treatment in the columns of his magazines, this idea was shattered the day before she married him.

Abide with Me opened November 21, 1935, at the Ritz Theater in New York City. Cissie Loftus and Earl Larimore headed a distinguished cast. Clare's friends were all in the audience for opening night. When the final curtain came down, she misunderstood their applause, and hearing a few friendly voices cry "Author, author," she went out on stage to take a bow. *Abide with Me* was the story of a young woman married to a rich old alcoholic.

The New York Times's Brooks Atkinson described *Abide with Me* as merely "a gratuitous horror play about an abnormal family jaw." Richard Lockridge in the *Sun* said, "It was too horrible to be real." And the reviewer for the *Herald Tribune* declared:

Mrs. Brokaw's first step in the theater is stumbling. The unhappy predicament of her heroine married to a sadistic drunkard is authentic enough for any drama, but she has not let these protagonists reveal themselves in significant action. Having sat and chatted for most of two acts, they are suddenly galvanized into frenetic and rather ridiculous action. Where a neophyte might be pardoned for a good many slips in dramatic structure, it is not so easy to forgive sheer bad writing.

In all the reviews, the author was criticized for coming on stage to receive the applause of the audience.

Time's theater critic thought the play was bad but he knew his boss was going to marry the playwright. Should he speak his mind and let the chips fall? He took his far-from-complimentary copy into Luce, who read the review carefully, looked a bit grim, and then suggested, "Perhaps we should let Mrs. Brokaw see this."

The writer may have wondered what the boss would do if Clare insisted that *Time* be kind to her creation, but Clare read the piece and then volunteered to rewrite the review herself. She was too much of a pro not to know that the critics were right. The review she wrote was even more brutal than the *Time* staffer's. When Luce read her revision he said, "No play is *that* bad." The final copy was a compromise. But it didn't contradict the critics, and it said quite plainly that the play was an amateurish failure.

Clare and Harry were married the following day, on November 23, 1935, in Old Greenwich, Connecticut, and then went to the Caribbean on a private yacht for their honeymoon.

Baruch once described Clare's physical and mental charms in these words: "When she comes into a room she attracts everybody's attention by the glow that emanates from her. Her extraordinary spirit shines out of her eyes. When courage was given out, she was sitting on the front bench."

Luce, who was amazingly articulate when dealing with objective situations, could never find that same clarity of expression when dealing with any subjective relationship. But it was plain that he enjoyed Clare's company. Some members of his family and a few people who spent considerable time with Clare and Harry Luce have recognized that while Clare's beauty may have been the lodestone which first attracted Luce's attention, it was her mind, her ability to express her thoughts, and her talent for selecting the genuine from the phony which commanded his admiration and kept him enthralled over the years.

Both Harry and Clare were prima donnas, and each, in his own way, egocentric. Of the two, Clare was much quicker and more intuitive, while Harry laboriously thought things out to a safe, if not brilliant, conclusion. Consequently they didn't always reach the same judgment.

In the early years of their marriage most people thought it would founder. How could two such competitive, strong personalities share the same roof happily for long? The attitude of Luce's family in the beginning was reason enough to predict this trouble for the newlyweds. Luce's sister Elisabeth, married to Texas-born Maurice Thompson Moore, a member of the New York law firm of Cravath, Swaine and Moore, general counsel for Time Inc., was deeply interested in working for righteous causes, and was mistrustful of society, especially people in the theater. Like all the Luce children, Mrs. Moore was a devoted Calvinist.

Harry's older sister, Emmavail, was married to Leslie Severinghaus, the conservative and religious headmaster of Haverford School, a Main Line boarding school near Philadelphia. A handsome woman, Emmavail was even more conservative than Beth. If her appearance was somewhat plain, her militant Presbyterian moral standards were shiny bright, and by these standards divorce was immoral.

Luce's younger brother, Sheldon, was a somewhat unhappy employee of Time Inc. Dr. and Mrs. Henry Winters Luce, living in retirement with the Severinghauses, were deeply distressed by their son Henry's divorce and remarriage. Clare was a divorcee, beautiful, chic, rich, and a habitué of that segment of American society which the missionary Luces regarded as "the world and the flesh," if not the devil. They were offended when Clare's comings and goings were noted in the gossip columns of the New York papers. They were mistrustful when her clothes attracted comment. The woman who had broken up Harry's home did not in any way recommend herself to this clannish Presbyterian family.

Lila Hotz had been a social butterfly, but she had never threatened to distract Luce's attention from his career. The Luce family did not altogether approve of Lila either, but they were comfortable with her. Lila's father had been a solid Midwest manufacturer and merchant. When the family business—they manufactured wagon and farm machinery—began to lose out to Detroit's trucks and cars, he had made a success of a second career in real estate and investments.

One of Luce's distant relatives describes the family reaction to Clare: "No one in the family ever put it in exactly these words but I think at first they were afraid of Clare because she was such a strong individual. They could see Harry was devoted to her. They thought she would distract him from his career, lessen his devotion to the church of his father."

Tex Moore was two years older than Luce. He had earned his law degree at Columbia in 1920 and achieved a respected position as a partner in a powerful law firm. In between looking after their two young sons, Thompson and Michael, his wife found time for her church, the Y.W.C.A. and numerous other good causes. Mrs. Moore was, and is, a very much admired woman. Clare boasts of her sister-in-law, "If Beth had been a man, she would have been an even more brilliant success than Harry."

Beth was Luce's favorite in all the family. In a peculiar way, she was always "the other woman," the person he turned to for advice, counsel and comfort. She was the standard to which he compared all women, including Clare.

Tex and Beth, who lived in New York City, were not quite as shocked by Harry's divorce and remarriage as were the other members of his family. They could understand and appreciate Clare's accomplishments. They also recognized that Harry's first wife had not provided the intellectual companionship he craved and needed in his career.

Emmavail Severinghaus never bothered to conceal her feelings about her brother's divorce and remarriage. Her husband, Les, was having his greatest problem as a schoolmaster in dealing with children from broken homes. They both believed marriage was a contract to be kept for life. "Vail" was probably the only member of the family who hadn't been aware of the fact that Harry's first marriage was on the rocks long before he met Clare.

As Luce's bride, Clare was determined to accomplish two things: be a real helpmate and bear him a child. Nature denied her the second, but almost everyone agrees that she was a generous contributor to the happiness and success of their life together. If his first wife did not sparkle at the other end of the dinner table, perhaps she just didn't want to; with Clare it was just the other way around. In the early years of the marriage many more people came because of Clare than because of Luce.

94

But later the combination of Harry and Clare made an invitation to dinner with the Luces at their Waldorf Towers apartment, or later on at their houses in Greenwich, Ridgefield, Mepkin and Phoenix, a social and intellectual banquet.

When Harry tended to monopolize the conversation, Clare would intervene—and vice versa. She would draw him into spritely discussions of controversial viewpoints with their guests. She made everyone in the room feel clever and therefore comfortable. Baruch once observed, "When Clare asks you a question, you know she will value your opinion, even though she disagrees with you. When Harry asks you a question, he might be setting you up to overwhelm you with his superior knowledge."

Luce enjoyed parties, but he didn't like staying up late. He was an early riser. He no longer felt compelled to personally direct the development of every story published in *Time,* but his magazines were probably the most influential—and criticized—interpreters of America to the world and of the world to America. This was a responsibility Luce never accepted casually. He said he disapproved of personal journalism, but at the same time he was probably the most personal of all journalists. He never regarded the magazines as merely a commercial, money-making property.

Perhaps God hadn't really commissioned Harry Luce to lead his people forward into a better world, but his attitude was still that of a Christian zealot. There is little doubt he loved America. He harbored a lingering resentment over the fact that he had not been born in this country and used to say wistfully that he would give anything to be able to claim some hometown in the United States. (When this remark was published he was invited to become an honorary citizen of Oskaloosa, Iowa, and he accepted.) He suffered over what he thought were his country's failures. When he exposed what he considered its mistakes, his reproach was that of a loving reformer.

Clare wanted to make a home where Harry would be comfortable, where their children would feel welcome, but she could never quite gear herself to the role of the adoring, acquiescent wife. Some of the qualities which had made Harry most attractive were also the most vexing. His aggressiveness and self-confidence could sometimes be irritating. He

95

knew so much about so many things, there were times when life was like being married to the Encyclopaedia Britannica. He cared very little about creature comforts or his physical surroundings. What he ate and what he wore were unimportant. At the dinner table he would be too interested in the conversation to remember to pass the salt or to serve himself from the dishes the butler held out to him.

Nineteen thirty-five was a year of significant events in the life of Clare Boothe Brokaw Luce. Her first husband, George Brokaw, died on May 28, leaving the bulk of his estate in trust for his second wife. One recital of his will declared: "I have made no provisions for my two children [Frances' daughter and Clare's] as they have been abundantly provided for in the will of my father, Isaac V. Brokaw, and my daughter Ann Clare Brokaw is provided for in a settlement made with her mother."

George died in a Hartford, Connecticut, sanatorium where he had been committed as an alcoholic. Fifteen months later his widow Frances, who inherited an estimated $4 or $5 million, married a young Omaha, Nebraska, actor named Henry Fonda, and subsequently became the mother of the current screen stars Jane and Peter.

When George Brokaw died, his estate owed Clare about $100,000 cash in still-unpaid moneys due on the settlement. Frances threatened to sue the first Mrs. Brokaw in order to make her pay an inheritance tax but the threat never materialized.

In November of that year Clare's first play, *Abide with Me*, was something less than spectacularly successful, and her second marriage got off to an auspicious start. On the honeymoon Harry agreed to investigate seriously the possibility of starting a picture magazine to tell the news in photographs.

Many years later Henry Luce told this writer that the second time he ever saw Clare she tried to persuade him to start a picture newsmagazine, adding with a smile, "Of course our experience with *Time* made *Life* possible, but it was Clare's idea originally."

Clare didn't tell Harry about the prospectus she had prepared for *Vanity Fair*. She thought that if he knew Condé Nast had rejected the idea it might dampen his lukewarm acceptance of the project. And when some months later he told her he had discovered he could buy the defunct *Life* humor magazine for $80,000, and he thought it would make a great title for the new project, Clare says, "I still kept my mouth shut. It was no time for the new bride to say 'I thought of that two or three years ago, when *Life* could have been bought for much less than half the price you are now willing to pay.'"

When Clare was urging him to start a picture magazine, she quite naturally expected there would be a place for her on the editorial staff. She didn't think it necessary to get any guarantees that this would happen. She was confident enough of her own ability to know she could successfully compete with any of the *Time* staffers.

Luce, responding to Clare's urging, assigned two of his senior editors, Ralph Ingersoll and Dan Longwell, to the project. Ingersoll was a Yale man and he had come to Time Inc. as an associate editor of *Fortune* in 1930. One year later Luce promoted him to managing editor, and then made him general manager and vice-president of Time Inc. Dan Longwell had left a position as publishing manager of the trade-book department of Doubleday, Doran in 1934 to become a special assistant to the president of Time Inc. and ultimately the first executive editor of *Life*.

The fact that Luce assigned Ingersoll and Longwell to work on the new magazine shortly after his marriage is a measure of the seriousness of the intent. He told them to put aside their other chores. He didn't want a slick-paper *Police Gazette,* but he did recognize that girls, sex, crime, the outlandish, and the shocking were immensely appealing to American secret appetites.

The camera invades privacy in a way denied to the printed word, and the public seems to have an insatiable desire to be on the inside of things. Harry knew that behind every personality, every success, every governmental action, the public believes there exists a secret, one which is kept hidden through the operation of a tacit conspiracy.

Longwell and Ingersoll came up with a host of possibilities for a name. They proposed *Look, Scoop, Eye, Parade, Click, Pick* and *Flash.* Luce didn't think any of them was just right for what he had in mind. Clare kept in the background. "I thought for a new bride I had done rather well to get Harry to look into the picture magazine. I certainly didn't want him to get the idea that I intended to run his business."

As format and policies were being formulated, Clare began to understand that if the *Time* staff had anything to say about it, there would be no place in the organization for Mrs. Henry Luce.

Communication between a husband and wife is a fragile thing, frequently limited by all sorts of inhibitions. Perhaps Clare didn't want to test her position in Harry's life by insisting that she have a place in the new venture. Perhaps she was afraid he would say no and didn't want to risk the division this might create. Judging from remarks Clare has made to friends and the things she has told reporters, Luce's decisions always remained as mysterious to her as they did to many of his editors. He did not like to have them questioned, and she tried not to question them.

The magazine was an instant success—something which no one had counted on and a circumstance which cost Harry Luce more than $5 million before *Life* began to show a profit.

The advertising rates had been predicated on a modest circulation of two hundred and fifty thousand copies. In order to cover the newsstands the first print order was for four hundred and forty-six thousand, but no one really expected to sell that many.

The public embraced *Life* with a passion. Some magazine stands began reserving all the copies they received for their favorite customers. Others just charged two or three times the published price of ten cents. At the end of three months the demand reached the one-million mark and the advertisers were getting four times the circulation they were paying for.

In all of the advance planning, the research, the market testing, the hours of debate with the staff, no one had ever suggested such a possibility.

The money received from subscriptions and newsstand sales for any magazine is never enough to meet the costs of paper, ink, distribution and editorial expense. The advertiser pays the freight. Space is usually contracted for long in advance of the publication date. The price is determined by the publisher's estimate of circulation. Harry Luce was delighted with the popularity of *Life* but the dilemma he faced was unique in the publishing world. He could cut the print order until the advertising rates could be increased, but if *Life* was suddenly unavailable, the public might turn to something else. The alternative was to absorb the loss. Luce put $1 million of his own cash into the first issue. He wasn't disposed to let the baby die.

The readers who wanted *Life* were going to get it. The print order was increased, new subscriptions were accepted, and Luce borrowed $4 million, pledging his Time Inc. stock as security in order to pay the deficits.

In retrospect, *Life* came out of the starting gate a winner, but planning the first issue was a long and arduous process. During this period, Ralph Ingersoll indicated that he and Longwell wanted an evening conference with the boss and his wife. When Clare asked her husband what Ingersoll wanted, Luce replied proudly, "I think they are going to ask you to take an editorial post with *Life*."

After a pleasant dinner in a restaurant, they adjourned to the Luces' apartment. Ingersoll came directly to the point. The project was suffering, he said, because Luce himself wasn't devoting enough personal attention to it. Not once in six months had the boss stayed later than five o'clock in the editorial offices.

The implication, which Longwell seconded, was that Luce was devoting too much time to his bride and not enough to *Life*.

"I don't like to have to put it this bluntly," Ingersoll said, "but, Harry, you just can't make a success of *Life* with your hands tied behind your back."

Clare came to her husband's defense. "Harry Luce," she said, "could publish a better magazine than Ingersoll or Longwell with both hands tied behind his back." Luce remained silent. Finally he said, "Go upstairs, Clare, and let me discuss this quietly with Dan and Mac." Clare went to her bedroom and burst into tears.

If Luce had fired Ingersoll or even indicated his disagreement, Clare might possibly have felt better about it. But that night she realized that if it came to a choice, the magazines would always be first with Harry. She resolved to make, once again, a career of her own. And after this episode she also resolved never to set foot in the Time Inc. building unless Luce specifically invited her to.

Clare sat down and wrote another play.

In July 1936 Max Gordon announced via the Broadway gossip

columns that he had purchased a new play by Clare Boothe Luce with an all-female cast—"thirty-eight women and no men." Ilka Chase, Betty Lawford, Margalo Gillmore and Audrey Christie would all play leading roles, and Clare was back in the headlines.

After a tryout in Philadelphia, The Women opened in New York on December 26, 1936. It has been suggested that George S. Kaufman actually wrote the play. His response to that rumor was "If I had written it, why would I have signed Clare Boothe's name to it?"

The characters in The Women represent that small segment of society which is overrich, oversexed and underoccupied. It is a play about men, without a single man in the cast. Clare says she got the germ of the idea from a conversation she overheard in a ladies' powder room at a hotel where she and Luce had gone to attend a party.

The girls' conversation was apparently earthy and frank. Clare, who had never been overly fond of the idle members of her own sex, was disgusted by these poisonous powder-room personalities. In the introduction to the play that she wrote for the published version, Clare calls the play "a clinical study of a more or less isolated group projected perhaps in bad temper, but in good faith."

The play's heroine, Mary, loses her husband to a very designing, sexy blonde, Crystal Allen. At the end of the play, Mary, by an intelligent ruse, exposes her rival's infidelity to Mary's ex-husband, and wins him back.

Clare points out that if the play has a moral it must be "Be intelligent, fair maid, and let who will be good." She also says, "The women who inspired this play deserved to be smacked across the head with a meat ax and that, I flatter myself, is exactly what I smacked them with. They are vulgar and dirty-minded and alien to grace, and I would not, if I could, which I hasten to say I cannot, cross their obscenities with a wit which is foreign to them and gild their futilities with the glamour which by birth and breeding and performance they do not possess."

Producer Max Gordon read the first draft of that script and decided to buy it. One story has it that Baruch, whose money connections could be very useful to a theatrical producer, pressured Gordon into making the purchase. The truth is that Gordon had known Clare when they both served on the NRA Theater Code Committee.

Clare has never claimed *The Women* to be a great play or even a good play, but she does feel the critics who reviewed it in New York after its Philadelphia tryout were much too harsh.

Brooks Atkinson said:

Miss Boothe's alleycats scratched and spit with considerable virtuosity . . . but *The Women* is mainly a multiscented portrait of the modern New York wife on the loose spraying poison over the immediate landscape. . . . Miss Boothe has compiled a workable play out of the withering malice of New York's most unregenerate worldlings. This reviewer did not like it.

For thirty years audiences have disagreed with Mr. Atkinson. *The Women* ran out the season and through the following year. It grossed more than $900,000. Two movie versions were made of it, and a television special. Scarcely a week has passed since the play was written that it is not being performed by some amateur or road company. It has been produced in England, France, Germany, Italy, Spain, the Scandinavian countries, in Ceylon and Thailand and Hong Kong, and in South America. Only recently in New York, it was performed at the United Nations by forty United Nations diplomatic wives from various countries. All together *The Women* has earned the author more than $2 million dollars.

Concerning its Broadway success, the New York *Morning Telegraph* said, "*The Women* outstrips by a wide margin any figure established by a contemporary play in the same period of time in the last twelve months." Hubert Griffith of the London *Observer* called it the best play of the (London) season and described Clare as "a woman with the brain of a demon."

In one scene of the play, the character Crystal Allen takes a bath on stage. Thirty years later such goings on had become commonplace, but at the time it was a shocker. The gossips quoted one line of Miss Boothe's dialogue to prove that Clare, a bride of less than a year when it was written, was beginning to regret her marriage to Harry. Crystal says to her maid, "Helen, never marry a man who has deserted a good woman. He is as cheerful as a man who has murdered his poor old mother."

Almost every other aspect of Clare's life as the new wife of Henry Luce equaled or exceeded her expectations. Clare was quite happy with the apartment at the Waldorf, but Luce, who never behaved as though he were rich or spent money recklessly, was uncomfortable as a rental tenant. A house of his own was essential. He wanted a place where he could escape the social and business demands of New York City. Six months after they were married he found a location he liked on the banks of the Cooper River at Moncks Corner near Charleston, South Carolina.

The old plantation, called Mepkin, comprised seven thousand two hundreds acres, with kennels, stables and tenant quarters. The property had once belonged to Henry Laurens, a hero of the Revolutionary War who had been President of the First Provincial Congress in South Carolina and a member of the Paris Peace Commission following the colonies' successful revolt.

The plantation house was on a bluff overlooking the river at the end of a mile-long driveway shaded by old moss-bearded live oak trees, camellias and azaleas. The main house was adequate but not ostentatious. It contained five double master bedrooms, living room, dining room, reception room and kitchen. About a tenth of the land was in rice fields abounding with duck, partridge, wild turkey, dove, snipe and woodcock.

Luce paid $150,000 for Mepkin Plantation. Clare engaged New York architect Edward Durell Stone to survey the plantation and submit sketches for developing guesthouses and improving the old residence.

The Luces in later years occupied many other houses—the one on King Street in Greenwich, a big place at Ridgefield, Connecticut, the house on the grounds of the Arizona Biltmore Hotel in Phoenix, Arizona. When Luce died, they were in the midst of plans for a new home on the island of Oahu in Hawaii. None of these other places challenged the house at Mepkin for their affections. The plantation became the center of family life. It was here the Luces gathered—Emmavail and Les Severinghaus, Beth and Tex Moore, Sheldon Luce and his wife, and all the Luce offspring.

It was of the plantation that Tom Moore, Clare's nephew, says there was a magic about Mepkin. "All of us, I mean the second generation, looked forward to our Christmas, New Year's and Easter vacations in South Carolina. Aunty Clare taught all of us how to shoot and ride. She took us quail hunting on horseback. She's the best woman rider I've ever known. And the evenings at the dinner table are easily the most cherished memories of my childhood."

Clare left the old house virtually untouched. Moncks Corner was to be a rural hide-out, a place for vacations, family and friends. She added three guesthouses and named them Claremont, Washington and Strawberry. They were tied into the old place with a long, open-faced brick wall, and each guest cottage was roomy enough to accommodate a family, or, as it usually happened, the nephews in one place, the nieces in another, and any adults who might be visiting in a third.

Luce's two sons by his first marriage, Peter Paul and Hank, and the Moore boys, Tom and Mike, usually wound up in Strawberry, so named because of the printed wallpaper. Ann Brokaw and any chum she might have invited would be next door, with the Longwells or the Moores or the Severinghauses or the Sheldon Luces in the cottage nearest the principal residence.

When Margaret Case Harriman in her *New Yorker* profile alleged that Clare baited the birds at Mepkin by scattering grain, she was deeply hurt. Dan Longwell rose to her defense in a letter to *The New Yorker,* in which he said:

To my certain personal knowledge this statement that Mrs. Luce baits ducks is untrue. I have visited Mepkin often and have shot with the Luces. I am an old friend of Mepkin and you wrong the plantation as well as Mrs. Luce. Hunting customs are scrupulously followed. Mrs. Luce happens to be a rather good shot, she doesn't have to bait game to hold her own.

The routine at Mepkin during the holidays was, according to Tom Moore, a combination of glorious days in the field and delightful evenings. "There was a big bell in the back yard. About six o'clock or some-times a bit earlier, the bell would ring to warn us that we had an hour to get ready for supper. That meant clean up and dress up, shower, clean shirt, necktie and jacket.

"Aunty Clare would sit at one end of the dining-room table. There would be fifteen or twenty of us, mostly youngsters and only a few adults. She would get us in to discussions of news, philosophy, religion, athletics, sex, and ourselves. No one was ever left out. She had a way of drawing us all into the circle and drawing us out. If things were dull, she would invent a game to play. Sometimes she understood us as well as our own parents, or so it seemed to me then. When Uncle Harry was there he seemed to soften under her influence, particularly when there weren't any other adults present."

Moore says that in New York Luce was tense, preoccupied and constantly involved in some aspect of his business. "I know he discussed things with my dad, but I can't remember a time when Uncle Harry talked shop with Aunty Clare."

Moore's observation that his uncle didn't talk shop to Clare is supported by an episode which developed about a year after *Life* ap-peared on the newsstands. Harry called Clare from his office to say he would like an early dinner because Tex Moore was coming over and they had a matter of urgent importance to discuss. When Clare admitted her brother-in-law to the apartment that night, he was, she thought, more agitated than she had ever seen him. When she inquired as to the nature of his business with Harry, he replied, "My God, hasn't he told you? Don't you know Time Inc. is about to lose a hell of a lot of money?"

He explained that two photographers, the Bruehl brothers, were suing Harry and *Time-Life* for millions of dollars in damages for what they alleged was his plagiarism of their idea for a picture newsmagazine. They had submitted their dummy for Luce's consideration some months before *Life* came on the stands. But Luce, it seems, had no recollection of ever having seen the proposal. The submission was probably con-sidered by someone on the lower echelon of the *Time* staff and was re-jected. The resemblance between the dummy of the magazine sent by the Bruehl brothers and the existing *Life* could not be ignored.

The lawsuit was to be tried before Judge Ferdinand Pecora. As things stood, it was Moore's opinion that the plaintiffs would be successful in their litigation.

Clare listened to this dismal recital, then she asked to be excused for a moment. In her *Vanity Fair* files she found the dummy of the picture magazine she had prepared for submission to Condé Nast years earlier. It too was titled *Life*. In preparing the dummy according to Clare's prospectus, the art director of *Vanity Fair* had used two of Condé Nast's other employees, the Bruehl brothers.

She brought the dummy into the room. Moore was pacing up and down when she handed it to him. "Would this," she asked, "be of any help in proving that the concept of a picture magazine was not originated by the men who are suing Harry?"

Moore studied the dummy, and smiling, took it away with him.

A few days later, Clare Boothe Luce in a chic, tailored blue dress, a smart white hat and immaculate gloves took the witness stand in Judge Pecora's court. Tex Moore offered the dummy as an exhibit in evidence for identification, and handed it to the judge.

Pecora studied the dummy for at least thirty minutes while Clare fidgeted and waited on the stand. Then he leaned down from the bench. "Mrs. Luce, did you prepare this dummy for Condé Nast before you were married to Mr. Luce?"

"Yes," Clare replied, wondering why he had to make the obvious inquiry if he had studied the dummy.

"Were you acquainted with Mr. Luce when you prepared this dummy?"

"No, I wasn't. Of course I knew who he was but we had never met."

"Did you have any help in the development of this project, Mrs. Luce?"

"Yes, I did. The Bruehls were working for Nast. Doctor Agha told them what we wanted in the way of photographs for that dummy."

Judge Pecora called the plaintiffs' lawyer to the stand and handed him Mrs. Luce's dummy. The case was dismissed.

Tex Moore patted his sister-in-law on the shoulder. She had, he indicated, helped save *Life* magazine and Time Inc. a good many dollars.

Clare rushed home to report the good news to Harry. He listened to her recital, asked one or two questions, and then suggested it might be well to forget the matter. It was all, he said, a little embarrassing to Time Inc.

5

Before the Storm

In every aspect of Clare's life from 1929 to 1939 there is evidence of a questioning uncertainty, a compulsion to experiment—personally, politically, professionally. This impression is supported by the record of her failures and her successes. If she had in fact married George Brokaw for his money, she had accepted a very modest settlement when she divorced him. Although she speaks of her mother nowadays with loving admiration, this relationship didn't provide much satisfaction. David's attempted career in the stock-and-bond business had been embarrassing and costly to Clare. Harry Luce was no George Brokaw but this second marriage somehow failed to give Clare the fulfillment she was seeking.

Perhaps her trip up the ladder at *Vanity Fair* had been too quick and too easy. Perhaps that intuition of hers had warned the magazine could not survive (it ceased publication in 1936). Her try at newspaper columns for Paul Block and the Hearst syndicate was disappointing. On the surface her second marriage was a tremendous triumph, but any hope that being Mrs. Luce would open doors for her at *Time* was quickly dispelled. She was indeed pleased that Luce had acted on her suggestion to publish a picture magazine, but that idea was taken away from her and given to others to implement and control.

Politically Clare had moved from no interests and no opinions to become a strong supporter of F.D.R. and the New Deal. Baruch, who is popularly pictured as a great supporter of the Democrats during this period, actually disapproved of the Administration's fiscal policies, the enlargement of the Presidential authority, and the burgeoning bureaucracy. And his thinking eventually influenced Clare.

During this period, however, Clare's politics were moving toward the left. Her friendship with Helen Brown Norden, her co-worker on *Vanity Fair,* led her into a flirtation with Communism, for Mrs. Norden had married Jack Lawrenson, vice-president of the militant National Maritime Union.

Working conditions for American seamen in the Merchant Marine were deplorable enough to arouse the sympathies of any well-meaning citizen. On the West Coast, Australian-born Harry Bridges was waging a successful fight against low pay, unsafe vessels and indifferent shipowners. Seamen sailing out of the Atlantic ports and longshoremen working on the Eastern docks revolted against the leadership of the International Seamen's Union. Joseph Edwin Curran adopted Bridges' militant tactics and formed the National Maritime Union, and Helen Norden's husband became the Number Two man in the organization.

In the spring of 1936 Curran and Lawrenson led the Atlantic dock workers in a walkout. The I.S.U. didn't give in without a struggle and there was a period of violent warfare between the rival organizers.

Clare was a frequent visitor at the Lawrenson home on Charles Street in New York's Greenwich Village. Her sympathies were with Lawrenson because of her affection for his wife. She met all the leading firebrands in the Maritime Union and listened thoughtfully to their indictment of capitalism. She also met Harry Bridges and Joe Curran.

Curran was a tough-minded, violent man. The record of this period reveals that many responsible commentators and Congressmen held the suspicion that Curran was a Communist, a charge he vigorously denied and one which has never been proved. Until the Nazis marched on Russia, Curran was an advocate of peace and opposed our support of the Allied cause. When Hitler's attack brought Russia into the war, Curran reversed his field and earned the approval of many United States Government officials, including Leon Henderson, for the N.M.U.'s record of no strikes, no work stoppages until the war was won.

The same charge of Communist Party membership has been made against Harry Bridges. The Government attempted to make a case against the West Coast leader in 1939 in a series of hearings presided over by Harvard law professor James M. Landis on Alcatraz Island in San Francisco Bay.

Landis ruled that the Government failed to prove its case, but Clare Boothe Luce says that on the two occasions when she talked at any length with Harry Bridges he attempted to convert her to Communism.

Others have testified to the magnetism of Bridges' personality. Like a revivalist preacher on the sawdust trail, he must have appealed to Clare's humanism and aroused her compassion for others. When he was ill in a New York hospital, Clare went to see him. When the Abraham Lincoln Brigade was formed to fight in the Spanish Civil War she contributed $1,000.

Nothing is more paradoxical about the Communist Revolution than its appeal to wealthy capitalists. Competent United States agencies have established beyond doubt that in the decade of the thirties many prominent Americans were seduced by Marxism. Clare was no exception. Despite all the Government programs, the Depression had dragged on and she felt a sense of guilt because of her own affluence. She was disturbed by the poverty and misery about her. As the editor of *Vanity Fair* Clare had participated in many bull sessions with thoughtful, responsible writers trying to explore and develop a new governmental and social structure which would eliminate poverty and war.

Describing her near acceptance of the doctrines of Marx, she says, "I suspect now that the appeal of Communism for many young people and for me lay in its religious aspect. Communism was a complete, authoritarian religious structure, and the 'liberal' mind had grown weary and confused defending the 'inalienable right' to disorganize and exploit society according to its own notions of liberty. This had led to Hooverism and 'rugged individualism.'"

Luce had no such temptations. Communism was antithetical to Christianity. His stern Calvinistic upbringing automatically protected him. In this area Clare felt markedly inferior to her husband. The daughter of unchurched parents, moral judgments were a problem for her; they were easy for Luce. He had a solid sense of belonging, of being something. Luce questioned the Christian religion at times, but he never doubted it.

Whatever the factors which led Clare to very nearly accept the doctrines of Communism, her conversations with Bridges and the doctrinaire Marxist whom he brought to see her led her to the realization that for all the prattle about idealism, the hard-core Communists were committed to violent overthrow of the Government of the United States and dedicated to the use of compulsion and force to achieve their ends.

The turning point came one evening when an admitted Communist agent invited Clare to join the party and work with him. Clare, who despised Fascism because it employed bayonets to destroy freedom, was equally repulsed by the brutal compulsion inherent in Communism. She dropped her do-good role and again applied her talents to the theater.

In January 1937 Reliance Pictures paid $125,000 for the movie rights to *The Women,* and Clare was engaged as a consultant on the screenplay at a salary of $3,500 per week. Following this assignment, MGM put her under contract to write a screenplay from Norman Krasna's original story "Turnover," and she stopped in Hollywood en route to Honolulu for a conference with the producers. Luce, his brother Sheldon, Sheldon's wife, and Ann Brokaw joined her for the trip to the Islands, where, according to her publicity releases, she planned to work on a new play to be titled *Kiss the Boys Goodbye.*

Margaret Mitchell's romantic and overlong novel *Gone With the Wind* had become a dramatic best seller in 1936, and the studio's widely publicized search for an unknown actress to play the lead in the picture version was a topic of household conversation. What Clare provided in the play that Brock Pemberton produced was a satirical spoof of this flamboyant movie promotion. *Kiss the Boys Goodbye* opened in New York on September 28, 1938. The playgoing public found it lively entertainment.

That same week Luce purchased a sixty-acre estate on King Street in Greenwich, Connecticut. There were twenty-five rooms in the main house, two guest cottages and other out-buildings.

The critics were not entirely enthusiastic about *Kiss the Boys Goodbye* but it ran for two hundred and eighty-six performances and was included in the Burns Mantle annual selection as one of the ten best plays of the season.

Playwright Luce should have been content to let the work stand on its own feet for what it was—a deftly constructed, amusing lampoon of the overblown Hollywood talent for promotion. She wasn't. When Random House published the play in book form, she wrote an introduction claiming *Kiss the Boys Goodbye* was a political allegory about Fascism in America, saying, "We are not, perhaps, sufficiently aware that 'Southernism' is a particular and highly matured form of Fascism with which America has lived more or less peacefully for seventy-five years."

Those who had seen *Kiss the Boys Goodbye* and those who came to see it later on were unaware of any such social implications. But ideology was beginning to take hold in America. Perhaps Clare did have in mind using her Southern characters to call attention to the evil of the Third Reich. If so, her subtleties escaped the public. Another explanation for that rather startling preface might be found in the fact of Clare's disillusionment with Communism. Perhaps she hoped in retrospect to give her writing a social significance.

At this point in history Adolf Hitler's militaristic National Socialism was threatening the peace of the world. *Time-Life-Fortune* was a world-wide enterprise. Harry was required to make frequent trips to Europe, and he took Clare with him. Her contacts with the *Time* staffers convinced her that until Nazism, Fascism and Communism were all destroyed, the future of the world would be filled with dangerous uncertainties. Never content to play a passive role, she undertook to do something about it personally, and what she did was to write a truly ideological anti-Nazi play, *Margin for Error,* which was produced by Richard Aldrich and Richard Meyers at the Plymouth Theater in New York City on November 3, 1939, two months after the thrust of Hitler's Panzer battalions into Poland.

Harry wrote the preface for the published version which appeared in 1940, and gave his wife credit for bringing National Socialism to the stage for examination.

If she expected her husband to speak approvingly of her work she must have been disappointed. Was it rigid honesty, critical conscience or just an automatic defense against the anticipated charge of prejudice which prompted Harry to say:

". . . for in all these years of failure the difficulty has not in fact been to get national socialism on stage. The real difficulty has been to get on stage a convincing rebuttal to national socialism. It is in this that Miss Boothe has half succeeded. I am still waiting hungrily for the theater to give me a believable, disinterested Democrat. Let us see a man without any particular ax to grind and not so very much better than any of us who will throw back in the face of that challenge an enthusiastic love of freedom, championing of truth and defense of justice. The dramatist who can vitalize this occurrence will have justified in himself all that has ever been claimed for a free art in a land of freedom. That dramatist, I regret to say, is not, at the moment, my dear wife, Miss Boothe."

Mrs. Luce says her husband never raised his voice in her defense when her life or her work became the object of criticism because it had been thoroughly understood between them from the first day of their marriage that his magazines would never compromise their editorial integrity by going to the defense of the boss's wife. This was a proposition she willingly accepted intellectually. It was not always easy for her to do so emotionally. And Clare's daughter, Ann Brokaw, never questioned her stepfather's position.

In November 1937 Ann Clare had been enrolled in the Foxcroft School in Middleburg, Virginia. She was a much better than average student, and the letters exchanged between mother and daughter indicate a close and warm relationship. One of these letters from Ann to Clare reveals Ann's feelings for Harry and his work. She begins:

Oh, I am so mad I could spit! I'm sitting in English class and listening to our English professor, who always thinks she's right, murder *Life*. She just said that *Time* is good, *Fortune* is good, but *Life* is bad yellow journalism. She is telling the class that *Life* is a magazine for morons. These are her very words, mama . . . oh, how I hate her . . . she's smug, she thinks she is always right . . . she's telling the girls in this class that the only reason *Life* is as popular as it is is because it appeals to the cheap people in the street . . . the editors print anything sensational. No matter what it is, it's just yellow journalism. I grant her that pop's magazine is easier to read than *Time,* but hell! She says that no really intelligent people read it because they can see behind the magazine's policy. Policy, my eye! A lot she knows about pop's good ideas, and I have to sit here quietly and listen to her. Oh, damn her hide! ! ! ! ! Gosh, I would give anything to squelch her and see that smug face of hers light up in surprise. She's the academic head of the school, too. But there goes the bell, I've gotta go to Latin now. I'll write you later. . . .

Like most of her countrymen, Clare did not want to believe the world would go to war. Emotionally, she belonged to the group which had buried its head collectively in the sand; but intellectually she realized there was no escape. As early as 1938 she started a letter to a friend with these words: *"God knows whether or not this may be the last letter from America, which you will receive in a peaceful world."*

Hitler's legions conquered Poland in the first three weeks of September 1939, following the signing of the ten-year nonaggression treaty between Nazi Germany and the Soviet Union on August 23. A majority of Americans were strongly isolationist. They had been lulled into believing there would be "peace in our time," after Chamberlain's visit to Munich. One public-opinion poll reported that seventy-eight percent of the people believed we had everything to lose and nothing to gain by supporting the Allies. *Fortune* magazine asked this question: "If it appears that Germany is defeating England, should the U.S. declare war on Germany?" Seventy-one percent of those who responded said no.

Harry Luce believed there was no way America could stay out. He didn't absolve the Allies of all guilt but it was clear to him that Germany and Russia were the aggressors. He wanted the United States to recognize reality and he urged immediate aid for beleaguered Britain.

Clare has frequently complained that the editors of *Time-Life* never treated her cordially. She resents the fact that *Time* never put her on its cover, but *Life* magazine gave her three successful plays feature treatment and in 1939, when she expressed an interest in going to Europe to "see for herself," Harry made her an accredited *Life* correspondent. She sailed for Naples on February 24, 1940. Edna Woolman Chase, her old friend and onetime boss on *Vogue,* went with her to cover the Paris fashion openings. It was the beginning of a trip which took Clare to Rome, Paris, London, Brussels, back to Paris, and then home by way of London and Lisbon.

In a very particular and special way, World War II from February to June, 1940, changed the mind, the thinking and the direction of Clare Boothe Luce. Until that time Clare had never been able to concentrate on a single activity or focus attention on a single objective for any great length of time. She had been an in-between, part-time playwright, a sometime hostess, part-time mother, indefatigable searcher for new truths and new understandings. She was regarded as bright, brittle and witty.

All of the errors in judgment, misrepresentations of Hitler's intent, the complacent optimism of the French, the optimistic inaction of the British, and the tragic uniform indifference of the Americans were being noted and reported by writers in Europe. Being an eyewitness to all this was a profound experience for Clare. The distance she traveled in her mind is more significant than the geography she covered.

As a correspondent for *Life,* Clare had entree to interviews with most of the political leaders in Europe. Through her old friend René de Chambrun she arranged to visit the Maginot Line and came away with the depressed feeling Hitler was fighting a war of movement. It was, she concluded, stupid to believe the Germans would attack the Maginot when the route through the Low Countries was open and relatively un-protected.

In England, Clare visited her old friends American Ambassador Joseph P. Kennedy, Winston Churchill and Lord Beaverbrook. Ambassador Kennedy, who had been undiplomatically critical of Britain's failure to prepare for war, told her, "Remember this, we Americans can live quite comfortably in a world of English snobbery and British complacency . . . but we can't live in a world of Nazis and German brutality." Churchill, out of power and out of favor, believed Britain would respond before all was lost.

It didn't require clairvoyance to recognize that the Germans were only waiting for better weather. Clare sent a cable to Luce: "Come, the curtain is going up." He joined her and they were in Brussels when the Panzers started their drive to the Channel. They escaped by car to the French border ahead of the German tanks and dive bombers.

Luce went to New York immediately. He intended to arouse the conscience of the American people. Clare followed by way of Lisbon

two weeks later, to record all that she had seen and heard in a book—
Europe in the Spring, published by Alfred A. Knopf in September 1940.
It wasn't the first, or perhaps the best, account of the events which
made World War II inevitable but it was reprinted eight times. André
Maurois, Walter Lippmann and Arthur Krock praised its style and content, and it does offer insights which are still of interest. And her con-
cluding paragraphs reveal that at least Clare could resolve any doubts
in her own mind. She says:

The situation as it stands in America is just about as it stood in the spring in
Europe. You see few people here in America who really care very much
about living a Christian life in a democratic world. But I am glad that I
went to Europe in the spring because there I found out what I went to
find out: I found out what I, anyway, mean by Democracy. I mean what
the Declaration of Independence meant by it: "Liberty and justice for all."
And when the Declaration of Independence said "for all," it did not mean
merely for United States citizens; it was written before there was a United
States of America, before there were Americans. Then we were a people
who had left the Old World in order to redefine and live a Christian way
of life, and who found that one of the principles of a Christian way of life
was "Liberty and justice for all." So we fought for it, and that is what made
us Americans. And out of that revolutionary belief, by the grace of God,
we made of ourselves a great and mighty nation, so mighty that we could if
we would, again by the grace of God, set out on a program for a thousand
years of world democracy and world Christianity.

But I think if we no longer believe what we believed then and are no
longer willing to fight for it, it is very likely that our "Christian Democracy," like this book, is at last finished.

These are the good old days now.

The war dominated public thinking, yet all the questions it provoked were political. Luce believed that F.D.R. had failed to arouse the
American people. He and Clare went to the White House for a private
conference with Roosevelt. The only other person present was Harry
Hopkins. Luce wanted the Government to give immediate aid to Britain
and undertook to promote public approval for lend-leasing some of
our destroyers to help the Allies combat Hitler's submarine fleet. In

Luce's view, Roosevelt's reaction was overcautious, but the President did say he would take action if he could be convinced the voters would approve.

Baruch told Clare that in his opinion the New Deal domestic policies had prolonged the Depression. He criticized the Administration's neutrality and was particularly concerned over Roosevelt's refusal to prepare the nation for war.

Clare believed that Roosevelt had determined to seek a third term and was playing politics with freedom's destiny but she didn't understand the extent of Harry's determination to change American foreign policy by changing the identity of the occupant of the White House. She was so busy writing and rewriting *Europe in the Spring* that she was out of touch with the American scene, and particularly with her husband's activities.

The Luces were spending that summer of 1940 in the house on King Street in Greenwich. When Luce telephoned from New York to ask Clare if she would like to have dinner with the Davenports and the Willkies, she agreed as a matter of course. She knew Russell Davenport, the editor of *Fortune,* and his wife Marcia, a novelist and biographer, but she had never heard of Wendell Willkie, and as they were driving to the Davenport home in Westport, Connecticut, that evening, she asked Harry about the Willkies.

Her husband was dumfounded. Didn't she know that Willkie was a Horatio Alger folk hero who had been elected president of the great Commonwealth and Southern utility system in 1933 when it was almost bankrupt and turned it into an expanding ten-state operation? He told her that Willkie had been born in the little town of Elwood, Indiana, that he had been graduated from the state university, entered law school, and built a very substantial practice in Akron, Ohio. Willkie had, Luce went on, worked in the wheat fields in Minnesota, dressed tools in the oil fields of Texas, and fought in World War I.

What Luce didn't tell her was that in the period she had been out of the country, a small but powerful group of New Yorkers had decided Willkie should be nominated on the Republican ticket to oppose Roosevelt's third-term aspirations.

So far as Mrs. Luce was concerned, the dinner was just another pleasant social occasion. She discovered that Willkie was roughhewn, very frank in his opinions, and like everyone else, he talked about the war.

After dinner, their conversation turned to politics. Clare concentrated on her needlepoint. She had learned that in situations such as this one, Luce liked to dominate the conversation. She remembers hearing Willkie asking Luce if he thought either Taft or Dewey could defeat Roosevelt. Luce said he didn't think so.

Willkie then began to describe his conception of the kind of candidate it would take—a businessman with broad experience, one who traveled throughout the United States and understood the people, a new face, a man who had been successful in his own business or profession, but with a nonpolitical background. The implication was that the man Willkie had in mind would be someone just like Luce.

Over the years, a number of national columnists had accused Luce of having political ambitions, implying that he thought the people would be very fortunate indeed if he would consent to serve as their President. Clare couldn't see Luce as a candidate. In her view, he was too reserved to appeal to the masses and too dogmatic to get along with the politicians. She said, "Now, Mr. Willkie, you know better than to think that any businessman in this international age can get nominated and elected President of the United States."

Luce kicked his wife's ankle under the cocktail table, jumped up, took out his watch and announced they must leave.

When they were in the car, Clare expressed her bewilderment. "On the way over here you told me that Wendell Willkie was a great guy. Now you know yourself, he must be an absolute fool to sit there and try to persuade you to run for President." Describing what followed, Clare has said, "I think it was one of the few times in our life together when Harry was truly furious with me. He said that until that moment he cherished a foolish notion that I was an intelligent woman."

"Wendell Willkie doesn't want me to be President," Harry said. "He wants to be President himself. All that talk about a successful businessman was just his way of opening the conversation."

Then he told his wife that Russell Davenport had taken a leave of absence from *Fortune* in order to devote his energies full time to the Willkie candidacy.

Clare had been to political conventions. She knew that a rank newcomer with no political base didn't have the chance of a "snowball in hell" of being nominated. She thought that Harry and Russell Davenport and all the others were just "whistling in the wind."

During the next few weeks Clare discovered there had been a very subtle campaign on behalf of Willkie, supported by *Time-Life-Fortune, The New York Times* and Wall Street.

The convention met in Philadelphia on Monday, June 24, 1940. Governor Thomas E. Dewey of New York and Senator Robert A. Taft of Ohio were the preconvention favorites. Beneath the surface there was some sentiment for Senator Arthur Vandenberg of Michigan. No one in the party appeared to take the Willkie candidacy seriously.

Clare went to Philadelphia with Harry, and Republican Joe Martin, Permanent Chairman of the convention, invited her to sit on the platform.

In 1940 the Republican Party was represented by an even one thousand delegates. New York with ninety-two was the strongest state, Pennsylvania with seventy-two, Illinois third, and Ohio fourth. Ex-President Hoover addressed the convention on Tuesday. There was an eleven-minute demonstration when he concluded. The platform, declaring "the Republican Party firmly opposed to involving this nation in a foreign war and against a third term for any President," was adopted Wednesday afternoon, June 26, and Chairman Martin ordered the nomination of candidates for President.

New York delegate John Lord O'Brian placed the name of Thomas E. Dewey before the convention. Grove Patterson of Ohio nominated Senator Robert A. Taft and Charles Halleck of Indiana asked the delegates to choose Wendell L. Willkie. In addition to the principal contenders, seven favorite sons were nominated. The process consumed so much time that the first roll call of the states was delayed until 4:30 on Thursday afternoon.

The results were inconclusive but Dewey was in the lead with 360 votes, Taft next with 189 and Willkie third with 105. The rest were divided between the favorite sons.

As the secretary started calling the roll for the second ballot, Clare noticed that Joe Martin was keeping a running tabulation. When Dewey lost seven in Illinois and Willkie picked up five, he winked at Clare and showed her the figures. Dewey continued to drop, one in Kentucky, one in Louisiana, four in Maryland, one in Minnesota, eight in Missouri and nine in Nebraska. Just before the vote of Puerto Rico was recorded, Martin showed Clare his totals. Dewey had lost twenty-two; Willkie had gained sixty-six. He told her the figures proved that Harry's candidate was gaining and said what the Willkie forces needed now was a little time to work on the delegates.

Clare asked how that could be done.

Martin said, "Everybody's tired. I could recess the convention for a couple of hours."

Everyone who has watched a national political convention on television now knows how simple it is for the chairman to declare a recess when he wants one by recognizing some delegate who is clued in advance to make the motion, calling for a voice vote and interpreting the response to suit himself. But Mrs. Luce, who still had a great deal to learn about politics, didn't understand. She does remember telling Joe Martin that if he thought a recess would help Willkie and there was any way for him to call one, she personally hoped he would do so.

When the results of the second roll call were announced, Martin pounded his gavel and announced that he would recognize Governor Aiken of Vermont for the purpose of moving a recess until 8:30 P.M. Then he called for the vote and declared the "ayes" victorious.

When the convention reconvened, Willkie was nominated on the sixth ballot. Perhaps he would have won without that recess, but bachelor Joe Martin gallantly told Clare that he wouldn't have recessed the convention if she hadn't asked him to do so, that this was the key to Willkie's victory.

Mrs. Henry Luce had no intention of participating in the campaign after that convention; she was provoked into doing so by newspaper columnist Dorothy Thompson. Miss Thompson, a lifelong Republican, and a forceful critic of the New Deal, had been beating the anti-Nazi drum for more than five years. Clare had first met her during the *Vanity Fair* period. A friendship developed based on mutual respect and the fact that in 1938 and 1939 playwright Boothe and columnist Thompson were trying to reverse the apathetic attitude toward Hitler. But Clare was outraged when Dorothy Thompson, in early October, announced via her column that she was deserting the Republican candidate, Wendell Willkie, who was also her dear, personal friend, to vote for Roosevelt, whose re-election, she said, was essential to the future of America and the world. Miss Thompson dismissed the anti-third termers as being the victims of sentimental tradition.

Clare wrote a strong letter to the New York *Herald Tribune,* publisher of Miss Thompson's column, condemning her friend for deserting principle in favor of expediency.

Luce showed the letter to Willkie before it was mailed and the Republican nominee suggested it would be more effective if Clare expanded the letter into a speech and delivered it before an audience. Luce thought well of the suggestion. Clare says when she appeared before a "Work for Willkie" rally at the Manhattan Center on West 34th Street, October 15, it was the first time in her life she had ever made a public speech.

Willkie had gotten off to a slow start. The Hoosier businessman was not a very compelling speaker. He quickly overtaxed his vocal chords, and the resultant hoarseness and the habit of shouting rather than talking into the microphone all added up to a rather dismal image, particularly when his performance was contrasted with the great voice and seasoned campaign techniques of F.D.R.

Clare went to work on Dorothy Thompson, whom she described as "a woman with a great heart and a fine brain, who had fallen victim to an anxiety neurosis because she had not been able to arouse the nation to physically do battle with Hitler."

"Miss Thompson," Clare said, "became the victim of that emotional disease called acute fear. If there were a doctor in the house, he could tell you better than I the psychology of fear."

She reminded her audience of the attacks Dorothy Thompson had made on Roosevelt and the New Deal, and then likened the Thompson flip-flop to a girl in an apache dance team who succumbs adoringly to her partner's brutal treatment.

The newspapers loved it. They called it a catfight and cheered the girls on to greater efforts.

Dorothy Thompson responded with a personal attack on Bruce Barton, a Willkie supporter, who, she said, "believes that everything in this world has been put over by advertising, including Jesus of Nazareth." She said:

Miss Boothe is the "body by Fisher" in this campaign, she's the Brenda Frazier of the Great Crusade, she's torn herself loose from the Stork Club to serve her country. Miss Boothe has everything to pull in the orders, the Powers model face, the recommendations of Lady Whoiswho, whether from her lovely apartment in the Super-Ritz or from the exquisite little yacht that was a gift from Lord Peevesh, she says to you "I use only Willkie."

I've met you before, Clare, in various costumes and under various hats, I've met your type in the Cliveden set and the last time I saw you the eternally repeating type of you, the lady Kingmaker, was in the apartment of the last Prime Minister of France.

The newspaper *PM,* in its cover story, reported that CBS had fifty telephone calls in response to Miss Thompson's speech. The audience, it said, was deeply offended by her flippant remarks about religion and her vicious attack on Mrs. Luce. To go with the story, the newspaper ran two photographs: Thompson in a stern, straight-on, unflattering pose and Clare a three-quarter demure and smiling face. Clare was in politics. She challenged Dorothy Thompson to a debate and Miss Thompson responded with the following wire: "Warmest congratulations on your wonderful performance of *The Women* and your offer of a part in the cast. Fear, however, role doesn't suit my type."

Clare's forthright stand for Willkie (she made more than forty appearances) produced a sharp division in the ranks of her old associates. She received thousands of letters and telegrams. Condé Nast wrote, "Congratulations on your speech. I like particularly the parallel you draw between the leadership which led France to its ruin and our own present leadership." Her nephew Clifford Brokaw wired, "I am proud of you and your stand under most important crisis in the history of our beloved country." And Frank Crowninshield said, "Congratulations. Coronor just leaving Thompson residence, declares it a murder. Calls it assault with intent to kill."

Walter Winchell cracked that when he encountered Clare and Dorothy in the same room at a night club he warned them, "Ladies, ladies, remember there are gentlemen present."

Clare was sincere in her criticism of F.D.R. and the New Deal. It was obvious to her that America would have to enter the war and she regarded Roosevelt's promise to the mothers and fathers of America that he would never send their boys to fight in a foreign war as the ultimate in self-serving political dishonesty. She learned that friendship has no bearing on politics. Herbert Bayard Swope sent her the most critical wire she received during the entire campaign, and General Hugh Johnson, supporting Roosevelt, had appeared on the same platform with her to contest her endorsement of Willkie.

As soon as the ballots were counted, and it didn't take long to determine that F.D.R. had won his third term, Clare sent a congratulatory telegram to Dorothy Thompson, ending with a plea that despite their political differences they could continue to be friends.

Vincent Sheean, who wrote Miss Thompson's biography, found the telegram among her papers, and the first draft of Miss Thompson's reply, which consisted of a bitter rejection of the olive branch Clare had offered. The first wire was never sent. Dorothy Thompson had scratched out all the ugly words and merely said, "Of course, Clare, we'll always be friends." They were too. And when Clare became a candidate for Congress two years later, Dorothy Thompson was one of her strong supporters.

Clare says now that her participation in the Willkie campaign taught her one great truth: Men can disagree violently and the press will acknowledge the possibility of a reasonable difference of opinion. If women disagree, it immediately becomes a catfight, a fingernail-scratching or hair-pulling contest—and she resolved never again to engage in a public dispute with another woman.

When Helen Gahagan Douglas was elected to Congress from California, she was pushed as the Democrats' answer to Clare Boothe

Luce. When Mrs. Douglas came to Washington, Clare made it a point to see her. She says the conversation went like this:

"I told Mrs. Douglas that if she said it was a nice day and I happened to observe that it looked like rain, the press would blow it up into a great big dispute. I wanted to make an agreement with her . . . we would never discuss the same subject on the same day, and we wouldn't under any consideration comment on what the other had said."

The new Congresswoman from California agreed to the ground rules. Douglas of California and Luce of Connecticut almost always divided on their votes, but they never gave the press an opportunity to use the terms "catfight" or "hair-pulling" contest in relation to their remarks or their votes.

In the spring of 1941 public attention was focused on the war in Europe. Both ethnically and historically the American people identified with the warring nations across the Atlantic. Luce's emotional ties with China and his belief that American interests were jeopardized by the Sino-Japanese war caused him to attempt to do something about it personally. On April 28 the Luces left San Francisco for Chungking, China, to visit Generalissimo Chiang Kai-shek's temporary capital on the Yangtze River in the mountainous province of Szechwan. En route they stopped in Honolulu, Manila and Hong Kong.

Clare and Harry both shared the general assumption that the U.S. fleet based at Pearl Harbor could successfully defend our Pacific outposts. In the Philippines, where they spent three nights, they discovered an underground uneasiness. They visited with General Douglas A. MacArthur, who had been detached from the American Army to serve as commander in chief of the new independent Philippine forces, and Rear Admiral Thomas C. Hart, commander of the U.S. Navy's Far Eastern fleet.

Francis Bowes Sayre, who had joined the New Deal as an Assistant Secretary of State in 1933, was the U.S. High Commissioner in the Philippines. President Roosevelt, with the approval of Congress, had promised independence to the islands at the end of a ten-year waiting period. In the interim the Philippine Government under President Manuel Quezon was virtually supreme in matters of domestic authority.

The United States was still obligated to handle defense and foreign relations. The Philippine people were extremely nationalistic, and during this interregnum period the dual authority shared by Sayre and Quezon had created considerable tension.

When the Luces arrived, they discovered that Sayre and Quezon were engaged in a bitter public dispute over which Government should pay the cost of constructing air-raid shelters in Manila. The Philippine President insisted the United States should pay the cost. Sayre, just as adamant, said it was the responsibility of the Philippine Government. When Luce questioned Sayre about this problem, the Commissioner dismissed the matter as a trivial disagreement. The Philippine Government had been cutting its defense budget every year; the proposed bomb shelters had become a political issue. Sayre believed that all of the U.S. funds should go directly into military preparedness.

The Luces went on to China, landing first at Hong Kong and then flying more than six hundred miles (over territory occupied by the invading Japanese) to Chungking. The landing strip in use at the time was a portion of the river bed from which the Yangtze had receded during the dry season. Clare wondered what they did when the river was in flood.

Dr. H. H. Kung, head of the civil government of China, was their host at a breakfast reception in a house which Harry later described as consisting of "four rooms on each of two floors . . . the kind of home any missionary might have." They went on to Kailing House, the only foreign hotel in Chungking, to meet the American reporters covering the Generalissimo. The press corps consisted of F. McCracken Fisher of UP, Melville Jacoby of NGC, F. T. Durdin of *The New York Times,* and Teddy White of *Time-Life.*

White's dispatches to *Time* had been consistently critical of Chiang Kai-shek. He accused the "Gissimo" and Madame Chiang of enriching themselves and living in luxury. When Clare and Harry went to pay an official visit to Chiang, they were received in a very ordinary house, one which was similar to the quarters occupied by the American press contingent.

The Luces were anxious to visit the front lines. To get there they flew from Chungking in a single-engine Beechcraft to Sian in Shensi Province, then went by car and Mongolian pony to the theater of operations at Tungkuan on the Yellow River. Here the 167th Division of the Chinese regular army had been holding the Japanese at bay.

Mrs. Luce was the first American woman journalist to visit the Yellow River front. She interviewed the General and his wife for *Vogue* magazine, and her articles suggest that she shared her husband's enthusiasm for the Chinese cause. Luce was convinced the Chinese must ultimately be triumphant.

Originally the Luces had planned to return to the United States by way of Rangoon and Singapore. The realities of the military situation as explained to him by Chiang caused Luce to change his mind. The Japanese had already occupied Swatow, Amoy and Foochow on the South China coast, less than a thousand miles from the Philippine Islands. Japan was an Axis partner. If the United States should become a belligerent on the side of the Allies, Chiang was certain the Philippines would be attacked.

The Luces flew from Hong Kong to Manila and stayed in the Philippines from May 23 to June 4, 1941. Harry had a number of conferences with President Quezon. He emphasized his belief that any effective defense of the Philippines would depend upon the degree of cooperation existing between the two countries, and pointed out that excessive Philippine nationalism could alienate the American public and reduce the flow of supplies pouring into the islands from the United States.

The Luces went to Baguio, a summer resort north of Manila, to attended a state dinner as guests of Quezon, and the onetime insurgent rebel leader came into Manila to dine with the Luces, General MacArthur and Francis B. Sayre, U.S. High Commissioner in the Philippines. Clare admits she was greatly impressed by MacArthur's stern military professionalism and intrigued by the historical incongruity of MacArthur's presence in the Philippines. In 1901, when the U.S. troops had crushed the Philippine insurrection, the young rebel commander, Manuel Quezon, had surrendered his sword to the American Military Governor of the Philippines, General Arthur MacArthur, Douglas MacArthur's father. And now, thirty-six years later, Quezon had asked that general's son to take charge of building the islands' defensive forces.

At one of the dinner parties Clare was seated next to Admiral Thomas Hart, and she channeled the conversation into a discussion of a possible Japanese attack in the Pacific.

Hart assured her the Japanese had their hands full in China. He was confident there was nothing to worry about unless the United States changed its policy.

Clare asked for an explanation.

"They can't continue to fight China without us," he said. "We supply the oil to fuel their military machines; we sell them the scrap iron they must have. Our people keep talking about supporting China from a moral standpoint, but we're not doing much to build the Burma Road."

Lieutenant Colonel Charles Willoughby, General Grunert's Chief of Intelligence, was seated next to Clare on the other side. She asked him to comment on the opinions Admiral Hart had expressed.

Willoughby responded that Hart's argument was sound up to a certain point. He thought that if Washington got the United States involved with Hitler and the Italians, the Japanese might have to attack. But he agreed with the naval man's basic assumption that so long as the Japanese were getting petroleum and steel from the United States, and the Chinese armies were cut off from the outside world, the chance of a Japanese attack was minimal. If it came to that, Willoughby thought the Japanese would try to follow the pattern of blitzkrieg Hitler set in Poland. It was his opinion that as long as our fleet was on station in the Pacific, the Japanese wouldn't dare move. But he warned that if we were to divert any of our present strength to the Atlantic, or permit any concentration at Pearl or Cavite, they were sure to take advantage of it.

Mrs. Luce waited for a convenient moment and then asked President Quezon for his opinion. Clare admits that her memories of some of the events which took place so long ago have been dimmed by time, but her conversation with the Philippine President that night casts some light on the tragic event which catapulted the United States into World War II.

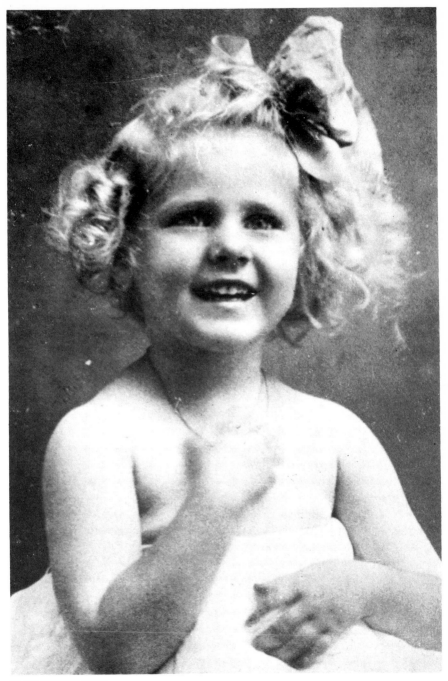

Baby Clare.

The Boothe family on the steps of the parsonage in Port Chester, New York. Left to right: John Walter Boothe; Sarah Boothe Pryor; Mr. Woodall, husband of Laura Boothe; Laura Boothe Woodall; Mrs. William F. Boothe; William F. Boothe (Clare's father); Mrs. John W. F. Boothe; Rev. John W. F. Boothe; Charles Boothe; Edwin Boothe; Lillian Boothe Munn; Grace Boothe Maloney; Madeline Boothe Reed; Mary Boothe Banks.

RIGHT: Schoolgirl Clare and her mother.

BOTH PAGES: CLARE BOOTHE LUCE

Mrs. George Brokaw on the beach.

CLARE BOOTHE LUCE

LEFT: Millionaire George Brokaw and his wife.

Clare Brokaw and her very good friend Bernie Baruch.

RIGHT: General Chiang Kai-shek, Madame Chiang, General Stilwell, Chinese officer, Clare Boothe Luce, May 1940. TIME INC.

Henry R. Luce and Clare in a cornfield at Mepkin.

Candidate Luce speaks to the Connecticut state convention of the Republican party, 1942.

Republican Presidential nominee Wendell Willkie, supported by Clare Boothe Luce.

Ambassador Luce and Henry R. Luce leave church in Rome.

Scuba diver Clare Boothe Luce.

LEFT: Vice-President Richard M. Nixon and Clare Boothe Luce at the Vice-President's birthday party in 1956.

RIGHT: Congresswoman Luce and her good friend the Honorable Winston Churchill. He encouraged her amateur painting. PUBLIFOTO-ROMA

Congresswoman Luce visits the front in Italy. U.S. ARMY

CLARE BOOTHE LUCE   Clare and Henry Luce.

Quezon didn't think of the Japanese as enemies. He didn't believe his islands were in any danger of being attacked. But if he was wrong, if he had miscalculated the Japanese intent, he would be warned long before an attack could take place.

Quezon told her he had secret agents occupying confidential positions in the Japanese Government. One of them was in the Japanese naval headquarters. The fleet, he assured her, could not move against the Philippines or Hawaii without his knowledge. He did not share the U.S. view of Hitler and Mussolini, and his representatives were at that moment engaged in talks with the Japanese Government concerning the future development of Asia.

When Clare reported this conversation to Luce, he told her that in all probability Quezon was telling the truth about his spy apparatus. He thought it would be most unusual if the Philippine Government had not developed an elaborate intelligence network. He also believed the Japanese had their observers in Manila and Hawaii.

The Luces arrived in San Francisco on June 4, 1941. They had spent twelve days in Manila. Harry's report of the trip was published in *Life* on June 30, and Clare wrote two pieces for the same magazine, "Destiny Crosses the Dateline" and "Wings Over China." Neither Harry nor Clare wrote anything to indicate they believed American interests in the Pacific were in danger. But privately they thought the U.S. commanders were underestimating the situation.

In August Clare Luce went back to the Philippines as a *Life* correspondent. It was obvious that Douglas MacArthur would become an increasingly important figure in world events, *Life* magazine should have a close-up, and Clare wanted to write it. She had another reason for believing the Philippines might soon be on the front pages. The United States had embargoed aviation fuel to the Japanese, halted the export of scrap iron, and renewed its earlier promises to open the Burma Road. The three conditions Admiral Hart had prescribed as essential to a Japanese move against the United States had been fulfilled.

On August 31 Clare flew to Manila. She contacted Colonel Willoughby, who she discovered was a great admirer of MacArthur, and made arrangements for the interviews necessary to complete the *Life* story. Then she looked up Admiral Hart and put the question to him point-blank, "When would the war come to the Pacific?"

She quoted his earlier conversation, reciting the conditions he had postulated as essential before the Japanese would think about an attack on U.S. Pacific bases.

Hart's reply was, "You have a very excellent memory, Mrs. Luce. I may have told you something like that, but as of now I don't want to either repeat it or deny it."

Mrs. Luce asked General MacArthur if the islands were defensible. He told her they would be, provided they had enough time.

"How much," she asked, "would be enough?"

The spring of 1942, late March or early April, if the material promised to him was delivered by then.

Clare says she found MacArthur a difficult man to interview. He resented every minute taken from his work. If, as some have said, Mac-Arthur was publicity conscious, he didn't give her that impression. At one of their meetings she did tell him of her admiration for Colonel Willoughby, and his competence, adding, "He's the only man I have spoken with on General Grunert's staff who admires you and doesn't resent the change in command." Clare's recommendation may have done nothing more than reinforce MacArthur's prior opinion of Willougby, but when Grunert returned to the United States, MacArthur requested that Colonel Willoughby be permitted to stay in the Philippines to handle military intelligence, a responsibility he discharged until the end of the war.

Mrs. Luce left Manila for Honolulu on October 7, 1941, and went into a hospital with what the doctors diagnosed as an acute fever, exact cause unknown. When she was discharged she spent two or three days with Doris Duke at the American heiress' estate on Oahu, and it was there she wrote the first draft of her MacArthur close-up.

The editors of *Life* liked Clare's story on Douglas MacArthur. They agreed that the new commander of USAFFE was colorful enough to merit special treatment in the magazine, but they didn't accept Clare's prediction that if the Japanese moved against the Philippines at all, they would do so before the spring of 1942.

Mrs. Luce's correspondence from Hawaii sheds considerable illumination on the articles she wrote about MacArthur.

In a letter to Noel Busch, who was then an editor of *Life,* she said:

You will see at once that it is a very laudatory article. It is in fact a big "build-up" of MacArthur. There are quite a few unpleasant things to be said about the man. I have avoided saying most of them, and for a good reason: In the whole Far East American military prestige is now indissolubly linked with the military (and personal) prestige of the General. He said in his own rather lurid words, "on the eve of a great battle." Anything which might tend to destroy his prestige in the eyes of his troops, the Filipinos, or for that matter, the British at Singapore, the Dutch, the Japanese, will inevitably weaken our military effort. The man is definitely *not* a "phony." Therefore, why point out that he really *is* a bit of a swashbuckler and overwhelmingly "ambitious"?

For the above reasons too I have left out of this record that he [MacArthur] had *really* had a terrible run around and had been given the gate as Field Marshal by that wily Malaysian Quezon, as late as June of this year. Quezon was sick of doling out funds to MacArthur, needed every last dime for his work of self-glorification, his "pyramids," "Quezon City" and Quezon bridges, buildings, etc. . . .

. . . At the General's own request I have omitted any mention of his salary as Field Marshal. He puts it at $18,000 a year. But with perquisites —that splendiferous penthouse and all the food he and his friends can eat, and with investments he's made in the Philippines (nothing improper was ever suggested by anyone about these) and with his salary as retired Major General ($6,000) and whatever he gets now, the General financially has done well by MacArthur. . . .

. . . Though enormously popular with the Filipino "Tao," the Americans on the Island have always disliked him. . . .

Clare went on to say that MacArthur was not an admirer of F.D.R., was critical of American foreign policy in the Far East, and "MacArthur, 'the prophet,' has also from time to time delivered himself of some arrant nonsense."

Clare said that most of the preparedness in the Philippines had been accomplished by General Grunert, and that MacArthur had reaped the benefit. She said that instead of the one hundred and twenty-five thousand well-trained soldiers MacArthur claimed, the Philippine forces probably mustered only about forty thousand.

The eight-page letter ended with this appraisal of the American military leader:

But, MacArthur, by prestige and brains, was just the better man of the two [better than Grunert], and—here is the crux of the matter: he had more vision, more far-sightedness, more savvy, and also he had a better military *plan* for the Island's defense than Grunert.

On the twenty-second of November *The New York Times,* which Mrs. Luce read in New York, carried a small story with a Manila dateline on an interior page. The dispatch briefly noted that President Manuel Quezon had made a very incendiary speech on the campus of the university over an island-wide radio hookup. He had renewed his attack on Francis Sayre. According to the *Times,* Quezon told his audience that if the Philippines were bombed, he personally would hang Francis Sayre from a lamppost because it was Sayre who had prevented the construction of adequate shelters in Manila.

The item concluded with the information that following his speech, Quezon, who was suffering from tuberculosis, had been lifted into an ambulance and been driven to Baguio, in the mountains, about a hundred and fifty miles north of Manila.

Mrs. Luce's first reaction was one of regret over the fact that the old feud had broken out again. Then she reread the dispatch. Why had Quezon suddenly attacked Sayre? What could he hope to gain at this stage by doing so? Certainly such an outburst would not build the bomb shelters. Then it occurred to her that the only logical motive for such an attack would be an attempt on the part of the Philippine President to exonerate himself. Did he know an attack was coming? Had his sources informed him the Japanese were preparing to move? Were his words just for the record, to establish in the minds of his countrymen the fact that he, their President, had been attempting for months to procure the bomb shelters?

Clare tried to call Commissioner Sayre on the long-distance telephone. He wasn't available. She spoke to his aide, Navy Captain Bill Priestly. "What had happened to prompt Quezon to make such an attack on Sayre?"

Priestly said he thought the President had just gone off his rocker. "He's hysterical . . . probably got some bad news from his doctor. We're concerned about it but I can't tell you anything more."

When Luce came home that night, his wife showed him the item in the *Times*. "There can be only one explanation. When I was there he and Sayre had patched up their difficulties and were getting along famously. You remember what Quezon told me about his pipe line to Japan. Quezon must know the Japanese are going to attack and Sayre doesn't believe him."

Luce, who had never in his life done anything on impulse, took the night train to Washington, D.C. The next day he was received by a general in the intelligence section.

He reviewed the situation carefully and methodically, outlining all the information he and Clare had personally gathered in Manila. He emphasized Admiral Hart's opinion that the Japanese might be forced to military action if we cut off their supply of petroleum and scrap iron and opened the Burma Road.

Luce was an ardent and persuasive advocate when he believed in the cause. "The action of Quezon attacking Sayre cannot," he said, "be explained in any other way. The President of the Philippines must think an assault is in the making."

The Government's intelligence officer listened patiently, then politely expressed his admiration for the publisher of *Time-Life-Fortune*, made some flattering remarks about the publisher's wife, and concluded by asking a question of his own. In essence, didn't Mr. Luce really think the intelligence agencies of the United States Government were a little more reliable than his wife's intuitive judgments? The Government should depend on its established sources, although Mrs. Luce, he admitted, was a very beautiful woman.

When Luce was asked about this incident twenty-five years later, he said, "That general made me feel very insignificant. I almost asked him to excuse my impertinence, and went home with my tail between my legs."

There is some support for Mrs. Luce's contention that she anticipated the Japanese attack on Pearl Harbor. In a letter she wrote Captain
Bill Priestly on December 1, 1941:

From here it looks as though your Christmas might be an unusually
hot one, even for Manila. I don't think Washington is out of the talking
state yet. By and large, it still intends to win this war with blank checks,
maps and volumes of newsprint. At any rate, Washington has once again
presented Japan with its "basic principles"—and piously leaves the next
move to Tokyo.

Unless the Japs jump the gun, I doubt Washington will. Of course,
many people who ought to know say "Time is working against Japan any
way." I saw Time work against Germany all during the "phoney" war in
Europe too! If they are right, then the Japs know it and will declare war and
take the initiative. Oddly enough, the American people would "go" for a
Jap-American war. And they still won't for a German one.

And on December 6 she wrote a letter to Elizabeth Sayre, conclud-
ing with this postscript:

. . . Nobody in the U.S. would be the slightest bit surprised if we
went to war with Japan tomorrow, *but* if we did go to war with Japan tomorrow, *everybody* would fall flat on his face with astonishment. That's
about the clearest description of public opinion I can give you.

On Sunday, December 7, 1941, the Luces were entertaining at a
large luncheon party for the Chinese Ambassador to the United States,
Dr. Hu Shih. Among the guests were John Gunther, Ambassador Rhine-
hardt, Vincent Sheean and a number of other correspondents. The Luces'
butler had standing instructions never to summon Mr. or Mrs. Luce
from table for a telephone call. At 1:30 the butler came in, hesitated for
a moment, and then in a whisper said, "Madam, I don't know whether
I should disturb you, but this seems to be a rather urgent message from
your husband's office." He handed her a slip of paper. It said, "Japan
has just bombed the Philippines, Pearl Harbor, and San Francisco."

Clare grabbed a spoon and rapped on her water glass. "Listen to
this, please."

When she finished, the guests laughed as though it were a practical joke.

Luce cut through their disbelief. "She means it," he said. "Please read it again, Clare."

Each guest left his half-finished dessert on the table. Thinking of her daughter Ann, who was then a student at Stanford University, Mrs. Luce tried to make a long-distance telephone call. The operator told her there were no lines open to the West Coast, but she did give Clare some reassurance—the first report of a Pacific Coast bombing was false but the fleet had been wiped out.

That night Vincent Sheean asked Clare to make a guest appearance on his radio program, and she went into the studio in New York. When she returned to Greenwich at midnight, Doris Duke was waiting for her in a very agitated state. "You and Harry know everything, Clare. Tell me, did they destroy my swimming pool?"

Life magazine scored a world journalistic beat by publishing "Mac-Arthur of the Far East," by Clare Boothe Luce, on December 8, 1941. The cover picture, which Clare had taken, became a symbol of American hope.

6

War Correspondent

The Japanese attack on Pearl Harbor severely damaged or destroyed eighteen ships of the U.S. Pacific fleet, one hundred and twenty-seven U.S. planes and killed three thousand, four hundred and thirty-five Americans. It also destroyed any pretense of neutrality on the part of the United States. War was declared on Japan, Germany, Italy, Bulgaria, Hungary and Rumania.

The United States recovered from its momentary hysteria but the mystery of Pearl Harbor is still unresolved. There have been at least eight official investigations designed to fix responsibility for that tragic event. The Roberts Commission, convened in December 1941, blamed the military commanders and particularly Rear Admiral Husband E. Kimmel.

We now know that U.S. Intelligence had broken the Japanese naval code some weeks, perhaps months, before Pearl Harbor. The intercepted messages clearly indicated an attack was in the making.

Clare Boothe Luce, who arrived at her conclusions by deductive reasoning, based on what she learned in the Philippines, is one of those who does not discount the theory that someone in the Roosevelt Administration seeking an excuse to take the nation into war may have deliberately withheld vital information from the military commanders in Honolulu.

Years later, in 1944, when President Quezon was in a hospital dying of tuberculosis, Clare Luce, a first-term Congresswoman from Connecticut, went to see the exiled President of the Philippines.

Describing the scene when she entered Quezon's room, Clare has said, "It was plain to me that he was dying. There was a little paper bag pinned to the bed sheets. He was literally coughing his life away and spitting his lungs into the bag. He seemed glad to see me.

"I said our medical men had made great strides toward conquering tuberculosis. He smiled his appreciation, but I knew he obviously didn't believe me.

"During our visit, I recalled our conversation in Manila . . . his angry speech denouncing Commissioner Sayre. I told him that when I had seen the item in the paper, I had concluded he must have known the Japanese were going to attack. I said it mattered a great deal to me to know my supposition was correct.

"Quezon nodded his head. Yes, he had known. His agents in Tokyo had informed him the Japanese fleet was planning to attack. He didn't know whether they intended to strike the Philippines or Hawaii first, or perhaps both simultaneously."

The Congresswoman asked Quezon if he had communicated this information to anyone in the U.S. Government. He told her he had informed Commissioner Sayre in Manila and that he had telephoned Washington and given the information directly to President Roosevelt. The President had replied that he was talking peace with the Japanese envoys in Washington, that he knew the Japanese fleet was out on maneuvers, but he assured Quezon the Philippines would not be attacked.

Before Mrs. Luce left, Quezon made her promise she would not reveal what he had told her until the war was over, or—the implication was plain—until he, Quezon, was dead.

Clare kept the secret. Many years later, after the war was won and Quezon was dead, she asked the Philippines' representative at the United Nations if he thought Quezon had told her the truth that morning. The man replied that although the event had taken place many years before he entered the political life of the islands, he thought she could believe Quezon had told her the truth.

The defense of the Philippines got off to a bad start and the situation rapidly worsened. Eighteen of the thirty-six B-17's based in Manila were destroyed on the ground by Japanese bombers. This, in spite of the fact that Lieutenant General Lewis H. Brereton, the American Air Commander, had been given seven hours advance warning.

General Douglas MacArthur was notified of the attack on "Pearl" at 3:40 A.M. on Sunday. All units of the Philippine defense force were immediately notified. When the Japanese planes came in from the sea at 10:40 A.M., Brereton's bombers were still on the ground being loaded.

In his memoirs MacArthur has accepted some of the blame for this error in judgment. The first report from Hawaii contained very little solid information. Pearl Harbor and the airfield at Hickam were defended by the most modern antiaircraft guns in the world. MacArthur mistakenly believed the U.S. defenses would be more than a match for the Japanese. Perhaps they should have been.

On December 22 the Japanese entered Lingayen Gulf with seventy-six troop transports supported by cruisers, destroyers and auxiliary craft. Two days later twenty-four more troopships entered Lamon Bay on the east coast of southern Luzon. MacArthur declared Manila an open city and retreated to the Bataan Peninsula. On December 25 Brereton with his few remaining big bombers flew out of the Philippines for Java.

The Japanese occupied Manila and the naval base at Cavite on January 2, 1942.

Clare felt a strong personal identification with MacArthur's cause. She managed to continue her correspondence with Colonel Charles Willoughby even after the American forces had been driven to Corregidor. Employing the same deductive reasoning which had caused her to anticipate the first attack, Clare concluded from his letters that MacArthur would ultimately move to Australia and begin the reconquest of Southeast Asia from that far-off base.

Life had scored an important journalistic scoop with Mrs. Luce's story about MacArthur. The editors agreed to let her play her hunch. She planned to go to Australia but there was no civilian transport available across the Pacific. The only way to go was to take the long way around, through Africa, Egypt, India, Sumatra and Java.

The Germans were beating the British in the Libyan Desert. The Japanese were threatening to occupy all of Burma. There would be plenty to report en route to Australia.

Clare's accounts of these early months of the war were published

in *Life* magazine in the spring and summer of 1942. She left New York
Harbor on February 11 aboard a camouflaged Pan-American Clipper.
The other passengers were all military men bound for reassignment.
Because there was a war on, she didn't identify her fellow travelers by
name in her first dispatch printed by *Life* on March 30.

We met at 8:00 A.M. at the Pan American Airport at Marine Base in
New York. The big waiting room was full of brown-uniformed men who
were going to faraway places—Cairo, Rangoon, Chungking, Darwin—
where the great job of the world has to be done. There is a big covey of
Colonels and Lieutenant Colonels, a brace of Brigadier Generals, one Major
General, several junior aides, a handful of non-coms and soldiers who are
technicians of one sort or another.

(The Major General was Joseph Stilwell en route to Burma. One
of the colonels was Frank Dorn, the handsome Chinese-speaking aide
to Stilwell. Another was Colonel Frank Roberts, who made the long
walk with his commanding officer on the retreat from Burma, and still
another was Colonel George Townsend.)
For a war correspondent assigned to the Burma theater, it was a
most fortunate passenger list. There is no doubt that *Life* editors knew
in advance that "Vinegar Joe" would be on the flight.
Pan American's route to Europe, dictated by the limited range of
the aircraft then in service, went south to Miami, Florida, crossed the
Caribbean to South America and ran along the northeastern coast of
that continent to Natal, Brazil. From here, the overwater distance to
the West Coast of Africa was only about two thousand miles.
Two hours out of Miami, Florida, on the second leg of the flight,
the Clipper encountered engine trouble and had to turn back. The next
morning a similar problem developed—the date was Friday, February
13. Spare parts were flown down from New York. Two days later the
flight was resumed. At Natal the passenger list was cut to twelve and the
Clipper, loaded down with extra fuel, started the night crossing to land
in Lagos, Nigeria, on February 18. The thickness of a continent separated Clare Luce from Cairo. Later, after interminable uncertainties, she
managed to get to Cairo and from there to Karachi and on to Delhi,

India, where Major General Brereton was attempting to put together an American-Far Eastern air force.

Mrs. Luce had met Brereton's aide, Colonel "Rosie" O'Donnell, in the Philippines. At the moment, the General had only six airplanes at his disposal. O'Donnell had time on his hands. He and Clare bought a secondhand automobile and explored India, or at least that portion adjacent to the old city.

Clare's article on General Brereton and his brave, minuscule air force was published in *Life,* the first account of an attack by American Flying Fortresses on Japanese-held territory. Clare said the mission's historic importance lay in the fact that it marked America's entrance into the war in the Far East, the first time American bombers, flown by American pilots, under American command and flag, had struck against the Japs in the Chinese theater of war. It was also the first U.S. bombing flight on record to be led by a general officer.

Clare's objective was to reach Australia ahead of MacArthur and she kept trying, but in Calcutta she learned the Japanese thrust to the south had cut the traffic lines from Ceylon to Sumatra and Java. There was no way she could reach Australia, but the Burma front was active. From one of her military friends she learned that all was not well at Allied Headquarters in Maymyo. "Vinegar Joe" Stilwell had wanted Brereton to move his bombers to the Burma front. When the air General refused, there had been bitter words. Stilwell was at odds with Chiang Kai-shek and resented the fact that the British commander, H. R. L. G. Alexander, outranked him. The Gissimo was coming to Maymyo to try to make peace. If the present stubborn uncooperative attitude continued, the British and Chinese forces in Burma would be forced to retreat.

On Easter Sunday, April 5, at the Dumdum Airport in Calcutta, Clare climbed aboard a twin-engine Douglas CNAC Army transport for the five-hour flight to Lashio, the nearest airport to the Irrawaddy and Toungoo fronts still in Allied possession.

There were only seven passengers—six Chinese soldiers and Clare. The rest of the space in the cabin was taken up by bales of American and Chinese currency destined for Chungking.

There were strict prohibitions against civilians taking up valuable space on the only transport between the outside world and Chungking. Clare has never revealed just what kind of pressure "Rosie" O'Donnell exerted but it was enough to cave in the regulations. She was on her way for what she later described as the "most gruesome airplane trip I have ever taken in all my life."

Fifteen minutes after take-off the plane encountered turbulent weather over the Bay of Bengal. The Chinese soldiers obviously had never been in an airplane before. The ventilation in the cabin was poor, the plane began to bounce around, the Chinese became airsick.

Clare helped them unbuckle their seat belts and all but one lay down in the passageway and vomited on the floor. The Chinese soldier who was still on his feet produced a can of the most popular all-purpose remedy in the Far East named "Tiger's Balm," guaranteed to kill any ailment. He passed it to his suffering companions and the Chinese smeared the greasy stuff on their faces. Suddenly Clare noticed a great purple stain begin to spread over the man's chest. For a moment she thought he had been shot or stabbed and was hemorrhaging, then she saw the cap of a European fountain pen in his jacket pocket. Apparently no one had told him that fountain pens regurgitate their charge when subjected to a change in altitude.

The odor of vomit and "Tiger's Balm" was too much for the lady war correspondent. She scrambled over the cargo and the outstretched soldiers to the pilot's compartment where she asked permission to ride up front for the rest of the trip.

Clare Luce was greeted in Lashio that Sunday evening by Colonel Haydon Boatner, who told her she was the luckiest journalist in the Far East. Generalissimo and Madame Chiang had just arrived from Chungking and would be leaving early in the morning by car for headquarters at Maymyo for a powwow which he predicted would patch up the difference and permit Stilwell to give his undivided attention to the war against the Japanese. He drove Clare to the two-story wooden building which served as a military center.

In her subsequent *Life* dispatch, she said:

I insinuated myself into the upflowing stream of officers, Chinese and American who were clumping up and down stairs. I found General Stilwell leading a Sino-American flight of officers down. He was wearing an overseas cap on his close-cropped, grizzled hair, smoking his interminable cigarette in its long black holder and chewing gum rapidly. "Hello, hello," he said brusquely, "Burma is no place for a woman." I started to give him an argument but he was already half down the stairs. At the bottom he turned, "Tomorrow at dawn, I'm driving to Maymyo. If you can get up that early, you can join me," he said with a half snort, half laugh, "on the road to Mandalay."

At five o'clock the next morning they were on their way in a very old Ford touring car driven by a "brown skinned, hook-beaked, somewhat ragged looking civilian." The sun was high in the sky by the time they reached Mandalay, where Japanese bombers had struck the day before.

Among the many things about the war in Burma which puzzled Clare had been Stilwell's recent promotion to command of the Chinese armies. She wondered why after four and a half years of leading his own troops in battle Chiang had asked for the services of an American commander. There were many able and trusted generals in Chiang's army, veterans of Changsha and Hankow and Taiuan.

Stilwell spoke excellent Chinese. He had a long history of service in the Orient and was familiar with the complexities of Chungking politics. She couldn't see why any of this made it logical to appoint an American chief of staff in active command of the Burma front. There was still another element. Stilwell had never been a partisan supporter of Chiang's regime. His critical attitude toward Chiang was widely known. Clare wondered if Chiang had asked F.D.R. to appoint Stilwell to the Burma post, hoping this promotion might temper the American General's attitude. Whatever the reasons, she was sure there would be a showdown at Maymyo and, thanks to her friends in India, she was there.

In her dispatch which was printed in *Life* Clare avoided any reference to the personality clash between Chiang and Stilwell. There were, she said, some good reasons for "Vinegar Joe's" assignment and one of them she described in these words:

I found part of the answer to my question about Uncle Joe, or rather saw it in the face of a boy . . . the bland, moon face of a Chinese guard who came stiffly to attention. So rigidly and smartly did he bring his bayonet up across his sturdy breast it almost slit the tip of his flat nose. His eyes glittered suddenly, brightly, happily. His young mouth fought against a wide and friendly smile as he saw U.S. General Joseph Stilwell alight from his car. This was "Uncle Joe" who had lived at the front with his Chinese brothers, ate their food, shared their dangers and would, if need be, shoulder their defeat. This was "Uncle Joe," a hostage to fortune, a flesh and blood offering, representing in his person and in the persons of his staff of officers and technicians, all the goodwill of a mighty but late-starting nation and the planes, the tanks, the supplies and even the doughboys would come someday.

However illogical militarily this Stilwell command in Burma might be, I thought, however useless in this collapsing area of war all Stilwell's professional skill may seem, the smile on the face of the guard at the Baptist mission proved this: Franklin D. Roosevelt and the "Gissimo" understand their peoples well. They dramatized in the person of Stilwell the fact that from here on out Americans will fight side by side with the Chinese.

She fought a small battle with her conscience before writing this. But America was at war. Two years of blundering had produced Pearl Harbor and the defeat in the Philippines. Was it necessary . . . would it be helpful to tell the American people that we were losing in Burma and that thanks to Stilwell's presence it would be regarded as one more defeat for the United States?

American military headquarters in Maymyo were located in a two-story mission house which had been built by the Evangelical Baptists. The building was surrounded by a pleasantly landscaped garden, a compound wall, and a forest of trees beyond. Clare's room on the second floor contained an iron bed covered with netting, a desk, two chairs and a rickety dresser. The common bathroom was equipped with a dented tin basin, one spigot out of which the best she could get was a dark-brown, lukewarm trickle of water, and an iron tub with one spigot out of which no water flowed at all.

Maymyo was the American military command post for the Irrawaddy front. There were about thirty officers on Stilwell's staff. Most of the Americans had been her companions on that Clipper flight across the South Atlantic. At 1:30 that afternoon Stilwell and four of his aides went off for the impending showdown with Chiang Kai-shek and the British commander, General Sir Harold R. L. G. Alexander. At three o'clock *Life* photographer George Rodger came to the mission headquarters in a jeep and asked Clare if she would like to see Mandalay. "It's still burning," he explained. "It's only about thirty miles away." In her report of that visit which appeared in the June 15 issue of *Life,* she said:

Yesterday what did I know of Mandalay? Yesterday to me it was just a Kipling song, an empire sound . . . but what do most Americans really know of Mandalay except this perhaps, "from Moulmein to Mandalay the course of empire took its hot triumphant way" . . . when Kipling was a war correspondent given to writing wondrous jungle jingles before this century began. I knew of course a few scattered facts that impinged themselves on my mind through the years; population 150,000, predominately Buddhist, famed for its temples and crowded market places. For tonight there is no Mandalay.

Tonight what do I know of Mandalay? Well not more than yesterday.

I smelled it before I saw it. My eyes were fastened on the blue thrust of the lazy pagoda-sprinkled peaceful northern hills above its outskirts. Then suddenly the smell brought my eyes down from the hills. Down to the leveled ruins that rushed upon us as the jeep tore into town. It was to me a smell not totally unfamiliar. I remembered one hot summer when I was a child, a dog died under our veranda porch. For some reason it was several days before anyone cleared through the porch vines to cart it away. It was that smell . . . but a thousand times magnified until it seemed as we whirled through the streets all creation stank of rotting flesh.

Now and again we saw something still standing. A great blackened pair of temple elephants or giant sacred marble cats and the miles long, six foot high, red brick walls of Fort Dufren that enclosed Government House and Thebaw's wondrous palace were still intact. But in the long moat that surrounded the fort where lazy lotus pads drifted in the hot green scum there floated many strange and hideous blossoms culled by the hand of death. The green little bottoms of babies bobbing about like unripe apples. The grey naked breasts of women, like lily buds, and the bellies of men with all their limbs trailing like green stems beneath the stagnant water. Neither Rodger nor I pointed a camera at these fearful indecencies.

On Tuesday, April 7, Clare interviewed Stilwell. The session lasted more than an hour. As she commented afterward, her questions evoked a great many words but almost no answers. The General did tell her that he had settled all points of difference with Chiang Kai-shek, that he expected there would be no more problems of policy to interfere with the actual fighting. He denied they had discussed a withdrawal from Burma.

On Wednesday, April 8, the Japanese bombed Maymyo. If they could kill the "Gissimo" and "Vinegar Joe," the Chinese will to resist might collapse.

Clare went into a slit trench with the others and watched the sticks and strings of high explosives come floating through the sky. For some of the officers present it was their initiation under fire. Clare's friend Colonel Roberts, for whom it was an old experience, told her to watch the reactions of the men who would now see death descending on them from above for the first time.

The bombs didn't hit the mission but after the attack all the Burmese servants left. The water supply failed. The officers' mess fell back on K rations. Clare described her reaction after the bombers had gone in these words:

My insides had not stopped quivering but my hands had when we came out of the trench on the all clear. The Colonel was right. The officers who had their first baptism by bomb were quite different men now. They were smiling, yes. They kidded a bit, but they were not really gay anymore and as you looked from one face to another you saw that they knew at last that they lived in a world where men are mortal. Until you have heard death scream in a shell or bomb through the insensible air, impersonally seeking you out personally, you never quite believe that you are mortal.

The nearest the Japanese came to General Stilwell and Generalissimo Chiang Kai-shek was one bomb that fell fifty yards from their hideaway. Clare in her mudstained slacks went off to keep a luncheon engagement with Sir Harold Alexander whose residence and headquarters were on an estate farther out of town. Alexander served a gin drink with real ice in it and dismissed the bombing with one question, "Everything all right your way?"

General Alexander had survived the evacuation of Dunkirk. He had gone through the Battle of Britain and the Blitz in London. After a tour of duty on the Libyan front, he had been assigned to a command in Burma. The British, he told Clare, would hold Burma as long as they could but he had only seven thousand troops. His men had been in the front lines for three and a half months without relief. They had no air protection, no supplies except those which were on hand when the war started. The Burma campaign was hopeless—he admitted it. The primary battle, he said, was being waged in Europe. "We have only so much air power and manpower, now, today, and we've got to beat the Hun first. He's the real enemy. Never forget that."

The Japanese bombers came over again the next day and once more Clare waited in a slit trench for the all clear to sound. That night she went to a party at the Maymyo Country Club. Her British hosts managed to give everyone there the impression that all was well—the air raids nothing much.

By Friday of that week, it was apparent that the Allied forces were making plans to retreat. Lashio and Maymyo could no longer be held. Once the airfields were lost any civilians would have no choice but to march out with Stilwell's men. Colonel Roberts drove Clare to Lashio and luck was with her. A CNAC plane bound for Chungking had just landed to refuel. It would depart in thirty minutes but Clare's ticket read to Calcutta and the aircraft was already loaded with all the passengers it was supposed to carry. Roberts and Boatner took her out to the airfield. It would be up to the pilot, they said, whether she could go or not. If he said no, then her best chance was to return to Maymyo with Roberts and try to escape overland. The pilot had gone into the operations building while the plane was being serviced. Reporting this encounter in her story on the Flying Tigers, which was published in *Life*, correspondent Luce wrote:

When I found him, he was an American with a handsome dark face, slick black hair, underlined by black eyebrows that made one straight line over his heavily lashed eyes. He was a character famous to millions of Americans, Dude Henrick, of *Terry and the Pirates* fame. His real name is Higgs and his letters out of China to an old friend Milt Caniff, the comic strip artist, had inspired many of the adventures of the Dragon Lady in Burma.

I said, "Hello, Dude, my name is Burma Boothe and I am a lady in distress which I gather is your specialty."

He said, "Well, beautiful, if you are in distress it's probably your own damn fault for being in China. What am I supposed to do?"

"Take me to Chungking. It's the only way I can get out of here and then from Chungking bring me back to Calcutta."

He said, "Have you got a ticket on this plane?"

And I said, "Obviously not or I wouldn't be in distress, would I?"

Higgs told her he thought he could get the airplane off the ground with an additional one hundred pounds and told her to climb on board.

When she said goodbye to Colonel Boatner, he asked her if she had gotten her story. "You will tell them the truth, won't you, Clare? The American people want to know. They've got that right, haven't they? I'd like to know it too. Tell me in three words."

Clare answered, "*Veni, Vidi, Evacui.* Which means, Colonel, we got the hell out."

Clare didn't go to Chungking. The plane touched down at Kunming, base of the famous Flying Tigers, and she stayed to get their story. Her dispatch, which ran in *Life* on July 20, was one of the best accounts of these courageous mercenaries commanded by General Claire Chennault. At full strength Chennault had a hundred pilots and fifty-four obsolescent P-40 pursuit planes. The men had ostensibly been recruited by the Central Aircraft Manufacturing Company of China to make planes for the Chinese Government. They were paid a salary of from $600 to $750 a month plus a bonus of $500 for every Japanese plane they destroyed in the air. Their contracts permitted them to resign at any moment the United States entered the war since most of them were on reserve status with the Army, the Navy or the Marines. The A.V.G. was disbanded as an independent unit on July 4, 1942, and the personnel was absorbed into the U.S. Air Force. But before this action wrote the final page of their history, the Flying Tigers destroyed two hundred and twenty-five enemy planes on the ground and two hundred and seventy-two in the air. In all they suffered only thirteen casualties.

The real accomplishment of the Flying Tigers was their demonstration that General Chennault's tactics for aerial warfare were spectacularly correct. The Tigers survived on teamwork. Three planes, six planes, nine planes flying in tight formation. No solo dogfights. No soaring off alone to become a sitting duck for the enemy. They kept their fire power concentrated and as a result they lived through the inferno.

One hour after Clare departed Lashio on the CNAC plane, the Japanese took the field. Colonel Roberts barely made it back to Maymyo and wouldn't have if the Jap snipers had been better shots.

Before Clare left the Allied headquarters one of the American generals handed her an automatic pistol. "You've got just seven shots," he told her. "Save one for yourself, don't use them all on the Japs. I've been out here a long time. When they get through with a woman prisoner of war, she's good for only one thing and that's the taxidermist."

Twenty-six years later when Clare was packing her things to move out of the Biltmore Estates house in Phoenix, following Harry's death, she found that pistol in the safe and her memories of the days and nights in Burma came rushing back to her mind.

The Flying Tigers had direct radio contact with a message center located on Treasure Island in San Francisco Bay. Clare transmitted her story on the American Volunteer Group for *Life* over this channel. She and "Pappy" Boyington, one of the famous Tiger pilots, are still close friends.

Privately she describes the mechanics and pilots of the A.V.G. as a "valiant, drunken, disorderly, chivalrous lot, who deserve major credit for denying the Japs a quick, easy victory."

From Kunming Clare flew to Chungking, where she was received by Generalissimo and Madame Chiang, who told her how the military situation had deteriorated in Burma. Madame Chiang did the interpreting for her husband, who couldn't speak English. Clare got the impression the feud between Stilwell and the Chinese ruler was still on.

She took the next available CNAC plane for India. In Delhi she discovered that General Brereton had made very little progress toward developing an adequate air force. He had, she concluded, made a serious error in the Philippines, where his planes were caught on the ground, and his superiors at home were reluctant to assign him any more of our very scant supply of B-29's. The Burma front, she concluded, would not become a major theater, and she flew on to Cairo.

With all the hard news going against the Allies, correspondent Luce was reluctant to join the chorus of gravediggers. She understood the enormity of the task, and where the men in command posts were doing their best, she thought it would be a disservice to write an account of their failures. When she departed from this policy and expressed her personal opinion of the command decisions being made in the Libyan theater, the resultant military and diplomatic flap threatened to upset the friendly relations between the United States and Britain.

In April 1942 General Erwin Rommel's Afrika Korps was at El Alamein, seventy miles from the British naval base at Alexandria and only one hundred and fifty miles from Cairo.

As correspondent for *Life* Mrs. Luce had spent nearly three months at the Allied outposts . . . she was ready to go home. Her husband's cables were becoming more and more impatient. But after two years of desert fighting, the Germans were very close to victory. She was determined to get that story.

General Sir Archibald Wavell had done very little to resist the first thrust when Italian Marshal Rodolfo Graziani and his troops crossed the Libyan border into Egypt. In December 1940 the British Eighth Army, under General Sir Henry Maitland "Jumbo" Wilson, began the campaign that pushed the Italians and Germans back to El Agheila, capturing more than one hundred thousand prisoners. Rommel replaced Graziani, made an end run around the British to occupy Benghazi and lay siege to the garrison at Tobruk. General Sir Claude Auchinleck replaced Wavell in Cairo, and General Sir Alan Gordon Cunningham replaced Wilson in the field.

In December 1941 the British attack reached Tobruk and liberated the garrison. Rommel continued to retreat. Cunningham pursued—with more speed than good judgment. His Eighth Army fell into the German's trap. The result was catastrophic. Auchinleck recalled Cunningham and gave the command to Lieutenant General Neil Methuen Ritchie, who chased Rommel all the way back to El Agheila, only to repeat Wilson's mistake of clinging too closely to the shoreline of the Mediterranean.

Rommel's divisions turned the British flank, recaptured Benghazi, destroyed Ritchie's tanks at Tmimi and Mekili, and charged forward to recapture Tobruk, Salum, Mersamaruth and develop their strong point at El Alamein.

This was the situation when Clare arrived in Cairo and secured permission to visit the front lines with a supply caravan carrying food and ammunition. Her escorts were two young colonels—Sir Arthur William Tedder and Air Vice Marshal "Mary" Cunningham. Tedder ultimately became a Field Marshal in supreme command of the RAF and deputy to General Eisenhower. Cunningham was in command of all Allied Air Forces in the final battle which drove the Axis powers out of Egypt and Libya.

Before she went to the front, General Ritchie invited *Life*'s representative to be "briefed" at a dinner in his field headquarters. He told Clare the German equipment was vastly superior to anything the British had, the Luftwaffe was magnificent. He didn't believe the British could successfully defend Cairo and Alexandria. He also indicated he didn't like living in field headquarters, explaining it was necessary for him to send his laundry back to Cairo to "get a decent shirt, you know."

The demoralized British units were so widely separated it was almost impossible to find the front lines. When the Germans attacked, the British gave ground, attempting to escape by outdistancing their pursuers. Clare concluded the disorganized, disheartened British were "just hanging on by their fingernails waiting for the promised American equipment."

Mrs. Luce returned to Cairo convinced that under its present command the British Army was no match for Rommel.

Author Fay Henle, in a book titled *Au Clare de Luce*, tells that

148

Mrs. Luce appeared in Cairo wearing freshly pressed silk slacks and jackets or sultry, long evening gowns. None of these items was in Clare's wardrobe. She preferred what she has described as a "sub-Wac outfit" —khaki trousers, khaki blouse and khaki jacket. This was what she was wearing when she attended a party at the residence of American Ambassador Alexander Comstock Kirk in Egypt.

Clare knew Kirk was an archeological dilettante and very proud of the view of the pyramids from his balcony. He had a reputation for ushering his visitors to the spot where they could see these ancient monuments, and then launching into a lecture.

Clare managed to reach the balcony ahead of her host. When he arrived she pointed innocently toward the pyramids and with great guile inquired, "Mr. Ambassador, what *are* those strange-looking objects?"

Clare says the expression on Kirk's face was worth a thousand dollars.

Clare went to Alexandria where six Italian frogmen had managed to sink two of Britain's great capital ships in the harbor. Her friend Florimund Duke took her to a pleasure houseboat on the Nile. He told her the boat, a very exclusive floating night club, was owned by some British officers and that a dozen such spots in Cairo would be doing a land-office business. No one seemed concerned about the war. Clare concluded that unless there was a change in command, the fall of Cairo was inevitable.

When she tried to file a cable to *Life* containing her impressions, the British censor refused to permit its transmittal. "The war," he said, "is going too badly to let you tell the truth." Mrs. Luce decided it was time to go home.

At the airport the British customs official asked Clare if she had any papers.

"I have a great many," she told him, "but you can do one of two things: destroy them all or put that official British seal on my bag and let me carry them home. All the information is in my head anyway."

At Lagos the only hotel which wasn't overcrowded with arriving military personnel was a well-patronized whorehouse. A Pan Am official arranged for the wife of *Time*'s owner to occupy a private villa owned by a Nigerian shipowner. The villa was small but new. There was a roomy, modern bathroom on the second floor. To Clare Luce it seemed luxurious. Her first act was to turn on the water and prepare for a lengthy, lazy soaking. The telephone summoned her downstairs. It was a Pan Am clerk calling to tell her that she was being bumped from the next flight to make room for a general. He said there might be a seat in two or three days or perhaps a week.

The prospect of spending a week in Lagos was something Clare wanted to avoid if at all possible. The conversation was a lengthy one, but finally the airline agent promised to try to get her a seat on the next flight out. Meanwhile she had forgotten about the water upstairs until she felt a drop on her head.

By the time she reached the bathroom it was too late. The floor was awash with what seemed to her like a foot of water. A few minutes later the entire plastered ceiling of the living room fell. Time Inc., of course, paid for the damage, but the war was almost over before the owner could get materials to complete repairs. She recalls this as the most embarrassing experience of her life.

With nothing to do but wait for a vacant seat on a westbound plane, Clare broke the British censor's seal on her notes and started writing a detailed report of all she had seen and heard. It was to be a confidential memorandum intended for Harry's eyes only. Clare still innocently insists she didn't realize the possible consequences, but she had been briefed on the necessity for censorship. And certainly the report she wrote for Luce contained vital information which might have damaged the war effort had it fallen into Axis hands.

Starting with the problems in Burma, she put it all down, including the impasse between Chiang Kai-shek and Stilwell. She didn't take sides because she could see the reasons which compelled each leader to support the policy he had adopted. Stilwell was determined to train and equip a first-class force of thirty Chinese divisions. Then he proposed to create thirty more. He argued that the troops were necessary, not only to defeat the Japanese, recapture Burma, and win a victory for the Allies in the Far East, but also to support the continuing dominance of the Chiang regime.

Chiang, on the other hand, had gained political power by winning the support of numerous independent war-lord generals. He knew these petty tyrants might become disaffected if Stilwell's program was implemented. If enough American supplies could reach China and be distributed to these semiautonomous groups, Chiang would be in a stronger political position.

President Roosevelt, acting on the recommendations of Lauchlin Currie (later identified as a member of the Nathan Silvermaster Communist group in Washington), had promised to give Chiang what he wanted with no strings attached. Stilwell, who understood the Oriental mind, wanted to bargain, to demand a *quid pro quo* for every shipload of supplies delivered.

It has been suggested elsewhere that Stilwell was sympathetic to the Chinese Communists. Mrs. Luce expresses a contrary opinion. She said Stilwell wanted to win the war and to establish China as a first-rate power. This, he believed, could never be achieved until the provincial rulers had been replaced by a tough, well-trained army under the absolute command of the central government.

Stilwell was no diplomat. Clare reported that in private he referred to Chiang as "the peanut" or "that bastard." The Burma campaign had been an ignominious defeat for Stilwell. He blamed the British and the Chinese and was extremely critical of General Claire Chennault.

It was Clare's opinion that Stilwell's insistence on reopening the Burma front was prompted by a desire to erase the memory of the defeat he had suffered in that area. She supported Chiang's contention that if thirty divisions could be equipped, they would be more effectively employed in other theaters. Clare, who was extremely air-minded, agreed with Chennault and Chiang, who were contending that air transport should be employed to supply China and that Stilwell's demand for the construction of the Ledo Burma Road would result in a wasteful undertaking.[1]

---

[1] Eventually the road was built, one hundred and seventeen miles of it at a tremendous cost in material and lives, but it wasn't open for traffic until 1945. By that time the American Transport Command was delivering seventy thousand tons of material a month over the Hump—as much in one day as highway transport could deliver in one month.

Mrs. Luce reserved her strongest criticism for General Neil Methuen Ritchie, who, she said, was worrying more about the starch in his shirts than putting starch in his soldiers.

She reviewed the entire Libyan campaign. She described the British general headquarters in Shepheard's Hotel where the officers and men gave the impression of just playing at war games, where every week-end there was some lively social affair. She had been to the front and she described the inadequacy of British supplies, the low morale of the troops, who, she said, were soft and lazy because their officers refused to demand anything else.

Clare packed the report and all of her notes in a briefcase. When the Clipper landed in Trinidad, the British customs officer examined her passport, looked at the briefcase, and asked to see her papers.

She told him they were just unimportant personal letters, one in particular she had been writing to her husband.

"I'll have to examine them."

"They really are very confidential, meant only for my husband, Henry Luce, the publisher."

The officer smiled. "I'll keep your secrets, Mrs. Luce, but I must examine the papers."

The officer read the first two pages of the report, and then courteously but firmly ordered Clare to a hotel. She should, he said, consider herself under house arrest.

Late that afternoon two American naval officers came to the hotel to report that her briefcase had been taken to the Joint Allied Security Control office in Trinidad. The British governor had read the report out loud to his staff and to the American representatives. The governor wanted to send a verbatim copy of Clare's confidential letter to Number 10 Downing Street by cable. He had been persuaded not to take this action for security reasons, but he was boiling mad.

The Americans asked Clare if she knew anyone who might be able to help her out. Clare did. She knew Colonel Bill Donovan, head of the American OSS. The Navy men wired Donovan, who in turn called Mr. Luce.

Donovan gave Clare a retroactive appointment as a member of

the American intelligence forces, but this didn't fool the British. They kept her in custody at Trinidad for five days, and then put her on board a plane for New York City in charge of a Queen's courier.

The courier was a grandson of Alfred Lord Tennyson. Clare describes him as an asthmatic, snub-nosed youth who took all her precious papers and put them in a big white bag which he flung over his shoulder.

Colonel Donovan and Harry Luce met the plane. The courier took Mrs. Luce's papers to Lord Halifax, the British Ambassador in Washington, D.C.

At the end of the week Lord Halifax asked Mrs. Luce to come to Washington. Luce offered to go with her, but she told him she had gotten herself into this mess and she would face it out alone.

The British Ambassador received his caller in his study. To her great relief, he was smiling. He indicated a chair across from his desk, made sure the door was securely closed, and said, "Mrs. Luce, I can't tell you when I've enjoyed a report as much as I have the one our people took away from you in Trinidad."

Clare said she hadn't enjoyed being treated like a spy, that it was her impression the Americans and the British were allies.

"We are, we are, Mrs. Luce," Halifax assured her, "but don't you realize that document could have affected the outcome of the war?" He said that she had very accurately described the weaknesses of the Allied position in the Near East. A copy of the report had been flown to Number 10 Downing Street where it was being studied by Winston Churchill who, incidentally, had that morning sent his regards to Clare.

"Our chaps," Halifax said, "are deucedly upset over the fact that you were able to stumble on to all this information. It might not be so embarrassing for us if you were not a woman. At any rate, if you do go back to any of the war zones, Mrs. Luce, I want your promise that you will never write a line until you are safely home in the United States."

There was no way of keeping the whole affair secret, particularly in Washington, D.C. The British Embassy had informed the State Department, and the State Department had told the White House, and Colonel Donovan had told the Pentagon—and the upshot of it all was that Clare had to go before the Joint Chiefs of Staff and be "debriefed." She may have been the first woman in history invited for a debriefing session before the high councils of the Pentagon.

Not long after this episode Churchill made a personal inspection of the Libyan front. Ten weeks later Churchill ordered General Ritchie removed and named Lieutenant General Bernard Law Montgomery to command the Eighth Army.

Montgomery moved headquarters out of Shepheard's Hotel into the desert. As a part of a general toughening-up policy, the troops were up and out of their tents at daylight for thirty minutes of vigorous calisthenics. Montgomery and his staff followed this same regime. American ships delivered tanks and guns and petroleum and ammunition via Suez. New B-25's of the Twelfth Bomb Group followed the Pan Am route across the South Atlantic to Africa and on to Cairo.

Beginning on the twenty-third of October, 1942, Montgomery drove the Axis forces out of El Alamein and back across the desert into Libya. Rommel's troops were destroyed. His tanks were driven into the sea, and the Allies had their first great solid victory of World War II.

The result of that change in command vindicated Clare's judgment and validated all of the opinions she had expressed in that confidential manuscript.

7

Congresswoman

When Dr. Albert Austin was elected to the U.S. House of Representatives from Fairfield County, Connecticut, in November 1938, Clare was too preoccupied to pay much attention to her stepfather's triumph. She and Harry had gone to London early in May, visited in France and Germany, returning late in June. *The Women* closed its Broadway run on July 9, 1938, after six hundred and fifty-seven performances—at that point only fifteen plays had exceeded the run of *The Women.*

In 1939 and 1940, with Ann attending boarding school in Virginia, Washington, D.C., was the most convenient meeting place for mother and daughter. Middleburg, a village of less than a thousand inhabitants, was only about forty miles from the nation's capital.

Clare was fond of Dr. Austin and when she was in Washington it was convenient to use his office as a place where she could receive messages and expand her contacts on Capitol Hill. Dr. Austin was immensely proud of his stepdaughter's success—his official biography in the *Biographical Directory of the American Congress,* put out by the Government Printing Office, begins: "Austin, Albert Elmer (stepfather of Clare Boothe Luce)." (Few of the other biographies mention a subject's children, natural or otherwise.)

It was on one of these visits to her stepfather's office that Clare met Albert P. Morano, a thirty-one-year-old second-generation Italian-American, who had played a leading role in securing the nomination and winning the election for Dr. Austin.

Clare's recollection of that first encounter is very hazy; Morano's, extremely specific. He says, "I knew who she was, all right. I had heard about her, but seeing her and talking to her convinced me everything I had heard was true."

With what may be hindsight rationalization, Morano says now that when he first met Mrs. Luce the idea flashed through his mind that she would make a magnificent candidate. In any event, Al Morano is certainly responsible for her entry into active politics as a candidate for Congress in 1942.

Dr. Austin was defeated for re-election in 1940 by a Democrat, Le Roy Downs, a newspaper publisher from South Norwalk, Connecticut. Morano lost his job in Washington and had to return to Greenwich. Dr. Austin died in January 1942. Morano was asked to help with the funeral arrangements, and particularly to be responsible for notifying the doctor's political associates. Morano sent Mrs. Luce a telegram advising her of her stepfather's death and giving the time and place of the funeral services. She replied with a message to Morano expressing sympathy and stating her intention of coming to Greenwich for the funeral.

A sudden snowstorm prevented Clare from making the trip to Greenwich. Instead of going to the funeral, she walked across to St. Bartholomew's Church, conveniently adjacent to the Waldorf Towers, and said a prayer for her stepfather. She wrote a note to Morano to tell him what she had done and why she hadn't been able to come out for the service.

Morano says he used this note, after a decent length of time, to re-establish contact. He asked for an appointment, saying he had a matter of great importance to discuss. A date was set. Clare broke the engagement "because she was going to China with her husband."

Morano, who subsequently became Clare's closest adviser during the period she served in Congress, says now that he thinks Mrs. Luce intuitively guessed what he had in mind and didn't want to talk about it. But at the time, he accepted her excuse at face value and determined to pursue the plan he had formulated in his mind at the earliest opportunity.

Morano had no real power in the Republican organization. He had fought the party leaders to win nomination for Dr. Austin in 1939, and when his candidate was defeated in 1940, the party pros blamed him for the loss. He had enjoyed his two years in Washington as Congressman Austin's clerk, and the salary had been more than he had ever made in his life before. He wanted to go back to the capital. Knowing his best chance for doing this was to find a candidate who could be elected, he put his heart into the campaign.

During the fall and summer of 1941 a number of potential candidates in Fairfield County floated trial balloons aimed at securing the nomination for Dr. Austin's old seat. Morano couldn't attach himself to any of the local contenders because of the animosity developed in 1938. These hopefuls were already surrounded by their corps of supporters. Morano had to find a fresh face. The more he thought about it, the more convinced he became that Clare Boothe Luce, if she could be persuaded to enter the race, was the key to his ambition.

When Mrs. Luce returned from Burma in May of 1942, Morano reopened the subject. He says, "Believe me, I was persistent. I wrote letters and called on the telephone until she finally agreed to see me at the King Street house on the eighteenth of May."

He says Mrs. Luce was noncommittal at that first meeting, but she did agree to think about it, and she did invite him to come back the following Sunday morning to discuss the subject again.

Morano admits he was overawed by the power, beauty, wealth and fame of Mrs. Luce. He was a nobody; she a celebrated somebody. When he went back to the King Street house Sunday morning, the maid told him Mrs. Luce was still in bed and asked him to wait. Then she brought him some coffee and a bottle of cognac. Morano says, "As I remember it, she kept me waiting more than an hour." He thinks the cognac gave him courage to argue fervently when the lady of the house finally received him in her bed-sitting room. "After I had given her all the reasons why I thought she could win, she called for Mr. Luce. It was the first time I ever met him. She said, 'Harry, Mr. Morano wants me to run for Congress. I will have him talk to you about it.' "

Morano says they walked through the garden and grounds for more than an hour. "Mr. Luce asked a lot of questions. I got the idea he didn't know the first thing about how a Congressional race was run, but the idea interested him. He told me Mrs. Luce would have to make up her own mind. They had an agreement, he said, not to interfere or give advice to each other. He did say he thought his wife would make an excellent member of Congress, but he didn't want her to run and be defeated.

"When we got back to the house, Mrs. Luce was dressed. She didn't exactly say she would be a candidate, but she led me to believe she would. When I left I was on Cloud Nine."

Morano's next move was to call on his friend Niver Beaman, editor of the Greenwich *Times*. Beaman was enthusiastic. On May 21 he ran a speculative story suggesting that Clare Boothe Luce would be a candidate for Congress, and quoting Republican State Chairman J. Kenneth Bradley and National Committeeman Samuel F. Pryor, both of whom said Clare would be an extraordinarily strong contender.

All of this furor astonished Clare a little. She wasn't sure she wanted to go to Congress. She wasn't at all sure she could win the election. When Beaman asked her about it, she equivocated. The Bridgeport *Herald* said, "Privately, GOP biggies have their thumbs down on CBL as a candidate, despite the fact they need somebody who can pitch lots of green hay into the party's loft."

During the month of June CBL refused to deny or affirm the rumors that she might try for the Republican nomination to oppose Le Roy Downs, the man who had defeated her stepfather. Morano, confident that he had a candidate, launched a quiet campaign to win the support of the Republicans who would be delegates to the state convention. Connecticut does not nominate in a primary. Party candidates are chosen by representatives of all the counties, meeting in state convention.

On June 21 the Washington, D.C., *Times-Herald,* reflecting the views of its publisher, Eleanor "Cissy" Patterson, ran an article on Clare's candidacy under this headline: "Luce neither hates nor loves anything. Publisher's only interest is self-interest. To serve that he sires hate and bitterness." And two weeks later columnist Helen Essary, in the same newspaper, forecast that Miss Vivien Kellems, owner of a Westport, Connecticut, industrial complex, would block Clare's ambition. Miss Essary said, "For a breathless while Connecticut knew only that Clare Boothe Luce was bound for the capitol of the U.S.A. ₹ '

the House of Representatives. Now it is Vivien and Clare—as quick-stepping, fast-murdering girls as any civilization, primitive or modern, ever stood up under. Vivien and Clare—what a battle! 'The Women' in real life."

On July 9 the Greenwich *Times,* quoting an authoritative source, said that Clare would definitely seek the Republican nomination from the Fourth District. The next day Mrs. Luce said the authoritative source couldn't be authoritative, that she would make her own announcements.

One week later the Greenwich Council of Women endorsed Clare and passed a resolution calling on her to become a candidate. And the Negro Republican League of Fairfield County went on record as favoring Clare's candidacy. Morano had things moving.

When CBL sent word to Morano on the fourth of August that she wanted to see him at the King Street house, he assumed she was ready to make her candidacy official.

When he arrived, Mrs. Luce's secretary handed him a letter addressed to State Republican Chairman Bradley. Morano says he read the last paragraph first and it burned him up. His "candidate" had written "that for the reasons recited above I have made an irrevocable decision not to seek the nomination."

Morano then read the letter from the beginning. It was a reasoned recital of what Clare Luce believed her political situation to be. She was, she stated, a legal resident of Fairfield County. It had been her child-hood home but for the past fifteen years she had spent most of her time either in New York City or traveling the world as a war correspondent. She argued that a Congressman should know his constituents intimately and be able to serve their needs and desires. She did not feel that she knew the Fairfield people well enough to represent them in the lower house.

In one paragraph Clare claimed that she was better informed about the problems of war than "anyone else whose name has been suggested." Then she said she "didn't feel the people of Fairfield County knew her well enough to vote for her."

Morano says, "I was annoyed, to say the least. Number one, at the decision, and number two, because she didn't come down herself to tell me." He says he sat on the couch reading the letter for almost thirty minutes until Clare came floating down the great circular staircase into the living doom. The truth probably is that Mrs. Luce wanted him to have time to master his disappointment.

"Well, what do you think, Al?" she asked.

"I think it's a wonderful letter," Morano replied. "It's beautiful."

"Let's read it over."

Morano read the first paragraph. Just right, he said. The second paragraph was good.

"What shall I do with it?" Clare asked.

"Send it, of course. It's addressed to Mr. Bradley, send it to him. But I would like to ask you to do me just one little favor. Take out that word '*irrevocable*.' "

Morano explained that her letter contained all the reasons why she thought she shouldn't run. "But," he said, "if the people want you after knowing all these reasons, then you may want to change your mind."

He remembers Mrs. Luce laughingly asked, "You mean they'll draft me?"

"No," he replied, "I am not saying that at all, but I don't think you have the right to make the decision for the people of Fairfield County if it should turn out that you are the one they want to run for Congress."

Mrs. Luce agreed to the change. Morano mailed the letter and then contacted his friend George Waldo, owner of the Bridgeport *Post*.

"You gotta protect me in this, but she's not going to run unless we can change her mind."

"What can I do?" the newspaperman asked.

"Get a copy of that letter. Ask Bradley for it; then you can answer her objections."

Waldo did. His editorial argued that all the reasons Clare had given for not wanting to run made her the best qualified of all candidates. She was honest about her political weaknesses. She was the best informed about the world situation.

Clare Luce might have stuck by her guns despite all the pressure. The idea of having to live in Washington while her husband remained in New York wasn't appealing. She had been quite sincere in her letter to Bradley when she said, "Therefore, humbled by the knowledge that the second, but no less important, part of the congressional aspirant's job . . . that of having served a long apprenticeship of neighborliness . . . is one I do not seem to possess today. I feel I cannot offer my name as a candidate for Congress."

Mrs. Luce left Connecticut a few days later to try out a play she was writing in the Barter Theatre in Virginia. Morano believes it was Vivien Kellems who changed Clare's mind. On August 15 Miss Kellems charged that Clare was not a Connecticut woman, and then implied that Clare's letter to Bradley had been a clever bit of political hypocrisy.

Miss Kellems said, "I do not subscribe to the artifices of politics. I do not indulge in clever moves, jockeying for position, letters of withdrawal which by some strange sleight of hand turn into an invitation to be drafted. Perhaps I am old-fashioned, but my actions have been forthright and my position is clear. No group of clever manipulators and influential politicians are back of me . . . no large fortune is at my disposal. No political boss sits in a swivel chair in New York City dictating my nomination. I can offer only one thing—myself as you know me."

The press described this as a "scathing attack against Clare Boothe Luce," and added, "the lady whose company is engaged in making cable clips and other devices for the War Production Board suggests Clare is running on a platform of sex appeal."

On August 17 *The New York Times* quoted Dr. Gregory Mason, head of the New York University School of Journalism, and former chairman of the local America First committee, as advising the Republican Party that the best way to insure the re-election of Democrat Downs would be to nominate Clare for Congress.

.Mrs. Luce suffers from two enormous political disadvantages, her connections with Willkie, and her husband, Henry R. Luce. She belongs to the narrow-minded, bitter and fast-dwindling Willkie faction which is determined to blacklist every American who did not agree with the Roosevelt foreign policy before Pearl Harbor. She is bound to be influenced by her husband, whose yellow journals are doing all they can to keep alive the disunity and acrimony which marred American discussion of foreign affairs before Japan's wanton attack on us.

There were five male candidates in the race for the nomination, but the attention seemed to focus on what the newspapers called a "rerun of *The Women*." If it was, Clare Luce was the silent member of the cast. She steadfastly refused to make the smallest comment on Miss Kellems' attacks. She remembered too well her encounter with Dorothy Thompson.

On September 1 the Greenwich delegates at the State Republican Convention unanimously voted to make Clare Boothe Luce their choice. She responded with a gracious note of acceptance and became officially a candidate.

Clare's apparent indecision, her letter of withdrawal, and her final announcement that because six delegates were for her she changed her mind, all seem to support the charge that she deliberately played hard to get, that Vivien Kellems was correct when she said Clare "had planned it all." If so, Mrs. Luce was a better politician than anyone suspected.

Al Morano doesn't agree with this reconstruction, but he was a partisan with a personal motive for wanting Clare to say yes. Harry Luce, who was perhaps in the best position of all to know the mind of the candidate or noncandidate, was so convinced Clare would not run that her announcement was quite a shock to him. Perhaps it was Morano's skillful manipulations behind the scenes which persuaded Clare that she could have sufficient support to win the nomination. Certainly he did a most effective job—the day after she became an official aspirant the Republican Party officials asked her to be the keynote speaker at the state convention, a spot on the program calculated to give her an advantage over every other candidate.

The charge that Mrs. Luce was nominated because of her husband's millions is one which the records clearly refute. She spent no money before the nomination. Harry's total contribution to the general election was $3,000. All together, her managers reported only $11,000 in expenses. But Henry Luce was helpful in other ways. He assigned *Time* staffer Wes Bailey to serve on Clare's strategy committee and take charge of all advertising and printing. Clare's papers covering this period, now on deposit in the Library of Congress, reveal that Luce wrote some of her campaign speeches and persuaded Stanley High of the *Reader's Digest* to help with others.

When Clare finally agreed to run, Morano expected to be named campaign manager. He was in for a disappointment. She called him on the telephone to say that she had decided to ask Bill Brennan, an Irish-Catholic politician from Connecticut, to serve in that capacity. It is true Clare never before ran for public office, but this first act indicated a shrewd understanding of local politics. She liked Morano. She knew he had been helpful and would continue to do so. But she also recognized that it would hurt her candidacy in certain areas of the party if she named him to lead her campaign.

Morano concealed his disappointment and promised to continue working in whatever capacity he could to help her achieve a victory. Later he said the selection of Brennan was a stroke of genius because it helped Clare capture the Irish-Catholic vote.

On September 14 the Republican convention, consisting of eighty-six delegates, cast its ballots—eighty-four for Clare Boothe Luce; two for Vivien Kellems.

Morano organized the factory girls for Luce with chapters in every industrial area of the district. He sponsored dinners, admission $1.00, filling the restaurants, and brought his candidate in to dazzle the working girls. Clare says she never worked so hard in her life. Her day started with a handshaking tour as the early-morning shifts came to the plants and ended after midnight, with five or six speeches in between.

Because there had been so many references to the Luces' wealth, Brennan wanted Clare to dress down to the occasion. She refused to take his advice because she felt the voters would recognize such a course as deliberate deception. When she appeared she made the most of her clothes, her face and her figure.

The nomination had been easy. The campaign was hard. In her very first speech Clare unwittingly made a statement which threatened disaster. Referring to the "rubber stamp representation" which Le Roy Downs had given the district—always voting the Democratic Party line —she used the term "faceless man." She didn't know that Downs had been wounded in World War I and that plastic surgery had been necessary to repair his face. The Democratic incumbent seized upon the phrase as a personal reference to the injuries he had sustained fighting for his country.

It was this innocent error which caused Clare to adopt as one of her political principles: "never explain." There was nothing she could say and she realized that anything she said would keep the matter alive. After a week or so, when Downs's charges brought no response, the matter was dropped.

In her speeches Clare called for greater sacrifice on the home front and better organization in Washington to support America's fighting men. She accused the Roosevelt Administration of fighting a soft war, of being unwilling to tell the American public the truth about our early reverses, our inadequate production of war materiel, and what she called a lack of over-all war strategy.

Morano recalls that Clare lacked confidence in her ability to win. "I constantly had to reassure her," he says. "Whenever the day's activities were over—and it was usually about midnight—she would call my house to ask how she was doing. I'd tell her 'you can't miss . . . go to bed and get some sleep.' "

Clare's campaign organization benefited from an extremely professional approach. William H. Brennan planned policy. The committee organization was delegated to J. Kenneth Bradley, State Chairman. Mrs. Cecelia Murray was adviser on women's groups; Leonard Wood, press representative; Wes Bailey, advertising manager in charge of all printing and of Clare's speaking (which also meant her speeches). Pauline Mandigo of New York handled PR. There was a chairman for the Young Republicans, a chairman for the farm leaders, a separate chairman for each civic and religious division, with Al Morano officially in charge of all foreign-language voters. A memo in Mrs. Luce's handwriting states that "all written material, speeches, advertisements, pamphlets, statements, etc. must be submitted to the policy committee and manager Brennan before release."

Morano remained in the background, at least his name is rarely mentioned in the newspaper reports of the campaign, but he did drive Clare to rallies, and they spent a good deal of time together. On one of these trips she asked him what time it was. He confessed he didn't own a watch.

Mrs. Luce won that election by a margin of less than seven thousand votes out of the more than one hundred and twenty thousand which were cast. Morano remembers that the following day Clare telephoned him at home. She was, he says, in a very happy frame of mind. She said, "Good morning, Mr. Secretary Morano. Would you mind coming by my house some time soon?"

He understood this was her way of telling him that when she went to Washington he would become her administrative assistant. When he got to the King Street house, Clare handed him a package. Inside he found a handsome wrist watch with these words engraved on the back: "You can't miss. Love, Sis."

Al Morano has said that Mrs. Luce was never personally confident of victory in that first race for Congress. Some support for his conclusion can be found in the fact that in October Clare signed a contract with Warner Brothers to serve as technical adviser on a film they were making about China. She left Greenwich for Mepkin Plantation on November 6, returned to fill two speaking engagements the third week of November and then went to Hollywood. Had she lost the election, the movie assignment would have provided a convenient escape and a task to take her mind off defeat.

Clare stayed in California until the last minute, then allowing herself just enough time to make the transcontinental journey, she boarded the train for Washington and arrived weary and dusty and two hours later than scheduled. She didn't expect any kind of a reception committee or to be interviewed. Unaware that a crowd of reporters was waiting for her in the terminal, she slipped off the train unnoticed and took a taxi to the Wardman Park Hotel. It was not an auspicious beginning. When the pursuing reporters finally caught up with her, she was taking a bath and kept them waiting another thirty minutes. Most of those first-day stories suggested that the new Congresswoman from Connecticut deliberately ducked out. They called it temper or temperament, an obvious attempt, they said, to gain publicity. To support their charge that Clare was arrogant, they reported that she had somehow wangled space in the then *new* House office building and said she had been presumptuous enough to ask Speaker Joe Martin to assign her a place on the Foreign Affairs Committee.

It is true that CBL was the only freshman Congressman that year to be given space in the newer, more comfortable building, but Al Morano says he was responsible for this. "I knew how they gave out space. I just stood in line and waited until all the senior members had been satisfied and grabbed the remaining spot."

Clare had hoped to be named to the Foreign Affairs Committee because the war was the big thing and the one she knew most about. She does not think it was presumptuous for a freshman Congressman to make such a request and her right to feel unfairly attacked on this score is supported by the fact that five first-termers, Will Rogers, Jr., of California, Mike Mansfield of Montana, Howard J. McMurray of Wisconsin, J. W. Fulbright of Arkansas, and Andrew C. Schiffler of West Virginia, were named to serve on Sol Bloom's committee on foreign affairs. Rogers, Mansfield, McMurray and Fulbright were all Democrats. Schiffler was a Republican who had been elected first in 1938, defeated in 1940 and re-elected in 1942.

Al Morano has pointed out that not one of these five freshman members had any experience in the actual theaters of war or overseas comparable to Mrs. Luce's. She was, however, assigned to her second choice, the Military Affairs Committee, a position which in the wartime year of 1943 took on added importance. In the words of Morano, "It beats hell out of the Post Office Committee or the District of Columbia Committee or Merchant Marine and Fisheries."

Speaker Joe Martin told Mrs. Luce that freshmen should work hard on their committees and keep their mouths shut. She was determined to follow his advice. But her good resolutions collapsed early in February when an article by Vice-President Henry Wallace, calling for a policy of postwar freedom of the skies, appeared in the *American* magazine. Addressing himself to the problems of air transport, Wallace said, "When this war ends, we shall be only at the threshold of the coming air age. Freedom of the air means to the world of the future what freedom of the seas meant to the world of the past."

Clare, who was intensely air-minded, who had flown most of the then-commercial routes of the world, couldn't let this go unanswered. When a Congressman wishes to address the House on some subject other than a current piece of legislation, he does so under a "special order." This mechanism permits the member to make advance arrangements with the Speaker for a specific amount of time. By custom, such requests are granted when the legislative business for that day has been concluded. The presiding officer has to stay, the majority and the minority each delegate a representative to guard against any unanticipated parliamentary move. Usually these are the only members who remain in their seats and the freshman making a maiden speech can expect to address an empty chamber.

Al Morano says that when it became known Mrs. Luce would make her first speech on February 9, 1943, more than half the members stayed in the Chamber, but he admits, however, that they were probably motivated more by curiosity than by the thought that she might say anything of particular significance.

There was nothing very startling in the freshman Congresswoman's opening sentences. She thanked the people of Fairfield County for sending her to Congress; she acknowledged that both parties had recklessly charged the other with being unclear about postwar aims, when in fact, the uncertainty of the situation made it impossible to lay down any specific demands or proposals. She further said:

Let us pity and not condemn Mr. Roosevelt and Mr. Churchill lest they find themselves like us, floundering in a sea of uncertainty. Let us try to understand that in such a situation, they have no choice but to indulge in monumental generalities and noble catch-alls like the Atlantic Charter, and various platitudes like the Four Freedoms.

Then contradicting her own remarks, she launched into a very precise and particular definition of the future of air transport. She noted that the British Parliament had just engaged in debate on the same subject and concluded that it was necessary even in wartime to subsidize an expansion and extension of British Flag air routes. She said the world had operated historically on a policy of sovereignty of the skies, a policy

167

which had enabled the United States to become the greatest air carrier in the world, a factor now invaluable in our defense program. She said, "Until this hour, the sovereignty of the skies policy has stood us in excellent stead, both commercially and militarily, and I hope diplomatically." She then asked a rhetorical question, "Is that policy being challenged today? It is. By what and by whom? By the advocates of a new policy which we are beginning to hear a great deal about called 'freedom of the air'!"

Clare suggested that the members should read the article by Mr. Henry Wallace, Vice-President of the United States. She said she was a great admirer of some of Wallace's ideas. "He has a wholly disarming way of being intermittently inspiring and spasmodically sound and certainly in this magazine article, there is much that all men of good will must agree to." Two paragraphs later, she said, "But much of what Mr. Wallace calls his global thinking is, no matter how you slice it, still 'globaloney.' Mr. Wallace's warp of sense and his woof of *non*sense is a very tricky cloth out of which to cut the pattern of a postwar world."

All of the sound reasoning, the carefully documented historical truths in Mrs. Luce's maiden speech were obscured by that one flippant word. The next day, before a Senate committee looking into the same subject, Senator Millard Tydings practically repeated Clare's warnings, saying it would be reckless and premature for the United States to declare at this point for a policy of unlimited access to the skies above our territory.

The New York *Daily News* pointed out that Under Secretary of State Sumner Welles had taken a similar position in his arguments for a foreign policy of enlightened self-interest, but the Louisville *Courier-Journal* said, "Mrs. Luce goes further than even the most bigoted of isolationists has yet seen fit to travel along the road to economic isolationism."

The President had not indicated any support for Vice-President Wallace's theories, but politics being what it is, the Administration could not let Clare's challenge go unanswered. Freshman Congressman J. William Fulbright of Arkansas was delegated to refute the lady's logic. Mrs. Luce and Mr. Fulbright were on friendly terms personally, but this was a partisan chore. Fulbright said that Clare had inferred that the Vice-President's proposal would endanger the security of the United States, that she had inferred that the United States was working behind closed doors to develop a radically new air policy for the United States. Congresswoman Luce wasn't offended but she saw an opportunity to make the man from Arkansas a little uncomfortable and she took it. Fulbright had been a Rhodes scholar, the president of a university. In rebuttal, she said, "At several points the gentleman said that I had inferred this or that. I inferred nothing. I implied, and the gentleman from Arkansas did the inferring. Will the gentleman be good enough to give me the exact text?"

Years later, when Mrs. Luce was being interrogated by the Foreign Relations Committee after President Eisenhower had expressed his intention of making her the American Ambassador to Brazil, she discovered that Fulbright still remembered his embarrassment over this grammatical error. He started the day by saying, "I am implying certain defects and drawbacks I recognize in this nomination and Mrs. Luce can infer whatever she likes from my implication."

During the two years they served together in the Congress and in 1945 and 1946 when Fulbright was a freshman Senator, she enjoyed his friendship and company and never once suspected that her verbal thrust had punctured his ego.

In 1967 Senator Fulbright described his former colleague as "more mentally vigorous than a great many Congresswomen. She was a very beautiful and attractive woman and she used this feminine advantage in every argument or discussion we ever had." He admits there were many hours of friendly dialogue on the subject of American foreign policy. Much of the time there was agreement between them. Al Morano claims it was Mrs. Luce who first suggested the declaration which became famous as the Fulbright Resolution of 1943 and certainly she supported the Fulbright proposal when it was presented to Congress.

The text of that statement, "That the Congress hereby expresses itself as favoring the creation of appropriate international machinery with the power adequate to establish and to maintain a just and lasting peace among the nations of the world and as favoring participation by the United States therein," was consistent with everything Clare had ever said about foreign policy. (The Luce magazines vigorously applauded the proposal.) In supporting its adoption Mrs. Luce said:

By historic use, as well as by dictionary definition, the philosophy, the ethics, the morals, the principles, the sentiments of a nation are not the same thing as its policies; policy is, to put it another way, the pursuit of national or international ends by a choice of national means. A wise and honest nation will always demand that the international ends it seeks should be open and above-board, just and honorable; and so also should be the means to these ends.

What she envisioned was an association of nations possessing sufficient military power to keep the peace. She called for a nonaggression pact or military alliance with Great Britain, France and some of our other allies—an objective which was eventually satisfied when the North Atlantic Treaty Organization was formed.

In the 1943 debate which followed, she highlighted what she considered the ambivalence of American foreign policy. We had shipped petroleum and scrap iron to Japan while condemning that nation's war against the Chinese and publicly sympathizing with the Chinese people. We had, for political purposes, refused to admit the possibility of our interest being endangered by Hitler's aggression in Europe. We had supported appeasement at Munich. We had passed the so-called Neutrality Act.

The Democrats vigorously attacked Clare's claim that the United States had no foreign policy. They expressed resentment over the implication that the Roosevelt Administration was somehow responsible for America's state of unpreparedness. In her final statement on the subject Clare responded in a way to remove the charge that she was motivated by a blindly partisan feeling. She said, "Does the gentleman again misunderstand me? Because if he does, I want to correct him. I *am* against and *was* against both the isolationist and the interventionist, neither of which had a foreign policy."

Clare's "globaloney" speech wasn't the only good reason the Democrats had for regarding her with hostility. When the President invited the new members of Congress to the White House for the traditional social reception to be held on March 10, 1943, and for an exchange of views, Clare responded with a full-page letter questioning the President's conduct of the war on the home front and challenging the wisdom of the President's efforts to enlarge the power of the White House. She said that the new members of Congress were fearful

. . . that the conflict of the military program and the farm program may cause serious if not disastrous, food shortages. That the aggravating muddling of the Manpower Commission which does not seem to have done the elementary arithmetic of finding out how many men and women are needed by whom and for what, and where they can be got, may lead to a calamitous cramping of war industry, that the protracted wrangling and vacillating authority of the War Production Board may yet take its toll on the battlefield. And in all frankness, let me say, that to us in Congress has been transferred as if by swift contagion, the people's long-delayed fury against the swollen and wasteful Washington bureaucracies that have burgeoned through the years.

In her final paragraph she said, "Naturally, the Republicans hope that someday they will be the party really in power, not only because we do believe in the two party system, but also we believe in the political validity and human worth of historical Republicanism."

No one really believed Clare's explanation that she had honestly misconstrued this social invitation as a desire on the part of the President to explore the political thinking of the new members of Congress. To make matters worse, she released a copy of the letter to the press.

Presidential Press Secretary Steve Early responded with a curt note saying the meeting was purely social, not political.

In 1943, her first year in Congress, Mrs. Luce made only two major speeches on the floor of the House. Both of them dealt with American foreign policy and were generally interpreted to be anti-Administration and anti-Roosevelt.

Harry Luce had supported Clarence Streit's proposal for Union Now with his magazines and with some sizable personal contributions to help publicize the proposal. Streit, a veteran American foreign correspondent, had spent ten years in Geneva for *The New York Times,* returning to the United States in 1938 to promote his proposal for a federal union of the world's great democracies—the British Commonwealth, France, Belgium, the Netherlands, Switzerland, Denmark, Norway, Sweden and Finland. Clare thought the proposal utopian but impractical. She argued that a first-rate American foreign policy, one devoid of any ambivalence, would create the unity Streit sought to achieve without the great surrender of national sovereignty Union Now required.

There was nothing partisan in her criticism when she attacked the isolationists, saying, "Now the effort during the past forty years of millions of Americans in high places and low to avoid having any foreign policy at all has come to be known in our day as isolation." She blamed this attitude for our involvement in two foreign wars.

Congresswoman Luce had a flair for the use of words. She was identified in the public mind as a bitter and intemperate critic of the Administration. The major support for this contention is not to be found in the full text of her speeches, but rather in the colloquy with other members of the House following her endorsement of the Fulbright Resolution. Congressman J. Leroy Johnson of California interrupted to ask, "Out where I live we have a port. For five or six years before December 1941 out of that port went hundreds of thousands of tons of scrap steel, and the same thing out of San Francisco. It went to Japan. At the very same time we were shipping thousands of tons of steel, we were befriending or supposed to be befriending China. What kind of a policy was that?"

Congresswoman Luce replied, "That is the isolationist policy of Mr. Roosevelt which I am presently going to describe."

Congressman George Anthony Dondero of Michigan then interrupted to say, "I have a distinct recollection of the campaign of 1940 when some of us were charged with some of the things the lady is now announcing. Is it not true that even the President of the United States then announced that the boys of this nation would never fight on foreign soil?"

Given this opening, Mrs. Luce said, "It is perfectly true. As the gentleman from Michigan says, in the last election the President outdid

Mr. Willkie in telling the people of the United States their boys would never be put on troopships and sent overseas. What safeguarded his political position for him at that time was that the insiders all knew he was talking with his tongue in his cheek. Now it is one thing for a private citizen to talk with his tongue in his cheek, but it is quite another thing for the President of the United States to talk with his tongue in his cheek. Of the whole American people, Mr. Roosevelt was in reality an interventionist talking like an isolationist."

Clare thinks she had difficulty with the press, that she wasn't reported accurately, that the newspapers emphasized her minor points and ignored her major theme. This may be partially true, but her independence of mind, her refusal to conform to the Republican Party lines or to the majority opinion of her own class, made her appear unpredictable, if not undependable. She voted against the Smith-Connally Act, a bill designed to give the President more power to deal with strikes and work stoppages. She opposed the first version of the Carlson-Ruml withholding-tax proposal because it provided for forgiveness of all tax on 1942 income. Clare offered an amendment which would limit the tax gift to the first $25,000 of income. She said the wealthy didn't deserve such a windfall.

Her amendment was defeated in the House on March 30, 1943. On April 1 the Administration, using Clare's argument, managed to defeat the full bill by a vote of 215 to 198. Clare was paired in favor. In May she voted against a revived and revised version. Doing so, she was the only Republican from Connecticut to vote no.

When the Smith-Connally Bill was debated on the floor of the House on June 2, 1943, Clare, who had voted in favor of reporting the bill out of committee, told the House that she had made a mistake. "I shall not hesitate ever, I hope, to say when I have made a mistake, and I do not feel that two wrong votes are ever going to make one right vote. For that reason I am today opposed to the rule."

Clare had been vocally critical of Donald Nelson and his management of the War Production Board, but in this instance she gave as a reason for changing her mind the fact that the War Labor Board (headed by the same Donald Nelson), the National Labor Relations Board, the Army and the Navy were opposed to the Smith-Connally Bill.

On June 27, 1943, Mrs. Luce journeyed to Appleton, Wisconsin, to address the Republican state convention.

It is not uncommon for a Senator or a Congressman to be invited to keynote a state party convention, but the fact that the Wisconsin Republicans invited a freshman Congresswoman to fill this important spot on their program was an indication of respect for her opinions and her ability.

In the speech she referred to the Republican Administrations prior to the election of Franklin Roosevelt as "the Old Deal" and she said it was "in large part the failure of the Old Deal to give equal justice to every individual and group—above all, the farmer and the laborer—which finally overthrew the Old Deal and brought the New Deal to power." Then she predicted that F.D.R. would attempt to win an unprecedented fourth term, and that because his domestic policy had been such a total failure, the campaign would be fought over foreign policy.

She said:

This Administration has no coherent policy, or if it has, it is keeping it as secretly to itself as any dictator ever kept his. And let us get this clear —the Four Freedoms are not a policy. They are simply the expression of principles and sentiments—principles and sentiments which are totally incapable of application to the whole world. Indeed, they are only capable of application to parts of the world on the condition that our nation embrace a foreign policy vigorous enough to implement them, if need be, by force. Windy, high-flown talk of world councils, regional federations, world federations, world government, world police forces or even under the League of Nations, indeed, talk of inner machinery for so-called collective security is meaningless unless our statesmen first collect their wits and decide how America can best secure herself.

These are all dazzle-dust terms thrown into the people's eyes in order to be able to complain that the people do not see.

Americans, who were still on the losing end of World War II and wanted desperately to have confidence in their President, had accepted the Four Freedoms in the way most Christians accept the Apostles'

Creed. It is no wonder the press reacted to Clare's speech and her flippant, descriptive phrase "dazzle dust."

The *Daily Worker* declared Clare had "aligned herself with the defeatist forces in the country by stating that the New Deal was dead."

Time magazine said, "Representative Clare Luce keynoted a Republican convention at Appleton, Wisconsin. Her speech was a model of partisan politics."

Representative James P. Richards, Democrat of South Carolina, defended the New Deal on the floor of the House in rebuttal to Clare's Appleton speech, and said:

She has shrouded the issue in a maze of words which will most surely drive ordinary men mad should they make the futile effort to harmonize and interpret them. The gentlewoman has injected a bitter partisan tone which heretofore has been omitted from our discussions of this momentous step in our foreign policy.

Novelist Edna Ferber, one of Clare's Connecticut constituents, took exception to that part of the Appleton speech in which Clare said the United States had shunned its responsibilities by not opposing Hitler with more vigor prior to the 1940 elections. In a letter to *The New York Times* she wrote:

She [Mrs. Luce] does not represent me in this. Her most appalling staement to date. Far in advance of Pearl Harbor, I and millions of American men and women were strongly in favor of the United States taking its rightful part in the destruction of the Nazi regime.

If Clare Luce and those for whom she speaks were aroused to the necessity for action only after a handful of Japanese attacked Pearl Harbor, then she is a self-confessed condoner of Hitler, and the Hitler regime and the Hitler plan from 1933 to 1941, and for all I know, to this day.

Clare had always considered Miss Ferber her friend. They had been acquainted for many years and this unexpected attack was hard to take, particularly since she believed her play *Margin for Error* had been written as an attack against Nazism. Nevertheless, remembering the

Dorothy Thompson affair, Clare refused to comment in rebuttal. In 1948, after Clare was out of Congress, Miss Ferber wrote her an apologetic note saying that when she sent her letter to the *Times* she hadn't read the whole speech, and asked forgiveness on the grounds that she had been caught up in the hysteria of the moment.

In Salem, Oregon, the *Capital Journal,* a newspaper of limited circulation but great political influence in the West, editorialized on Clare's Appleton speech, saying, "In Representative Clare Boothe Luce of Connecticut the Republicans have found their ablest campaign orator, next to Wendell Willkie, and she is perhaps more subtle than the latter, a better master of satired invective and phrase-coiner—using the rapier rather than the broadsword."

Harriet Hughes Crowley in the Detroit *Free Press* headed her column with this bit of doggerel:

> "A lawmaker, wiley and fair . . .
> Wore bows on each side of her hair . . .
> Of velvet her clothes . . .
> And with voice like a dove's . . .
> She cooed as she knifed . . . c'est la Clare . . ."

The *New Republic* commented that Clare "blew hot and cold from liberalism to isolationism," speculated that she was probably genuinely sorry for the globaloney speech because it had laid such an egg. "A political career is a relatively new thing for Mrs. Luce and it is not surprising that she has made almost the classic fool of herself." Later on in the same article the *New Republic* revived the story that her request for a place on the Foreign Affairs Committee was an act of vast presumption, and implied that Russell Davenport at the time had actually written the globaloney speech, and then in his position as an editor of *Time* had been forced to criticize Clare for delivering it.

Bouquets or brickbats, catcalls or cheers, every line of comment added to Clare's national reputation. Seventeen newspapers, including *The New York Times,* the New York *Herald Tribune,* and the Washington, D.C., *Times-Herald,* ran lengthy news stories when she had trouble firing a domestic servant.

Apparently the maid found the job too hectic after a very short period of service on the Luce staff in Connecticut and went to a reporter with her complaints. In response to questions about the incident, Clare replied, "We have lost an old family retainer who has been with us for almost two weeks."

Shortly after Clare went to Washington, Major Fred Eldridge, editor of a service newspaper, the *China-Burma-India Round-Up,* asked her to do a column for the men overseas. She obliged under the title "Here the Gavel Fell." Despite its political heading, most of what Clare wrote was a rehash of her experience as a war correspondent on these fronts, generously larded with the names and exploits of the military men and the military units she knew something about.

After Clare's speech to the Republican convention in Wisconsin the War Department banned her writings as politically controversial and ordered Eldridge to discontinue the column. There were letters from readers of the service paper charging censorship, and partisan Republicans said the Administration was stifling criticism.

All of the press items in this period were not exclusively political. A national public-opinion poll found that after Marlene Dietrich, Congresswoman Luce was deemed to have the most beautiful pair of legs in America, whereupon Walter Winchell reported that when a member teased Clare with this question, "Don't you think it's beneath the dignity of this House to have one of its members voted among the six women in America with the most beautiful legs?" Clare replied, "Don't you realize, Congressman, that you are just falling for some subtle New Deal propaganda designed to distract attention from the end of me that is really functioning?"

The *Reader's Digest* alleged the following to be true: "Returning to her office from one of the sessions of the House, Clare had found a letter on her desk which it turned out later was intended for a Miss Luce in the Sanitation Department." She opened the envelope and read, "There are termites in President Roosevelt's swimming pool. Please take care of this at once." According to the *Digest,* Clare's comment was "Fourth termites, I presume."

On July 6, 1943, speaking before the Institute of Arts and Sciences at Columbia University, Congresswoman Luce called for the repeal of the Chinese Exclusion Act, which she said would go far to promote a better understanding between ourselves and the Chinese nation. She said:

These anti-Chinese laws put upon our statute books many years ago by Congress seemed to have anticipated and given approval to the whole Hitler doctrine of race theology. The next Congress will attempt to repeal them and put the Chinese people on the regular, long-established quota system. That quota would allow the entry of exactly one hundred and five Chinese a year—hardly a threat to American labor markets, the American way of life, or even our so-called white civilization.

In a speech at the University of Rochester on November 18, 1943, Clare accused Britain of hanging on to India for reasons of commerce and empire. After recognizing that British rule had maintained the stability necessary for the peace of the world, she said:

The heart cries out and the head argues too . . . that three hundred and ninety million men who want to be free and self-providing and prosperous must be free and self-providing. If it is not good that they should be free and prosperous, then all notions of progress and freedom are lies. And religion itself is a lie, and surely all the great spiritual things we claim we're fighting for in this war are lies, and that just cannot be so.

Clare did say the United States should be prepared to compensate Great Britain for the commercial loss and be willing to assume responsibility for the military defense of Asia against aggressive nations. But the main thrust was for Indian independence and that's the way the newspapers reported it.

Two days after the speech Clare received a six-page cablegram in purple prose disputing her logic, condemning her sentimentality and contradicting all her assumptions. The cable had been transmitted on the regular commercial wires and was signed "Churchill."

Clare assumed that the Prime Minister's son Randolph had sent it and promptly consigned the critique to the wastebasket. Surely if the Prime Minister of Great Britain had wanted to communicate with her, he would have used the more conventional diplomatic channels.

Many years later when the Luces were visiting Sir Winston in the south of France, he observed over a cup of tea that Clare was the only lady to whom he had ever sent a lengthy cable and received no acknowledgment whatsoever.

8

The Private Woman

The image of Clare Boothe Luce as a happy, successful sophisticate was widely accepted by her contemporaries. The profile in *The New Yorker* by Margaret Case Harriman [1] titled "The Candor Kid" paid tribute to Clare's beauty and talents, but left the reader with the impression that a cold and calculating mind had directed her climb to fame and fortune. In public Mrs. Luce radiated self-confidence. Only a few close friends —her second husband was not of this group—were permitted to see the softer, less assured self. In many ways she regards her personal life as a series of tragic disappointments. In her relationships with both her first and second husbands she failed to achieve the warmth and mutual dependency usually associated with a successful marriage. . . .

> "Though I go by with banners, oh never envy me . . .
>   These flags of scarlet flying, this purple that you see . . .
> Was all that I could save . . . of love that had an ending . . .
>   And hope that had a grave."

Margaret Widdemer's sentimental verse might have been written to describe the strikingly beautiful blond girl from the wrong side of the tracks whose personal and public achievements made her the object of envy on the part of those who didn't know.

Perhaps Clare didn't marry George Brokaw for his money, but

[1] Published 1941.

everyone *thought* she did, including her mother and her brother David. She believed she was truly in love with Harry Luce, but there is too much evidence of Harry's preoccupation with his magazines not to suspect that Clare was often lonely in a way her close friends could not compensate for.

Harry and Clare were more like partners in power than they were like bourgeois married people. This may be why Clare has always over-dramatized her lack of blood relations and why she always displayed such tenderness for her brother David.

When Clare married George Brokaw, David enjoyed having a multimillionaire brother-in-law, and he also turned the situation to his financial advantage. About the time his sister finally made up her mind to file for divorce, David gave up the stock-brokerage business, rejoined the Marines and went off to fight or frolic in Nicaragua. In 1931 David came back to New York with an honorable discharge from the Marines and formed a new partnership with Romero Petronino, a stock salesman he had known earlier. The new firm leased an office from Kuhn Loeb and Company at 54 William Street in Manhattan, and Clare paid the rent.

David took over as the business manager for the investments his sister had acquired in her settlement with Brokaw. The record isn't clear as to how much leeway Clare gave him in the management of her portfolio, but as her fiscal agent David did preserve the principal and provide Clare with a satisfactory income. One of his reports, dated July 15, 1936, shows Clare's holdings were worth approximately $490,000. Her investments were fifty percent in Government securities, twenty percent in railroads, fifteen percent in utilities and fifteen percent in common stock—a good conservative position considering the state of the market at that time. Eventually David Boothe managed to lose most of his sister's money in the market.

Perhaps David Boothe never quite made the transition back to civilian life after his early experience in the Marines. At any rate, when the shadow of hostilities appeared on the world scene in 1939, he told his sister he wanted to go to flying school and become a pilot.

This interest in aviation might have had quite a different inspiration. After Clare married Harry she bought a sizable amount of Canadian-Colonial Airways, Inc., stock with the understanding that David would become an executive with the company. Apparently this didn't work out but there is nothing to indicate whether the failure was due to David's financial ineptitude or the result of the changing world situation produced by the war.

Clare continued to exhibit an almost maternal interest in David's welfare. As late as 1940 she was writing him notes to remind him to keep a dental appointment with a Dr. Heiser. "I can see there is going to be a race as to which falls out of the plane first—your teeth or you. Enclosed is enough to get you in and out of town for the dentist appointment. If you use this for any other purpose, so help me God, I'll come down the street and personally brain you . . . Love, Clare."

David enrolled in the Ryan School of Aviation in San Diego in early December 1940, and for Christmas the Luces sent him a new wrist watch. Explaining how useful it would be, he said in a letter to his sister:

In these open planes it is impossible, for me anyhow, to reach for the time. Better if the time has to come to you. My seat belt is always fastened so tightly that my old watch is practically in dead storage. If I unfasten my safety belt to get at the time, I will probably hit a bump and get thrown clear of the plane. If I don't get the time, I will run out of gas and come down in a hurry. The moral is: Never contemplate aviation unless you have a good wrist watch.

Then he added:

Since December 11, the day I soloed, I have been without friends. You must solo to understand this reaction. At that time I corraled my moneys in company with some other aviators and did a little debauching. Remember no matter how long you live you can only solo once.

The Ryan School gives each solo artist some gold wings. Enclosed herewith are mine. If you manage to outlive me, which I doubt, place said wings on my coffin. This relieves Dr. Austin of the responsibility of covering my abdomen with a white Masonic apron. Anyhow, where I'm going wings won't be the vogue.

David indicated a desire to be accepted at Southwest Airways Training School in Phoenix. This civilian contract operation, offering basic training for military aides, was owned by John Swope and Leland Hayward. Clare was able to make the arrangements.

The losses Clare suffered as the result of money loaned to her brother apparently had no effect on her affection for him, but they were substantial. In August 1941 she wrote him a very gentle creditor letter beginning:

DEAR DAVID . . . As you know, at various times during the last three years I have made advances to you. Some of these were contributions I was only too glad to make . . . either at times when you needed money or to help you in business.

But as you know, I also made available to you substantial sums which you borrowed and which I have every reason to expect you to repay. These loans total $49,791.84 as follows:

Cash advanced on April 14, 1939, evidenced by your demand note bearing the same date, $12,609.50.

$31,000 principal amount, state of Arkansas three percent Series A Road District Bonds, due January 1, 1949, which were delivered to you on July 29, 1936, when their market value was $25,182.34.

Two thousand shares of American Colortype common stock delivered to you on May 17, 1938, when their market price was $12,000.

Total: $49,791.84.

These figures are correct according to my records, but I would appreciate your confirmation on the duplicate of this letter which I am enclosing.

The way things have gone for you, I don't see how you can possibly make any repayment. Hence, I suppose the best I can do is write it off as an income tax loss. Sincerely, CLARE

There was no love in that signature.

David's response to this letter indicates that the warmth of the brother-sister relationship would survive all sorts of vicissitudes. On many occasions Clare has confessed an inability to understand any mathematical problem by saying "I have to do sums counting my fingers and toes." But her request that David acknowledge an indebtedness of about $50,000 is so much an understatement it cannot be explained by saying Clare was a poor bookkeeper. According to the answer David gave his sister, the proper amount was somewhere between $250,000 and $500,000—which, he said, represented the true total of the amounts loaned and investments converted to his personal account.

Just one transaction—the sale of some Homestake gold-mining shares in 1934—had provided him with $175,000.

He concluded this letter with:

According to the accountant's figures, I got $250,000 in just four years, or $60,000 average per year, plus my own income. On the face of it, I am dumb, sister. Sorry I wrote you the other letter. It was a stinking thing to do. Something told me you didn't believe in miracles. Neither do I. Guess I'm like the counsel in your play—he was such a villain everyone hated to see him die so soon.

After Pearl Harbor David, with some help from Clare, managed to be accepted as an enlisted liaison pilot. He was much too old for such an assignment, but he worked his way through a barrier of red tape and served in the Asiatic-Pacific Theater.

David flew in New Guinea, the Philippines, Borneo and China. He was awarded a Presidential Unit Citation, the Air Medal, First, Second, Third, Fourth and Fifth Oak Leaf Cluster, a Purple Heart, eight Bronze Stars and the Richter Ribbon. He logged one thousand eleven hours of combat flight time. Clare was very proud of him, and she probably helped his career by writing to the officers on MacArthur's staff urging them to give David special consideration. But the honors and citations didn't come to him because he was her brother.

After he was mustered out, David couldn't seem to readjust to civilian life again. His violent, uncontrolled temper frightened his old friends. In a fit of rage or a seizure of combat fatigue, he very nearly killed one of the servants at Mepkin. He had no job and no income so he borrowed money from his sister and brother-in-law.

David Boothe brought an Australian bride to Connecticut and lived in a house Clare had purchased for him in 1946. He tried his hand at stock selling again, then when his wife divorced him he tried to get back in the air transport field, and finally moved out to California.

On September 8, 1948, David Boothe rented a small plane from Glendale School of Aviation at Grand Central Airport in Burbank. He flew out over the Pacific Ocean and never returned. Some members of a fishing party reported they had seen the craft crash. The plane wasn't found. David's body was never recovered.

In August 1943 the women's division of the Republican Party announced that Congresswoman Luce would make a four-week speaking tour of twenty states, commencing on September 28. After the tour had been planned and publicized she bowed out, on the score of ill-health.

When Congress recessed, she went to Mepkin to spend Christmas with Harry and all his nieces and nephews and her stepsons and her daughter Ann, who was then a senior at Stanford University. The tour was rescheduled to start in January 1944, with an opening speech to be delivered at the Los Angeles Biltmore Hotel.

The Luce party—Mrs. Luce, daughter Ann and husband Harry— left New York for California on the second day of January, accompanied by Miss Virginia Blood, a young Connecticut woman who had been elected to the state legislature and was anxious to expand her political activities. Serving as traveling secretary to Mrs. Luce would, it was thought, give her favorable publicity and strengthen her chances for re-election.

One of Clare's great gifts is an ability to concentrate, to devote all of her energy and attention to one subject or one individual at a time. She is like an actress playing three or four leading roles in as many separate theaters simultaneously, without letting either the audience or the supporting cast discover that she has any interest in life other than what she is doing for this audience in this theater at this moment.

During the Christmas holidays and on the Western trip she devoted all of her attention to her daughter.

Ann Clare was to graduate from Stanford University in June, three months before her twentieth birthday. She was a serious-minded, sensitive girl, not quite so beautiful as her mother or her grandmother, but attractive and more mature than most nineteen-year-olds. Despite the handicap of having lived in the shadow of a famous mother and an illustrious stepfather, Ann had developed her own philosophy of life.

Tom Moore, Mr. Luce's nephew, has described Ann as exceptionally mature, and a brilliant scholar. He says she was annoyed at the gossips who were continually hinting that her mother's sex appeal was the secret of her success. In order to be able to defend both Clare and Harry against their critics Ann read everything that was written about foreign policy and domestic politics. He remembers that she was greatly disturbed by an editorial which appeared in an International Teamsters Union publication just before Christmas, opening with the words "Clare Boothe Luce of Connecticut, the Congressional snake charmer, spread some more of her 'globaloney' recently." At Mepkin, Ann had shown him an article from the Danbury, North Carolina, *Reporter* which commenced with the statement, "Clare Boothe Luce is said to be very beautiful. She is a very beautiful liar unless, forsooth, she is short on information and is only innocently loose tongued."

(What had aroused the ire of the Danbury editorialist was Clare's statement that "the American people could never have been branded as isolationists if President Roosevelt and his State Department had disclosed to the nation the danger of which they themselves were fully aware. The Administration suppressed the facts because 1940 was an election year.")

Ann shared most of her mother's opinions of the Roosevelt Administration, its conduct of the war, and the world situation in general.

Traveling on the *Santa Fe Chief* to Los Angeles, Clare showed Ann a copy of the speech she intended to deliver at the Biltmore Hotel. In it she called for national unity to support the war effort and Republican strength to correct the errors of "drift and improvise" which she said were the chief characteristics of American policy at the moment.

Ann approved the speech and was delighted when the audience gave Clare a standing ovation and the Los Angeles newspapers applauded her statement.

On Thursday, January 6, Harry Luce returned to New York. Ann, Clare and Virginia Blood went on to the Mark Hopkins Hotel in San Francisco. Clare's next speaking engagement was in that city on Tuesday, the eleventh. Mrs. Luce had arranged it so in order to spend more time with her daughter Ann, who was not due back at Stanford until Monday morning, the tenth. Miss Blood would take care of any problems in connection with the tour, and mother and daughter would have an uninterrupted five days to shop and sight-see and visit friends.

On Sunday morning, January 9, Ann and Clare went for a walk. Halfway down the hill toward Market Street they passed a small Catholic church, and Ann suggested they go in.

Mrs. Luce agreed to what she thought was her daughter's impulsive suggestion inspired by the beauty of the morning. They stayed through the Mass, then walked on down to the St. Francis Hotel for their breakfast.

In retrospect, this seemingly casual attendance at that Catholic church becomes extremely important to any understanding of the greatest sorrow in Clare's life.

That night Clare and Ann went to a small dinner party given by Mrs. Hampton Cameron, who had been one of Clare's classmates at the Castle. When they returned to the Mark Hopkins they found a message from Virginia Lee Hobbs, one of Ann's school friends.

Miss Hobbs, the note said, would be driving down to Palo Alto early Monday morning. She would be delighted to have Ann go with her.

The Stanford campus is only about twenty miles down the peninsula from San Francisco. Mrs. Luce had been planning to get up early, drive Ann down in a rented car so she could register, and spend the day on the campus. It was agreed that Ann would go with Virginia; her mother would come down about noon. They would have lunch and spend the afternoon together.

Ann telephoned Virginia Hobbs to say she would be packed and ready and in the lobby of the hotel at seven o'clock Monday morning. Then mother and daughter spent a happy hour discussing the party, the holidays, Ann's plans for a career when she was graduated (she wanted to be a diplomat), and a great many other things, including Ann's new hairdo. It was after midnight when they finally went to bed.

Clare Luce was aroused from her sleep the next morning by two strong hands shaking her shoulders and an almost hysterical voice screaming "Wake up! You wake up! Your daughter is dead!"

In that half-conscious state Clare thought she must be having a nightmare. Then as the voice repeated the words "your daughter is dead" over and over, she jumped out of bed and faced Virginia Blood, her hysterical secretary. "What are you trying to tell me?"

"Ann's been killed. There was an accident. She was thrown from the car. She was dead when they got her to the hospital. Don't you want to go down there?"

There was a long silence. "I don't know what I want to do," Ann's mother replied, "but whatever it is I want to do it alone. Please get out of here."

She dressed slowly. Then she went into the other room and told Miss Blood, who had somewhat regained her composure, to put in a call for Mr. Luce.

"Aren't you going down to Palo Alto?" her secretary demanded.

"No, I'm not going down there. I'm going to take a walk and pray to God to help me to understand this. When you reach Mr. Luce, please tell him that I'll be back here in half an hour."

Clare went down the hill to the little Catholic church where she and Ann had worshiped the day before. She discovered the only prayer she knew or could say was "Our Father, Who Art in Heaven." She was, she realized, a stranger in God's house—not anti-Christian, not an atheist, not an agnostic, but she had no faith. Her grief turned to resentment against any God who could have permitted this to happen. Yesterday she and Ann had been here together in response to what she had thought was her daughter's whim. Had it been a premonition? What, she wondered, had Ann thought of God and church and life and death?

She went back to the hotel and talked to Harry, who had already made his reservation and would be on the plane within an hour. The thought of spending any time in the hotel room with or without Miss Blood was unbearable. Clare remembered that Colonel Townsend, the Army officer with whom she had shared a slit trench in Burma in 1942, had been at the Camerons' party. She found the Colonel's telephone number and called him. "I am in more trouble now, much more than we were in Burma. Will you come help?"

The Colonel didn't ask what kind of trouble. He just said he would be there in twenty minutes.

When he arrived Mrs. Luce told him what had happened. By this time she had the details. The two girls were in an open convertible only two blocks from the campus when Kurt Bergel, a refugee assistant instructor in an Army specialist training unit, drove his car out of a side street and struck the convertible from behind. Virginia Hobbs was only slightly injured. Ann was hurled from the car. Her head struck a tree and she was killed.

For more than two hours Colonel Townsend and the bereaved mother walked the hills of San Francisco in silence. The physical exercise, the Colonel's presence, all helped Clare over what she has described as the darkest hours of her life.

When they returned to the hotel and the Colonel had gone, Clare asked Miss Blood to locate the priest at the little church and say that she would like to see him. She wasn't sure what a priest could tell her, but she knew she needed help.

Telling Harry about it later, she described the visit as a disaster. "I said, 'Young man, I've got some questions to ask you and I want some straight answers.' I asked him why Ann was killed, and to tell me the meaning of life and death."

The bewildered cleric, obviously uncomfortable in the presence of this celebrated public figure, tried to respond but his answers failed to comfort her. They were, she says, too pat, too shallow.

Ann's death changed everything—Clare's attitude toward life, the world, the future and perhaps even toward her husband. In some subtle way she transferred her resentment over this tragedy to him. It seemed to her that Henry Robinson Luce had never suffered a defeat. There was nothing in his own experience which could help him understand Clare's situation.

The Luces took Ann's body to Mepkin to be buried in the little private cemetery of Strawberry Chapel. Later Clare Luce took the remains of her mother to rest beside those of her daughter. But she left a space for herself between the two headstones.

A measure of the affectionate relationship between Henry Luce and his stepdaughter is indicated by the notice in the obituary column of *Time* magazine, which reported "the accidental death of Ann Brokaw, daughter of Mr. and Mrs. Henry Robinson Luce."

9

Clare Finds the Real Reason

Clare stayed at Mepkin until February 2. She says now she lost all desire to be active in the world when Ann was killed, and there is ample evidence to support the belief that this tragedy did have a great impact on Clare's personal life and her attitude toward religion. But publicly and politically there was no perceptible change. Her critics continued their attacks and Clare responded in kind.

On February 6 Drew Pearson's "Daily Washington Merry-Go-Round" had this comment:

Representative Clare Luce probably never realized before she came to Washington how true to life is her sparkling play, "The Women." Her friends got a taste of it in a cocktail lounge in a conversation between Representative Winifred Stanley of New York, Mrs. Luce's chief competitor for Congressional "glamour girl" honors, and bewhiskered ex-Representative George Tinkham of Massachusetts.

Introduced to the blond Miss Stanley in the Carlton Hotel, Tinkham inquired if she knew Mrs. Luce, said he would like to meet her.

"I would be delighted to introduce you," purred Miss Stanley; "you like actresses, don't you?"

This floored Tinkham. A famous globe-trotter who used to hunt elephants in Africa, he tried to change the subject by commenting on Mrs. Luce's travels.

"Oh, yes," responded Miss Stanley, "Miss Luce is a well-known traveler. She spent fifteen minutes in Tokyo and flitted through most of the other capitals hunting for material for her writings."

That same week Fay Henle's *Au Clare de Luce* was published and more fuel was added to the fire.

Stephen Daye, reviewing this book in the San Diego, California, *Union,* said:

Mrs. Luce's life is one chapter in the contemporary American success story. So handled it might have told us much about our own social, economic and political standards. Unfortunately, this biography contents itself with drawing an intellectualized glamour girl in the first half and in the second with making her a sometimes ridiculous, always calculating public figure.

Clare came home to Greenwich on February 3 in time to read an item in the New York *Daily News* headlined "Green-eyed Males Bar Clare Luce as Delegate."

Writer Dick Lee said, "Connecticut's gift to the glamour department of Congress and the Republican Party—Representative Clare Boothe Luce—is being subjected to an attempted deflation by the male meanies among the powers that be in our home state. They have barred her as a delegate to the GOP national convention in Chicago."

The story went on to explain that the GOP Central Committee, meeting in Hartford on January 31, had passed a resolution declaring "No elective officials except the Governor of the State of Connecticut shall be eligible as a delegate to the Republican National Convention. This shall be construed to include members of Congress."

The Central Committee had indeed adopted such a resolution, but to report that it was aimed exclusively at barring Clare is a good example of the kind of journalistic emphasis which justifies Clare's belief that she was treated unfairly by the press.

In the Seventy-eighth Congress, Connecticut was represented by six members of the House and two members of the Senate. Seven members of the delegation were Republican. Only Senator Francis T. Maloney of Meriden was a Democrat, and the party action, which the news story said was aimed at Clare, denied a seat on the state delegation to five other Representatives and one United States Senator, John A. Danaher of Portland.

Party workers consider it a high honor to be elected as a delegate or an alternate to a national convention. Connecticut that year was entitled to sixteen delegates. By eliminating the seven members of Congress, the ruling would make it possible for some less well known members of the party to be chosen.

Mrs. Luce understood this. She issued a mild statement saying that she would leave her status as a delegate up to the Fairfield County Republicans. Then she returned to Congress and went back to work on February 15.

The country's problems—winning the war and then winning the peace—were still to be solved. President Roosevelt favored a National Service Act as a means of overcoming the manpower shortage. Congresswoman Luce introduced a bill calling for induction into the Army for limited service in essential war activities of between fifty thousand and two hundred thousand men previously classified as 4-F. Organized labor, fighting to break the Little Steel Agreement for wage controls, bitterly opposed her proposal to put men in uniform, receiving Army pay and under military discipline in the factories and foundries where workers were desperately needed. Some of Mrs. Luce's Republican colleagues accused her of joining the opposition.

In March, along with twenty-three other Republican Congressmen, she signed a letter to Secretary of State Cordell Hull demanding that the Government reveal its objectives in the war and its plans for peace. Hull met with the protesting members of Congress. Mrs. Luce came away from the gathering convinced the Roosevelt Administration had no plans and was drifting with the tide.

In Connecticut, State Chairman J. Kenneth Bradley was urging the Republicans to select Mrs. Luce as keynote speaker for the convention, and Clifford Prevost, writing in the Brooklyn *Eagle,* said of this suggestion, "Not in years have we had an attractive or even a really good orator open one of these conventions. Not professing to know just who Clare will support this fall, we venture to say she would wow 'em if given the job of keynoting at Chicago next June."

On March 5 it was officially announced that Miss Virginia Blood had completed her work as a temporary member of Congresswoman Luce's secretarial staff and would return to Connecticut. Mrs. Luce had forgiven the girl for her hysterical reaction at the time of Ann's death, but her presence in Washington was a painful reminder of that morning, and privately Clare was fighting her inward doubts about the meaning of death and life. She had lost weight and was neglecting her appearance. Her friend Arthur Krock was seriously concerned for her physical welfare. He knew Clare had been deeply influenced by a book on soul transmigration titled *A New Model of the Universe*. The author was a Russian mystic name Uspenski, who had fled to Constantinople to escape the Bolsheviks.

Much later Mrs. Luce described her philosophy of life at this period as Lucspenskyism—a foggy, indefinite belief in the resurrection of the body which "allowed the soul to spin time and again into the same though different body until spiraling up it perfected itself and became part of God, or spiraling down, destroyed itself and became nothingness."

In April the Connecticut Republicans reversed their earlier decision and elected Mrs. Luce a delegate to the national convention. Tom Dewey was front runner for the nomination, and his managers vetoed the selection of Clare as keynote speaker after making a deal with California's Governor, Earl Warren. The Dewey people wanted the support of the California delegation, and to justify their refusal to accept Mrs. Luce, they said she was committed to Willkie—an allegation which CBL promptly denied.

Willkie's conduct as titular head of the party after his loss in 1940 —his support of F.D.R. and his advocacy of a one-world government— was regarded as disloyal. Both Harry and Clare had become disillusioned. Harry had lost none of his desire to be a political kingmaker, but Tom Dewey was an established personality. He didn't need a build-up in *Time* or *Life,* and could afford to maintain an independent attitude toward its publisher and the publisher's Congresswoman wife.

The last time the Luces seriously discussed the 1944 nomination with Willkie was during a weekend at Mepkin. The 1940 Republican nominee outlined his plans for "one world," a vision which Mrs. Luce thought as utopian as Union Now. When Willkie asked her opinion, she bluntly advised him "to stop drinking, lose forty pounds and adopt a more realistic understanding of the Communists' announced plan to conquer the world."

The Republican National Convention that year met in Chicago on June 27. Possibly as a gesture of appeasement to the Connecticut forces, or to *Time-Life,* the lady from Fairfield was assigned to make one of the preliminary speeches on the opening day.

Once more her imagery with words and her bitter attack on F.D.R. aroused a storm of protest. She spoke of G.I. Jim, the soldier who had lost his life in the war, and his buddy, G.I. Joe. She recited that paragraph from Roosevelt's speech in which he had promised the mothers and fathers of America "again and again and again" that their sons were not going to be sent to fight any foreign war.

Those promises were made, she claimed, "for the wholly selfish purpose of winning the pending election, by a government that was elected again and again and again because it made them, and they, the promises, lie quite as dead as young Jim lies now. Jim was the heroic heir of an unheroic decade of confusion and conflict which ended in war —the Roosevelt decade."

The Republicans nominated Thomas E. Dewey on the first ballot and named Governor John Bricker of Ohio to be his running mate.

At the Democratic convention F.D.R. was "drafted" for a fourth term, but he dumped Vice-President Wallace and selected Senator Harry S. Truman for his Vice-Presidential candidate.

According to the newspapers, the convention leaders had told Roosevelt that Wallace was unacceptable and asked for suggestions. Many newspapers, even those supporting the Administration for a fourth term were publicly critical of the fact that Roosevelt had instructed his floor leaders to clear the Vice-Presidential selection with labor leader Sidney Hillman. When Congress reconvened, Clare requested unanimous consent to address the House for ten seconds.

The Speaker politely inquired, "Is there any objection to the request from the gentlewoman from Connecticut?" There was no objection. She made her speech.

"Mr. Speaker, clear everything with Sidney."

On August 9 Clare Boothe Luce announced for re-election, and Samuel Gruber, director of the CIO Political Action Committee for Fairfield County, Connecticut, told the Communist *Daily Worker* that the PAC intended to use cold calculation in its efforts to prevent her re-election.

The Democrats, apparently feeling they needed a woman candidate to oppose Clare, nominated Miss Margaret Connors, a twenty-nine-year-old Bridgeport attorney who had served as Deputy Secretary of State, special agent for the Department of Justice, and as counsel for the American Civil Liberties Union.

Miss Connors, twelve years younger than Mrs. Luce and quite attractive, announced that "with President Roosevelt on my side and some hard work, we'll beat the incumbent."

In her speech before the Connecticut Republican convention accepting the nomination, Clare warned against "Communist strangulation by underground American forces spawned, nurtured and encouraged by the Roosevelt New Deal misrepresentation."

Sidney Hillman, Earl Browder, Henry Wallace, Dorothy Parker, Quentin Reynolds, Orson Welles, Clifton Fadiman and Dorothy Thompson all endorsed the Democratic nominee.

The *Daily Worker* described Clare as "the lady with the dry ice smile, and an aristocratic contempt for the people who work for a living."

Clifton Fadiman, the New York author and radio personality, called her "an Elizabeth Dilling, redesigned by Bergdorf Goodman" —Miss Dilling being one of the more outspoken anti-Communists of the period.

In a speech in Philadelphia Congresswoman Luce prophesied the Republicans would restore unity and said, "After the election there will be nothing for Sidney to clear but his throat."

Mrs. Luce again named William Brennan to serve as her campaign manager. Most of the people who had assisted in the 1942 effort were re-enlisted, including *Time* staffer Wes Bailey.

There is little doubt that the staff on *Time* magazine viewed Clare's candidacy as a liability. On August 15, 1944, a personal memo to Henry Luce from Eric Hodges, chairman of *Time*'s public relations committee, said:

This business of the allegation that CBL owes everything to the enormous build-up she gets from publisher Luce's properties, when neither fact nor the implication behind the fact is true, does an injustice to everyone. So long as the wife of publisher Luce is also Congresswoman Luce, politics being what it is, I am afraid there will always be anguish enough to go around.

The memo went on to say that during Clare's first campaign Bailey had been kept in the background, but this time he could not remain anonymous. Hodges suggested that perhaps Bailey should take a leave of absence from Time Inc. without pay for the duration of the campaign and stay out of the *Time-Life* Building. Harry kept Bailey on the *Time* pay roll and assigned him to work full time on Clare's campaign.

Clifton Fadiman set the tone for the opposition in an opening speech when he said:

Republicans, Democrats and Independent fellow voters of Fairfield County, I am now a voter of Connecticut. That fact gives me a great privilege, a privilege of voting against Clare Luce.

Now generally when a man criticizes a woman he is supposed to be gallant and polite. My friends, today I propose to take gallantry and wring its neck. Mrs. Luce is a member of Congress. She should be praised or blamed in accordance with her record and her character. You did not elect her because she could charm a table of guests, but because you hoped she would make a good member of Congress.

The times are too perilous for empty compliments, but take a square look at Mrs. Luce . . . Mrs. Luce the Congresswoman, not Mrs. Luce the photographer's delight. After a careful study of her speeches, I am convinced that no woman of our time has gone further with less mental equipment—Mrs. Luce being the only lady in America who can skillfully make up two faces at the same time.

F.D.R. stopped his campaign train in Bridgeport to make a back-platform speech denouncing the Republican incumbent Congresswoman, and Vice-President Wallace spoke at seventeen different "Connors for Congress" rallies. For a woman whose mental capacity was alleged to be so sparse, Mrs. Luce challenged a good many "big brains."

Dorothy Thompson, who had supported Clare in 1942 following a rapprochement of their differences in the 1940 campaign, opposed her re-election. She and author Rex Stout, in a joint radio appearance at the end of the campaign, combined to attack Clare personally. Dorothy Thompson said, "Clare is not interested in this war nor is she disinterested in Fascism. Her appalling speech about G.I. Joe was used by Goebbels."

Dorothy Parker came to Bridgeport and made a speech in which she said:

While I am not a citizen of Connecticut, Mrs. Luce, who only visits the state at election time, serves to damage the cause of the United Nations throughout the country. [Mrs. Luce had come out for the United Nations but had warned her constituents that it would not save the world in the absence of a sound U.S. foreign policy.] Her retirement from public office is the concern of everybody who has the welfare of the nation and a desire for enduring peace close at their hearts.

Quentin Reynolds said, "Representative Clare Boothe Luce's charge that President Roosevelt 'lied us into the war' is not the first time a person named Boothe treacherously assaulted the President of the United States." Reynolds spoke on behalf of a "Broadway for Roosevelt Committee" headed by Fredric March, Jo Davidson, Moss Hart, Ethel Merman, Frank Sinatra, Jackie Gleason and Bert Lahr.

The most devastating published attack of that campaign was a two-page ad which appeared in New York's *PM* late in October. The piece was a put-together which took paragraphs out of speeches Mrs. Luce had made, articles she had written for *Vanity Fair* and editorials from the magazine, whether written by her or not. It was here that Clare Brokaw's lighthearted "Ananias Preferred" was offered as evidence of her devotion to untruths.

Ralph Ingersoll, the former *Time-Life* employee who had objected so strenuously when his boss married Clare, and then tried to keep her away from *Life*, was the editor of *PM*.

After Ingersoll's departure from *Life*, he had conceived the idea of establishing a newspaper which would be a journal of opinion in the tradition of the semi-literary newspapers of the past. The original capital had been quickly exhausted, but in Marshall Field he found a backer who took over the bankrupt newspaper and reorganized it, leaving Ingersoll as editor.

Clare says now that many, many years later, John Courtney Murray, a Jesuit theologian, asked her to come to the hospital to see a famous New York psychiatrist who was on his deathbed and had expressed a wish to see her before he died. She says he told her that he was the one who brought Ingersoll and Field together—as part of each other's therapy—an unlikely statement, since Field had ceased being the doctor's patient long before *PM* appeared.

In 1944 the Bridgeport *Herald* was owned and published by Lippmann Dannenberg. It was rumored that Sydney Carp, a brother-in-law of Vyacheslav Molotov, had financed Dannenberg's acquisition of the newspaper. In 1936 Madam Molotov had come to Bridgeport and stayed for a time with her brother-in-law using an assumed name. In September 1939 the House Un-American Activities Committee had secured from Carp an admission that beginning in 1936 he had brought Soviet cash to Bridgeport.

In the Bridgeport *Herald* Clare was accused of being anti-Semitic —this in spite of her speech supporting the Zionist movement—and anti-Negro—despite her introduction of a resolution calling for racial equality in the armed services and her condemnation of the D.A.R. for refusing its Washington hall to Negro singer Marian Anderson. Citing the *Vanity Fair* article which Jay Franklin had written titled "Wanted, a Dictator," Clare's opponents called her pro-Fascist and anti-Democratic.

Al Morano contributed the one touch of levity to the campaign. When it was announced that Henry Wallace would make repeated trips into Fairfield County to campaign for Margaret Connors, Morano had hundreds of small signs made and distributed in the rural areas. They said, "Hide your little pigs . . . Wallace is coming."

On election eve the outcome was very much in question. Franklin Roosevelt, speaking at Hyde Park to a press conference, said, "Mrs.

Luce is way behind. Her defeat would be a good thing for this country and it's a rough thing to say about a lady."

It was not only rough, it was wrong. When all the votes were counted, Clare had received 102,043 to 100,030 for Miss Connors. Four of the six incumbent Republican Connecticut Congressmen had been defeated, and F.D.R. had been re-elected for his fourth term.

On October 30, 1944—eight days before that election was held— Clare had written her husband a confidential letter beginning with these words:

DEAR HARRY . . . My original intention was to write this as a not-to-be-opened-before-November 8th letter, and to deposit it with Miss Thrasher [HRL's secretary] to be put on your desk November 8th just in case.

Such coyness results from the vanity of a would-be analyst who doesn't ˙ want to go out on a limb, yet on the other hand loves to be in a position of having always known it. The desire to be safe in either case is utterly damnable, and so am I.

Still, after long pondering, I stick to my initial intention. If I sent you this letter today I would merely display an annoying case of jitters and I wouldn't be helpful. Here I go out on a limb coyly:

This is the first national campaign in which I have participated knowingly and with a tolerable amount of information. I have gone through this campaign as a partisan. The net impressions of such a novice might be of some significance. . . .

As of today, October 30, I have the feeling that Dewey has lost the campaign, and for the last few days I have tried desperately to find out why.

The Republican campaign hasn't missed a single point. It was an able campaign, well planned and efficiently executed. Nor can I find a single major mistake as to rational articulation. After all, there was definitely a genuine trend away from the fourth term and toward the able young opponent.

So why shouldn't all that add up to victory? Here is the pretty banal conclusion I arrived at . . . the Republican campaign lacked warmth. The lack of warmth I'm talking about is something different from charm, personality, etc. The outstanding lesson of this campaign was to me that the opposition has no chance of winning unless it can impress the nation with being actually the nation itself. In less high-falutin language, the opposition had to show that it not only likes power, but also that it likes people. The Republican campaign was able, intelligent. It wasn't humanly attractive.

The lesson to be learned is that the Republican Party must acquire during the next four years a positive and humanly attractive record. Dewey was perfectly capable of licking Roosevelt, but he was incapable of licking the recent record of the Republican Party.

Possibly Clare put her finger on the Republican Achilles' heel—a lack of warmth. In the five succeeding Presidential elections, Dwight Eisenhower is the only Republican candidate widely regarded as a warm human personality. He is also the only Republican to win a Presidential election in that period.

Congresswoman Luce was generous in victory. Of the President's active opposition she said, "The purge that failed leaves us without rancor or malice, and we hope that we may all be given greater wisdom and courage to meet the task ahead." After her overpublicized catfight with Dorothy Thompson, Clare had vowed never again to criticize another woman, and during the campaign she studiously avoided any comments about Miss Connors. Of her opponent she said, "I wasn't running against Miss Connors but against the New Deal and the PAC."

There wasn't much doubt of that. John Meldon in the *Daily Worker* headed his account "The People and PAC Versus Clare Luce." The Greenwich, Connecticut, *Times* reported "CIO Political Action Group to Concentrate on Defeating Clare." Frank R. Kent in *The Wall Street Journal* noted *The New York Times* had first reported that Roosevelt had said "Clear it with Sidney."

CBL wasn't exactly silent. In the Bridgeport *Post* she is quoted as saying "PAC means Party of American Communism." In the New York *Mirror* one headline read, "Clare's cocker can lick any dem falla." It went on to quote Drew Pearson, who noted that Clare had named her dog "Mr. Speaker" for Sam Rayburn. All this produced a story in the Bridgeport *Post* headlined "Clare Luce Denies Training Her Spaniel to Battle Fala." It is interesting to note that the Atlanta, Georgia, *Constitution,* the Newport News, Virginia *Press,* the *Christian Science*

Monitor, The New York Times, and more than a hundred other newspapers great and small from coast to coast gave prominent coverage to Clare's campaign for re-election.

When the returns were analyzed, they revealed that her slim two-thousand-vote margin was a much greater victory than it first appeared, for she had received the bulk of her support from the industrial areas of Bridgeport, Hartford and Stamford. The working men and women of Fairfield County had ignored the orders of their union bosses. What Clare called the "Broadway-Browder Axis of carpetbagging New Deal celebrities" had failed in their efforts to convince her Connecticut neighbors that she was a perfidious, part-time obstructionist member of Congress. It also revealed that the station-wagon set had not been solidly for CBL.

In the aftermath of defeat Mrs. Luce's opponent charged that she had overpowered the voters with Time Inc. money, and had made a deal with Jasper McLevy, the Socialist mayor of Bridgeport, to enter the race and split the vote. The official report of expenditures filed on Clare's behalf by her campaign treasurer discloses that she spent a little less than $13,000. No single individual, Harry Luce included, had contributed more than $1,000. Miss Connors reported expenditures of approximately $22,000. But campaign reports, being somewhat imprecise, didn't reveal what it cost Harry Luce to have Wes Bailey work full time in his wife's campaign, or what other of her friends might have provided in services.

In the files from that campaign there is a memorandum from Wes Bailey, who had handled Clare's speeches, her advertising and her radio appearances. Thinking Clare might lose, Bailey had made a list of what he thought were her errors. They were:

1. Her charge that the President lied us into war. [She had said "lied us into a war into which he should have led us."]

2. The statement that she would like to see federal employees laid end to end quietly. [This was a distortion of a quip reported in Walter Winchell's column. What she actually said was "If all the Congressmen who dozed on the floor during the Surplus War Properties debate had been laid end to end, they would have been much more comfortable." It came out the other way during the campaign.]

3. Her G.I. Joe speech. [After that speech the term "G.I. Joe" supplanted "doughboy" as the name of our World War II soldiers.]

4. She thinks she is running against F.D.R. and not Connors.

5. She makes no defense of her absentee record. [The result of her daughter's death.]

6. She makes quips like "Back on relief with the Commander in Chief" and "My head is more American than Hillman's."

Mrs. Luce wrote two guest columns for Walter Winchell at the end of August. He specifically asked her to follow his style. The columns probably irritated the Democrats and President Roosevelt as much as anything she said on the platform. Some of her brittle remarks came back to haunt her years later—one in particular: "Senate nicknames for Harry 'Pendergast Machine' Truman and Mrs. 'Office Helper' Truman: 'Kickback Harry' and 'Overtime Bess.' "

When Truman became President after Roosevelt's death he flatly refused to invite Clare to the White House with other Congressmen.

After the outbreak of the Korean War, Clare wrote an article commending President Truman for what she called his courageous conduct. Harry S. Truman responded with a note of acknowledgment saying he had read the piece three times—first for the information it contained, second to be sure it had been written about him, and the third time to reassure himself that Clare had written it.

Two weeks after she had won re-election Clare was en route to the European Theater of Operations with sixteen other members of the Military Affairs Committee. The party landed in London and as usual Madame Luce landed in the headlines when Captain Gordon J. Berger, a twenty-four-year-old Army public-relations officer, told her she wasn't to talk to the press. Those were his orders from Washington he said. When the reporters asked Clare to comment on the trip and its purpose, she repeated what Berger had told her and refused further comment.

The Washington, D.C., *Times-Herald* topped a column with this: "War Department Denies Any Knowledge of Gag," while the New York *Mirror* gave it a three-column head: "Army Gags Clare Luce in War Zone; Permits Others to Talk."

Congressman Matthew Joseph Merritt, Chairman of the Military Affairs Committee, said "It couldn't be true. Every member was free to express his own opinion." Later, when he found out it was true, he said they had all agreed any official statements would be made by the chairman.

Some papers suggested Clare had contrived the whole thing just to get publicity. Young Captain Berger had made two mistakes: He underestimated Mrs. Luce and he failed to recognize that the reporters, confronted with sixteen male members of Congress and one female (and that female the celebrated and attractive Clare Boothe Luce), would naturally focus their attention on the lone Congresswoman. The resultant furor didn't benefit Clare or the committee.

In Paris, the next stop on the inspection tour, Mrs. Luce was quoted by INS as making a statement appealing to Americans to give more aid to the British, who were suffering from the effects of the V-1 and V-2 bombings. Then she made a tour of the Third Army front. All the visiting Congressmen had their pictures taken with General George S. Patton. Only the one with Mrs. Luce was published.

The committee went to Rome to meet with Major General Mark Clark. Alexander Kirk, the American Ambassador in Cairo whom Clare had spoofed about the pyramids, had been transferred to Rome. The Embassy gave a reception for the American Congressmen, and Clare was quoted as saying that the Italian front was being neglected.

On December 20 the committee came home without Mrs. Luce. The official reason for her absence was that she had got lost in the fog while trying to visit the troops and missed connections. She had deliberately stayed behind. Being at the front, where misery and death were a daily experience, was preferable to going home and spending the first Christmas at Mepkin or in Greenwich without Ann.

When Mrs. Luce came home from Italy she made half a dozen speeches in support of the effort on the Italian front. She called the nation's attention to the fact that Mark Clark and his armies were getting second-class materiel from those in charge of supplies. She questioned the wisdom of our preoccupation with the European front while we neglected the troops in the south.

In February 1945 the Military Affairs Committee held hearings on "an act to insure adequate medical care for the Armed Forces." The lady from Connecticut questioned the witnesses regarding the existing practice of segregation in the treatment of the Negro wounded. She brought out the fact that colored medical personnel were not acceptable in the Navy. The witness, a Colonel Ijams, argued the need of drafting nurses. Clare asked him, "Are you prepared to use in all your facilities all the available colored nurses there are without regard to segregation?" The Colonel refused to answer the question.

In the month of March, Field Marshal Alexander, aware of the increased support for Mark Clark's Fifth Army, perhaps as the result of Clare's speeches on Italy, invited her to return and visit the Eighth Army Headquarters. She was in Europe on April 11 when the American forces liberated the Buchenwald and Nordhausen concentration camps. She reported on the horrors she had seen and concluded with this paragraph:

America's frontiers tomorrow lie not on the shores of the Pacific or the Atlantic, nor even on the Rhine or the Volga or the Yangtze. America's frontiers of defense are where they have always been—on the borders that separate the concentration camp states from every liberty-loving country under heaven.

In the climate of anticipated victory which prevailed at the time Clare's strong anti-Communist position provoked the wrath of many members of Congress, newspaper writers and private citizens.

After the Yalta Conference, February 3 to 11, 1945, Clare's concern over American foreign policy increased. On February 16 she informed the House that the results of the Crimean Conference were by no means a victory for American ideals. In support of her charge she inserted a column by David Lawrence from the Washington *Evening Star* in the *Congressional Record*.

Lawrence said, "American idealism has been defeated as conspicuously at the Crimean Conference as it was at Paris twenty-six years ago."

Mrs. Luce's reservations about U.S.-U.S.S.R. relations are clearly expressed in the *Congressional Record* of June 7. She said:

Mr. Speaker, a few days ago several Democratic members of this House called upon the acting Secretary of State, Mr. Grew, to question him concerning this country's relations with the Soviet Union, which they feared had deteriorated sorely since the days of Yalta. They reported Mr. Grew as saying "this country is leaning over backward to avoid giving offense to Russia."

If one may judge by the complexion of mind of several members chosen to represent the United States on the United Nations Reparations Commission, now assembling in Moscow, Mr. Grew's reported remark is a correct analysis of our government's conciliatory attitude toward the Soviet Union.

Then she noted that one member of that commission, Dr. Robert Gordon Sproul, the distinguished president of the University of California, "has an excellent record of friendship for the Soviets and for Soviet groups in America."

She reminded the members that in 1943 Dr. Sproul extended the hospitality of the university to a congress of the Hollywood Writers' Mobilization—a three-day meeting at which greetings were brought from Russia by Dr. Mikhail Kalatazov, the agent of the Soviet motion-picture monopoly Sovkino.

Of Mr. Richard B. Scandrett, Jr., of New York, the legal adviser to Dr. Isador Lubin, also a United States representative on this delegation, Clare said, "Mr. Scandrett's record of avoiding friction with the Soviet Union goes back sixteen years to the time when he was associated with the law firm of Simpson, Thatcher and Bartlett, American legal representatives of Amtorg, the Soviet trade agency from 1919 to 1923." Then she outlined Scandrett's history of association with Soviet causes.

The full text of Clare's remarks about U.S. foreign policy, reprinted from the *Congressional Record,* and extending from May 31 through July 17, was reprinted in a twenty-six-page pamphlet and deals almost exclusively with the Communist threat to the free world. She describes the movement in Mexico and the increasing sphere of Soviet influence in Europe, and takes issue with all those who were predicting enduring Soviet-U.S. friendship, including one of her friends, Archibald Mac-Leish, who once worked for Harry Luce and Time Inc.

It was a statement MacLeish made in a State Department broadcast on May 26, 1945, which Clare found particularly offensive.

MacLeish said:

The facts speak for themselves, and what they speak are profoundly reassuring to any man who will open his ears and listen. The vital interests of the United States and the U.S.S.R. conflict at no point on the earth's surface.

However much they may differ in philosophy, and however they may differ in practice, they aim in their several and dissimilar ways at what they believe to be the betterment of the lot of their own people.

What underlies the current talk of inevitable conflict between the two nations . . . is nothing real, nothing logical.

MacLeish had been a particularly articulate and adamant critic of Hitler's Nazis. Mrs. Luce was dismayed that while her old friend could recognize the evil in Germany's totalitarianism he could be so blind to the dangers of Soviet totalitarianism.

She dug up one of MacLeish's earlier speeches in which he had condemned the Nazis for their brutal treatment of individuals. Wherever MacLeish had said "Nazism" in his indictment she inserted "Communism." Then she sent the speech to her old friend with a note asking why he never made such a speech about Communism, and why he couldn't recognize the similarity between the aggressive policies of the Reds and the brutal ambition of Hitler.

MacLeish didn't reply to her note.

In October 1945 Secretary of State James Byrnes, reporting on the failure of the London Conference of Foreign Ministers, said of the U.S. attitude toward Soviet Russia, "We are not unduly exacting." And Clare, in her extension of remarks in the *Congressional Record,* commented, "Today many competent observers of our foreign policy claim that our failure to be firm, precise and clear in our foreign policy expectations toward Russian rearmament and territorial and political demands in all quarters of the globe will result in an increasing drift toward world catastrophe." Then she asked to have the *Record* include an article by Walter Lippmann titled "Perilous Drift" and one by Dorothy Thompson.

Lippmann said, "The administration is not in control of its policy."

Miss Thompson called attention to the fact that in that same week the United States had signed a text of protocol to create the United

Nations Charter and President Harry Truman had demanded universal military training. Miss Thompson said:

There is something strangely ironic in this combination of events. On one day it is proposed the United States train all its male youths for the war; on the next the United Nations of the world solemnly covenant to live together in peace.

The reality is that at Teheran, Yalta, San Francisco and Potsdam our political leaders gave away the power that America had built up for the cause of justice, liberty and peace. The political leaders of the three great powers rejected at San Francisco the thesis that great powers must be subjected to any law governing their sovereign actions and in the name of war establish lawlessness for the powerful and servitude for the weak.

To Miss Thompson's old friend and opponent—Clare—it seemed we had indeed won the war, lost the peace, and were busily sowing the dragon's teeth for World War III.

On November 12 Judge Floyd Collins ruled that the entire estate of Ann Brokaw, bequeathed to her under the terms of the will of her grandfather, Isaac Brokaw, should go to Frances Brokaw, then fourteen and Ann's half sister. Because of the size of the estate (it consisted of one-fourth ownership in the New York Guarantee Trust Company and one-third of all the holdings in the multimillion-dollar Brokaw corporations) the newspapers gave considerable publicity to the judge's decision.

Mrs. Luce wasn't at all disturbed by the fact that her daughter's inheritance would pass to George's child by his second marriage. But the publicity revived all the events of Ann's tragic death, and Clare became very despondent.

Describing this moment in a series of articles for *McCall's*, Clare wrote:

Some time after midnight, alone in my room, all the doubts which I had ever felt concerning the dogmas and doctrines I had held in all the years before, all the futile and sterile relationships I had ever nursed or tolerated in pride or vanity, all the lacerations of the spirit suffered so helplessly in contemplating my meaningless world soaked in blood and violence, converged in a vast, sour tide within me.

I tasted at long the real meaning of meaninglessness; it is to believe that one is crawling to extinction unloved, unlovable and unloving in the same kind of a world.

Plainly contemplating suicide, she continued:

I now vividly remembered my four clever friends who had committed suicide so long ago. Riddles were still smoldering in their eyes, riddles that seemed to beckon me. I despaired of myself and for myself and of the world and for the world.

Five years earlier, after returning from her first trip to China, Clare had written an article about Madame Chiang's war orphans. Father Wiatrak, a Jesuit priest, had seen the article and written Clare to commend her for what she said. She had acknowledged his letter. Somewhat to her surprise and annoyance, he responded to the note.

Providence had brought her on that day a letter from Father Wiatrak, and in a *McCall's* series titled "The Real Reason," Clare wrote:

I opened the letter. It was very short. It asked me if I had read St. Augustine's confessions, and how one bright day in an Italian garden that brilliant, bold and famous man had suddenly burst into a torment of despairful tears, sick and tormented with the world's vileness and his own.

Clare wrote that she had searched for a Bible, but there was none. What she found was the telephone book and the number of the Jesuit mission house where Father Wiatrak was staying. This is how she reports the conversation:

"Father, I said I am not in trouble but my mind is in trouble."

He said, "We know . . . this is the call we have been praying for."

Then in the calm, practical voice of a doctor who recommends a specialist to a patient suffering with unusual disorders, he said, "We are not the priests for you. We are very simple priests. You think you have intellectual difficulties. They are spiritual of course, but you will not be persuaded of that until both have been properly dealt with. Father Fulton Sheen lives in Washington. No doubt you have heard him on the radio. I will make an appointment for you tomorrow. You don't have to keep it if you think better of it. No one is obliged to come home, so have a good sleep and God bless you."

Congresswoman Clare Boothe Luce kept the appointment.

Father Fulton Sheen, former Bishop of Rochester, says she was rebellious, questioning and defiant when he invited her for dinner with two other priests who lived in his home in Washington.

Describing what happened, Bishop Sheen says, "Clare wanted to discuss religion during the meal. I told her not at table. We went into my study after dinner and sat on opposite chairs facing one another. I said, 'All right now, Clare, we will begin talking about religion, and we will do it this way: I will talk to you about five minutes on the subject, uninterrupted. Then at the end of five minutes you may take an hour to talk.'

"I had been talking about three minutes and I mentioned the goodness of God . . . she jumped out of her seat, stuck her finger under my nose and said, 'Listen, if God is good, why did He take my daughter?'

" 'In order that you might be here in the faith.'

" 'Is that why you invited me to dinner?' Clare demanded.

" 'That is the reason,' I replied.

"From that point on we had regular meetings. I don't remember how often, but they were the most interesting discussions I ever had in my life on the subject of religion. I can remember one evening I said, 'Tonight I'm going to talk about Hell.' She often sat on the floor and I would sit in a chair, and she said, 'I can't accept Hell, Father.' I said, 'All right, I will give you as much time as you want to argue against it.' So she talked for an hour and fifteen minutes. I never heard such arguments against Hell in my life. And I said, 'All right, now I will have to take the same amount of time.' When I finished after an hour, she jumped to her feet and threw her arms in the air, looked up toward the heavens and cried, 'Oh, God, what a protagonist you have in this man!'

"When it came time to receive her into the church, I said, 'Clare, I will not hear your confession. I will get someone else to hear your confession. Whom would you like?'

"She quipped, 'Someone who has seen the rise and fall of empires.' "

Mrs. Luce was confirmed at St. Patrick's Cathedral on February 16, 1946. When she is asked why she became a Catholic her answer is "It's very simple . . . to get rid of my sins . . . to have my sins forgiven. This will not make sense to people who have never sinned."

Clare Luce's first-person version of her conversion to the Roman Catholic faith, printed in four parts in *McCall's* magazine under the title "The Real Reason," is still that magazine's most popular reprint.

Twenty-three years to the day after Ann's death this writer asked Bishop Sheen to describe Clare Luce—was she a woman, politician, writer, wife, mother?

"No," Bishop Sheen said, "none of these. I have not hit yet upon the answer. It has something to do with light. I have never met or talked with a more brilliant mind than Clare. She is scintillating. Her mind is like a rapier. It bursts foibles at a second and in that it stands out, and faith had to be the perfection of such a mind.

"In philosophy we distinguish between two kinds of knowledge. There is what is known as rational knowledge, then there is what is called intellectual knowledge. That distinction may be a bit too academic. The rational is slow. It goes from point to point. The intellectual actually is seeing a vision. It is intuition. Intellectual knowledge is something we have when we say for example 'the part can never be greater than the whole.' We can see that; we can never take it back. That is something like the angelic knowledge Clare has. She doesn't have a rational knowledge. She intuits. She sees things all at once. It would take a man six or seven steps to arrive at the same conclusion. That's why she infuriates men, because they are rational. They can't understand how she got there so quickly. They have to go upstairs. She doesn't go upstairs, she floats. The answer is she's an angel. She is an angel first of all in this unusual beauty of chiseled features but I am speaking of more of an angel in the sense that she has that kind of knowledge.

"No man could go to Clare and argue her into the faith. Heaven had to knock her over. It was about the only way it could get into her. I tell you it is the key to Clare and I have known her over the years."

In January 1946 Mrs. Luce announced she would not seek re-election to the House for "good and sufficient reasons which will become obvious in time." The reason was her decision to enter the Roman Catholic Church. There were, she knew, a great many Catholics in her Connecticut constituency. She believed many people would say that political motives had inspired her spiritual decision.

Harry Luce, who loved nothing better than to argue about theology, voiced no objections when he discovered what his wife intended to do. His friends insist that Clare's sudden interest in religion actually strengthened Luce's faith. Critics of *Time* have claimed that before Luce married Clare the magazine was somewhat anti-Semitic. No one has ever made the charge that either *Time* or Harry voiced any anti-Catholic sentiments.

Mrs. Luce's conversion put her in the news again. She received some angry letters from militant Protestants, but the press in general was tolerant and understanding. Clare Luce had never before enjoyed the kind of acceptance she received from the Catholic community. Until her conversion she always felt she was rootless. She thought the staff of *Time* was against her—a not irrational conclusion—and she had felt isolated by Harry's solid, unquestioning and unquestionable Presbyterian faith, a factor in their marriage which caused her to be deeply resentful.

Clare declares without any qualification whatsoever that her rediscovery of the goodness of God and her formal acceptance of the Christian necessity to be a public worshiper was the turning point in her life. It may have been that she found new confidence, or perhaps it was just a growing concern for what she considered to be America's blundering foreign policy.

The record reveals Clare was more active and more vocal during her second term in Congress than during her first. Despite all the publicity she received, her remarks on the floor and her insertions in the *Record* during 1943–1944 occupy less than forty pages in the *Congres-*

sional Record. During her second term her speeches and insertions in the *Record* occupy five times that space.

She introduced legislation to rewrite the immigration quotas and permit Polish refugees who fought on our side in the war to enter the United States; a bill to help veterans get Civil Service jobs; a bill to create a labor committee to study the subject of profit sharing as an answer to strikes; a bill to permit physicians, surgeons and dentists an income-tax deduction for the amount of time devoted to charity patients; a bill to eliminate discrimination in industry among workers who perform equal work with equal efficiency (this was aimed at employers who were paying Negroes less than they paid whites); a bill to create a governmental department of science to foster, promote and develop the study and spread of scientific knowledge; a resolution calling for the election by popular vote of the U.S. representatives to the United Nations.

In the fall of 1945 Marquis Childs solicited the opinions of certain American Congressmen as to what the United States should do in regard to the economic problems confronting postwar Europe.

On September 29 Congresswoman Luce sent Childs a letter in which she suggested we should first determine what was needed to prevent widespread European famine and how much additional aid would be required to prime the pumps of European and Asiatic economy. Then she said, "We should decide how much of our food, money and material would be needed: A. On an out-and-out charitable basis immediately to prevent famine and pestilence; B. To risk in the hope or on the promise of political or economic *quid pro quo;* and C. To invest in sound international business and trade principles."

Mrs. Luce pointed out that such a plan wouldn't work if attempted on a piecemeal basis. She thought food, clothing and medical supplies should be an outright gift of the American Government, to be distributed by American agencies and plainly identified as to its source in order to insure that the ultimate recipient would know the life-giving supplies had come from the American people.

She showed her letter to Congressman Everett Dirksen of Illinois. He was impressed and suggested the proposal should be introduced as a bill in Congress.

Clare said she didn't think her staff had the technical knowledge to draft a bill on such a complicated and comprehensive problem.

Dirksen replied that he would draft the bill and introduce it. He did. But no action was taken until June of 1947 when Secretary of State George C. Marshall proposed an almost identical approach to the problems of postwar Europe in a commencement address at Harvard.

In the book *Diplomat Among Warriors,* published by Doubleday in 1964, author Robert Murphy says, "The basic principles behind the Marshall Plan can be traced back to many men, including Henry L. Stimson, John J. McCloy and Lewis Douglas."

Apparently Murphy didn't know of the Luce-Dirksen proposal which was offered to Congress in January of 1946. As it was finally implemented, the Marshall Plan departed in a very major way from Mrs. Luce's suggestion—there was no attempt to make certain that the food, clothing and drugs paid for by the American taxpayers were always identified as coming from America. Billions of dollars were distributed without securing any "political or economic *quid pro quos.*" But the Marshall Plan did prevent a great many European countries from falling into the grip of the Communists.

When Clare Luce announced that she would not be a candidate for re-election to the House, without revealing her reason for that decision, the rumor went about that what she really intended was to become a candidate for the U.S. Senate.

The incumbent, Thomas C. Hart—the same Tommy Hart who as admiral of the U.S. Asiatic fleet had given her the tip-off which permitted her to predict the Japanese attack—had been appointed to fill a vacancy created by the death of Francis T. Maloney. Hart, who was sixty-nine, had written a letter to Governor Baldwin saying he would not be a candidate for re-election in 1946. He had also written to Mrs. Luce that he hoped with all his heart she would succeed him.

The two-term Congresswoman could probably have had the nomination merely by making herself available. This she refused to do, arguing that if her reasons for not seeking re-election to the House were valid, they were doubly valid for not attempting to move up to the U.S. Senate.

Because so many politicians say one thing when they plan to do another, Mrs. Luce's declaration of noncandidacy for Congress was not accepted at face value until midsummer of 1946. When the politicians finally became convinced that she would not be a candidate for any office, there was a flurry of trial balloons on behalf of aspirants for the seat she was vacating.

The Congresswoman's administrative assistant, Al Morano, wanted the post. "Sis" was sympathetic with Morano's ambition. He knew his way around Washington. He had been a very faithful and helpful supporter all during her two terms. But she believed that if he became a candidate, the opposition would attack him as a stand-in for Congresswoman Luce. He would be the target for all those who displayed their animosities toward her. She would be criticized as a kingmaker—and worse, he would lose.

She told Morano of her reservations. "This," she said, "isn't the time for you." Then she encouraged John Lodge, younger brother of Cabot, who had lived in Connecticut less than a year, to go after the Republican nomination.

The initial conversation on this subject took place on the terrace of the house on King Street. When Clare Luce said he ought to become a candidate, Lodge offered a number of objections. He had never done anything in public life; he had been a movie star; he had made films in Mussolini's Italy; his wife, Francesca, was Italian-born, and there was great prejudice against anyone who had ever associated in any way with the Fascist regime.

She reassured Lodge. "You come from a fine family. You're a handsome young man. Your wife is a lovely woman. Bring her over tomorrow afternoon and I'll give you a few pointers on how to go about it."

The Lady from Fairfield's prescription was a simple one: get acquainted with the community and the issues that bothered the average citizen. She told Mrs. Lodge to split up her grocery list. "Buy one or two items in one store and go on to another. And always introduce yourself. Just say, 'I'm Mrs. John Lodge . . . we live over at Westport, you know.' Ask questions, questions, questions. And smile, smile, smile."

She told Lodge, "When you ride the commuters' train to New York tell everybody you would like to be the next Congressman, because you know for *sure* that Mrs. Luce is not going to run. And let them tell you what they would expect of the next Congressman."

"But what will I do about this Fascist moving-picture thing?"

Mrs. Luce laughed. "Sam Rayburn," she said, "once told me that the five rules for a candidate are: 'explain nothing, deny everything, demand proof—don't listen to it—and give the opposition hell.' I've never been able to follow them, but maybe you can." (Francesca Lodge says John pasted these rules on his shaving mirror and read them every morning.) Mrs. Luce went on. "Nobody will believe I am not going to run at this point, and so you can get a head start. After a couple of terms in Congress you can run for governor, and after that who knows?"

Lodge told Mrs. Luce that it all sounded very simple, but he didn't think it would be that easy. He mentioned the fact that Al Morano was working for the nomination, and because of his long association with the party could probably get it. She told Lodge she had advised Morano not to run, and had secured his promise not to make the race, provided Lodge became a candidate. "He'll stand aside for you, John. In return, will you give your promise that when you *do* run for governor, and leave the House, you will support Morano for your seat?"

Lodge agreed. He was elected to the Eightieth Congress in 1946, re-elected in 1948 and became Governor of Connecticut in 1950.

Mrs. Luce fulfilled her pledge to Al Morano and helped him win the nomination for the seat Lodge vacated when he became a candidate for governor. John Lodge, however, ignored his earlier commitment. He did nothing to help Morano.

Both Morano and Lodge were victorious in the general election. Two years later, events caused Mrs. Luce to remember that politicians, even good friends, can go back on their word.

10

Eisenhower

The public explanation Congresswoman Luce gave for not seeking re-election was, perhaps, only part of the reason for her decision.

Harry Luce had never objected to her service in Congress, but the necessary physical separation was having its effect on both of them. The thrill of being a member of Congress had long since palled on her and she knew that Harry, inhibited by an awareness of his importance as the master of *Time-Life,* maintained an uncomfortable formality with even his closest friends when she was not with him.

John Kobler, in his biography of Harry, published by Doubleday in 1968, describes Luce's attempt to find companionship during this period, and says that Oliver Jenson, who was then the editor of *Life*'s entertainment pages, after spending several nights with Luce, decided that his boss was lonely. Kobler adds that *Life*'s publisher, C. D. Jackson, made the same discovery. "He craved easy, relaxed comradeship but he didn't know how to get it. He always put you on the *qui vive.*"

Mrs. Luce wasn't prepared to risk either her marriage or the years of effort a continuing career in politics would demand.

When her Congressional obligation was satisfied, Mrs. Luce went into seclusion at Mepkin to write the history of her conversion to Catholicism. Publication of her apologia in *McCall's* magazine in the spring of 1947 brought a flood of speaking invitations from Catholic groups around the country. She gave the $10,000 *McCall's* paid her for writing "The Real Reason" to a Negro maternity hospital in Mobile, Alabama. Immediately after the publication of the articles *McCall's* canceled her contract on the grounds that she had involved the publication in too much controversy. In the twenty years since the articles were written *McCall's* has continually been asked for reprints.

The development during the war of an airport near the King Street house had introduced both noise and traffic into that quiet neighborhood, and the Luces had moved to a handsome red-brick Georgian mansion at Ridgefield, a few miles north in Connecticut, which they christened "Sugar Hill." Decorator Gladys Freeman (sister of Clare's early *Vanity Fair* sponsor, Donald Freeman) supervised the redoing of the house to respond to Luce's interest in the Far East and Clare's practical requirements. Indicating that the former Congresswoman had no intention of retiring from life, the basement was filled with standard public-library equipment, so that Mrs. Luce and her secretaries could carry on their research.

Chinese porcelain and a portrait of Clare in a green mandarin coat, teakwood furniture in the dining room and private personal offices—Luce's finished in gun metal, scarlet and white, matching the cover of *Life,* and Clare's in beige and turquoise blue—all reflected the personalities of the owners.

Here the Luces entertained. There were some business guests and a great many old political friends, but Sugar Hill was a family home more than anything else.

Luce's nephew, Tom Moore, recalls that it was here he truly learned to appreciate his aunt's ability to make any informal social gathering an exciting experience by directing the conversation into specific and unusual channels. Uncle Harry was a great reporter and Clare was an intuitive investigator. She would get people started on subjects about which they had strong feelings. There was never a dull moment.

The war, Clare's service in Congress, and Luce's absorption with his business had all worked to limit social activities. Now for the first time in their marriage there was a real opportunity to enjoy some privacy. Luce was privately pleased that his wife had terminated her political career. He was also proud of the fact that she had twice won election on her own. Her experience in Washington had broadened her understanding of the world and its problems and he has described the years at Ridgefield as some of the most satisfying and exciting of his entire life. "I think that in those years we both acquired a better perspective of each other, our associates, and the world." He found some of the answers to the incessant *whys* which had plagued him all his life.

Congresswoman Luce had retired from elective office, but she was still a public figure. In April of 1947 she accepted an invitation to address the Chamber of Commerce of the state of New York—the first woman guest speaker since that organization was founded in 1768.

In June the Bridgeport Sunday *Post* published a copy of the Congresswoman's letter to Marquis Childs and publicly identified her as the author of the concept which became the Marshall Plan. Al Morano, eager to keep "Sis" alive as a public personality, may have been responsible for sending the Bridgeport *Post* this letter.

In November of that year Clare Luce went to Hollywood to make a screenplay from the book *The Screwtape Letters,* by C. S. Lewis, for 20th Century-Fox. When the project was scrubbed after three months she explained the reasons in a letter to Mr. Lewis.

The book she was assigned to translate into a movie consists of an exchange of letters between Screwtape, a senior Devil—presumably residing in Hell—and Wormwood, a sort of apprentice Evil Spirit on Earth. (Wormwood's task is to capture the soul of his subject. To help him in this, Screwtape sends Wormwood letters of advice.)

Her five-page letter to C. S. Lewis describes what happened to his book, and her screenplay, in Hollywood.

I knew, for example, that the movies are rightly called an industry because they are made like automobiles on the assembly belt. This requires numberless participants in the operation, so that neither author nor adapter would ever be permitted to play a truly creative part in the making of a picture. Yet I imagined that Screwtape was so original, and so unusual a work, and my enthusiasm for it so single-minded and faithful to its intent and spirit, that I could lick the system. I had even counted on Hollywood's indifference to an ignorance of Christian theology as a help.

Hollywood is Christian only in the most attenuated sense of the word Christian—as Christian as Christmas cards or Easter bonnets. In short, wherever it is box office to be Christian.

Most especially I erred in thinking that Hollywood has no ideas about the Devil. They had many. Some thought Screwtape should be a character "you love to hate" . . . an Al Capone type—brutish, brutal and thuggish, or a sadistic, paranoiac manic-depressive, first cousin to Frankenstein's monster. Others thought he should be a character "you hate to love"—the gay, suave seducer—diabolically charming, rather than diabolic. But all agreed on one thing: Screwtape's main job was to tempt "the boy" to get in bed either with the wrong woman for the right reason, or the right woman for the wrong reason.

From the beginning Mr. Zanuck insisted that Screwtape and Hell be offset by the invention of what he called a "deeply human and thrilling boy and girl story strong enough and interesting enough to stand on its own feet."

I shall always remember the expression of incredulity and pity on the face of Mr. Samuel Engel, my producer, when he first realized that I was, as he put it, "on the level about the Devil's existence." Perhaps my real difficulty dated from that hour. Thereafter, Mr. Engel was torn between dreadful alternatives: that I might be daft, or that he might be doomed.

When *Screwtape* was scrapped, Mrs. Luce wrote a movie called *Come to the Stable.* It was the story of the efforts of two nuns to found a hospital for crippled children in Bethlehem, Connecticut. Mrs. Luce gave all her earnings on this picture to the convent of Regma Laudes in that town.

Shortly after she finished *Come to the Stable* the San Francisco Forum invited her to appear as a guest on its lecture series. She asked a fee of $1,500. The director, Dr. Albert Rappaport, objected, saying, "Never in all our history have we paid any outstanding lecturers, such as Thomas Mann, Stefan Zweig or Sir Philip Gibson, more than five hundred dollars." Mrs. Luce's explanation of this was that she preferred to give away large sums.

She didn't go to San Francisco, but that spring she delivered the commencement address at Creighton University in Omaha, Nebraska; instead of an honorarium she gladly received an honorary Doctor of Laws degree.

The ex-Congresswoman's principal interests in the spring and summer of 1948 were Roman Catholicism and Republican politics. She spoke at dozens of Catholic gatherings and accepted an invitation to again address the delegates of the Republican Party at their June nominating convention.

Henry Luce was interested in promoting Thomas Dewey as the Republican candidate. His wife believed that Arthur Vandenberg was the man to lead the nation.

In April and May of that year, however, she began to question her own judgment. Vandenberg, who had earlier indicated considerable interest in the nomination, now refused to do anything for himself, or even to encourage any of his friends to mount a preconvention draft.

Dewey, who had lost to Roosevelt in 1944, Harold Stassen of Minnesota, and Senator Robert Taft of Ohio were the only active candidates. Mrs. Luce and U.S. Senator Henry Cabot Lodge of Massachusetts went delegate hunting in spite of Vandenberg's objections. They both believed isolationism was dead. As the most powerful nation in the world, they wanted the United States to assume a dominant role in world affairs, and they wanted the Republican Party to develop an aggressive foreign policy. Lodge, who had resigned his Senate seat to become a full-time soldier—the first Senator to do so since the Civil War—had been re-elected from Massachusetts in 1946.

When Mrs. Luce spoke to the opening session at Philadelphia on June 21, 1948, she deserted the emotional approach of her G.I. Joe speech. Referring to President Harry Truman, she said:

His time is short. His situation is hopeless. Frankly, he is a gone goose. But before he goes we should admit that we owe him several debts of gratitude.

We should be grateful to Mr. Truman that he tried to be Vice-President in 1944, and that with the gallant aid of the big-city bosses, Kelly and Flynn, Pendergast and Hague, he did not fail—providence wrote straight with crooked lines when Pendergast gave us colorless Harry Truman instead of Red Hank Wallace.

She described Truman as a "man of phlegm, not fire."

There were, she said, "three wings to the Democratic Party—the extreme right, or Jim Crow, group, led by lynch-loving Bourbons, sheet-shirted race supremists of the Bilbo ilk; the left, or Moscow, wing of the party, currently masterminded by Stalin's Mortimer Snerd, Harry Wallace; and the center, or Pendergast gang, run by the Wampum and Boodle boys."

On the issue of war and peace she said:

The Democrats are divided. Wallace says that Truman wants war at any cost. Truman says that Wallace wants peace at any price. Both may be right. But our party is not divided by what it believes. We believe neither in war at any cost, nor peace at any price. We Republicans believe that peace can be brought to a great section of the world by electing a President who will show the simple courage of saying what he means and meaning what he says, both to the people overseas and to us at home.

This was Mrs. Luce's criticism of our foreign policy. It was the ambivalence of our position from 1936 to 1940 which produced World War II, and our failure to face the Russian challenge from 1945 on which resulted in the diminishing of the free world nations.

She outlined a foreign policy which she believed Arthur Vandenberg would implement. The delegates committed to Taft and to Dewey were not particularly sympathetic, and the press reaction was divided.

The next day in the New York *Journal-American* Bob Considine said, "The boys in general learned a lot about television at the Republican Convention. Madame Luce, for instance, wore the wrong kind of outfit and war paint and showed up on the screen looking like a stand-in for the ghostly Lenora Corbett in *Blithe Spirit*."

Long before the nominating speeches were concluded, it became evident that while none of the active candidates had sufficient strength to win on the first ballot, Dewey would gain on the second. The only hope for Vandenberg rested in the possibility of persuading Taft or Stassen, or both of them, to switch their support to the Michigan Senator.

Mrs. Luce went to Taft first. It was obvious the Republicans were going to nominate Dewey again if something wasn't done. "You can't win it, Senator. Stassen can't win it. Can't you swing your delegates to Arthur Vandenberg?"

Taft replied in that rather cracky voice, "Mrs. Luce, there is no one who admires Arthur Vandenberg more than I do. Certainly I prefer him to Dewey, but once I release my delegates, I can't control them. They will go to Dewey. Why don't you talk to Stassen? His supporters are zealots. He might be able to control them."

In that response, Senator Taft voiced a truth which is frequently overlooked at convention time when reporters hint about swaps and deals. A Presidential candidate with any inherent strength can usually hold his own delegates, but he can't transfer his support at will to another aspirant.

Mrs. Luce found Stassen in a hotel sitting room surrounded by young people wearing huge sunflowers. "He was looking glassy-eyed, as he always did, when the Presidency was mentioned. He refused to release his delegates, and insisted the convention must come to him eventually."

She went back to headquarters and told Cabot Lodge it was no use.

Thomas Dewey of New York was nominated with Governor Warren of California as his running mate. The ticket was defeated by "give-'em-hell-Harry Truman," and Tom Dewey disappeared as a national figure.

Clare Luce left Philadelphia believing that if Arthur Vandenberg had made an effort he might have had the nomination. She was intensely disappointed by the aloof "I'll take it if it comes my way, but I won't seek it" attitude of the Michigan Senator.

When next they met, Vandenberg was in the hospital recovering from lung surgery. He greeted Clare warmly, then he asked her to open the drawer of his bedside table and read the manuscript she would find there. It was Vandenberg's acceptance speech written for the 1948 convention.

If the Senator had really wanted the nomination, if he had gone to the trouble of writing his acceptance speech, why in heaven's name hadn't he made a fight for it?

"I was leaving this one up to God," Vandenberg said. "I knew I had lung cancer. I couldn't seek the nomination knowing I wouldn't survive in office, so I left it up to the Almighty. If He wanted a sick man who would die in office, then I would be drafted and I would serve."

Arthur Vandenberg died in April 1951. At his funeral the minister read what he described as "the Senator's farewell address to his country-men." It had been written in the form of a personal letter to a friend and in it Vandenberg expressed his hopes for the American people. He had died before it could be mailed.

The clergyman stopped short of the end, saying there was one additional paragraph, but it was personal—intended only for the individual to whom the Senator had been writing and therefore he would not disclose the dead man's final thoughts.

When the service was over the minister gave Clare Luce the letter.

The final paragraph of the letter said, "They tell me, Clare, I am on my deathbed, but even if I am, if you decide to run for the Senate, I'll do something I never wanted to do again—I'll get up and campaign for you. We can win the next election with Eisenhower."

The pollsters and most of the nation's press predicted a Republican victory in the 1948 Presidential contest. The GOP had won control of both the House and the Senate in the election of 1946. The United States had speedily dismantled its military strength following V-J Day, and the intransigent position of the Russians had undermined public confidence in U.S. foreign policy. The agreements arrived at between Roosevelt, Churchill and Stalin at Yalta and Truman, Attlee and Stalin at Potsdam were under heavy attack at home and abroad.

In Mrs. Luce's mind Dewey's defeat was the result of that lack of campaign warmth which she had described in her letter to her husband before the outcome of the 1944 election was known.

In 1945 and 1946, as a member of Congress, she had predicted the Communists were determined to conquer the world by subversion if possible, by aggression if necessary. Russia's diplomatic and military moves in Europe and in Asia, and the conviction of eleven top U.S. Communists for conspiring to advocate the violent overthrow of the Government of the United States in the federal court, presided over by Judge Harold Medina, validated her prediction, all of which spurred her to new activities. She spoke to hundreds of Republican gatherings on the failures of Truman's Fair Deal. She appeared before business groups to urge more citizen participation in politics. Her main theme was that the Cold War was not an expression of political or territorial difficulties. The battle would not be won with planes or bullets or atom bombs. The theater of war was in the minds of men. Victory would be awarded to the protagonists with the strongest faith in their own system.

She resumed writing a monthly article for *McCall's* magazine, contributed to numerous Catholic publications, tried to write for the theater, and talked about a new novel.

In 1950 Connecticut Democrat William Benton, who had been appointed to fill a vacancy when Republican Raymond Baldwin resigned, became a candidate for the balance of his predecessor's unexpired term. There was talk in political circles that Mrs. Luce should oppose him. This rumor was still floating around when a reporter on *The New York Times* quoted Henry Luce as saying that he was considering seeking the Republican nomination. After a good deal of smoke and no fire at all, neither Mr. nor Mrs. Luce made themselves available.

Luce was too busy with his magazines. His wife seemed to prefer her career as a speaker and a writer. Probably the real reason for this Lucian reluctance was their friendship for former ad man Bill Benton. Both Luces were strongly partisan Republicans, but they had many intimate friends who were just as strongly partisan Democrats. Their affection and admiration for Benton made it difficult for them to oppose his election to the Senate. The ordinary party member doesn't understand these across-the-party-lines associations. But there is a power elite in the United States which cuts across party lines, and the Luces were members in good standing.

Many of Mrs. Luce's die-hard Republican supporters would have been horrified to know the truth of her close and warm relationship with Joe Kennedy and his family. As F.D.R.'s Ambassador to Great Britain at the outset of the war, Joe Kennedy had been outspokenly critical of the British military and political posture. When Mrs. Luce interviewed him in connection with her book *Europe in the Spring,* she discovered that this self-made Democratic millionaire shared many of her doubts about the wisdom of American foreign policy. Young Jack Kennedy had written to Clare from his PT boat in the Pacific when he learned of Ann's tragic death.

In 1948, when the Communists were threatening to overwhelm the De Gasperi forces in Italy, Clare and Joe Kennedy helped to raise $2 million from private sources in the United States to help the Christian Democrats win that election. This effort may have been more church than politics, but Mrs. Luce says the money was subsequently repaid in full by the Italian Government.

Arthur Vandenberg, in that deathbed note, had said the Republicans could win with Eisenhower. Harry believed *Time-Life* should have a hand in selecting a Republican President. On one of her trips to Europe Clare stopped at S.H.A.P.E. headquarters to visit the General. Ostensibly it was a "socialite-come-to-pay-her-respects sort of call." Actually, it was a part of the campaign Harry was forming in his mind to make the U.S. war hero the next U.S. President.

Clare has supplied an account of what happened based on the notes she made at the time.

General Jerry Persons received her. He told her Eisenhower had been detained a few minutes, took her into his private office and said, "I want to talk to you. We're having a stinker of a problem."

"You mean with S.H.A.P.E.?" Clare asked.

"No," Persons said, "with this Presidential thing. All these reporters keep asking Ike about his religion, and he goes through the roof. He has issued an order: No one is to ask that question again. He says a man's religion is his personal affair."

Mrs. Luce couldn't see anything wrong with that position.

"The trouble, Mrs. Luce," Persons replied, "is that Ike doesn't have any religion. That's why he gets so flustered when people ask him about it. You know what will happen to us if the reporters write a story saying Ike doesn't believe in God."

When Mrs. Luce finally saw General Eisenhower, she used the first few minutes making small talk. Then she struck out at the problem. "General," she asked sweetly, "I'm wondering, what's your religion?"

Eisenhower got red to the roots of his hair. "That's a personal affair, Mrs. Luce, and I'm not going to discuss it with you or with anyone else."

"But, General, a President's religion is not a personal affair. There isn't anything about a President that is a personal affair. Everyone in the United States has the right to know what your religion is."

Clare says Ike paced up and own the office and appeared to become increasingly agitated. Finally he turned to her and with that infectious grin, shrugged his shoulders and confessed, "I don't have a religion, Clare."

"Do you mean, General, you don't believe in God?"

"Of course I believe in God," Ike snapped. "Do you think I could have gone into any one of those great battles unless I had deep faith in the Almighty? Of course I believe in God," he repeated.

"Then what you are saying is that while you believe in God, you happen not to belong to any church."

"That's it."

"How does it happen you don't have a church?"

"Well, you see, my grandparents were Mennonites. They came from Germany. They settled in East Texas and there were no Mennonite churches. My father and mother read the Bible to us every morning and every evening. We said a blessing at the table, but I never went to any formal church services. I believe in God and I know my Bible, as well as the next fellow. But I don't belong to a church. And I'm not going to join one just to get votes. I'd have no respect for myself if I did that."

Clare nodded sympathetically, but didn't give up. "Now look, General, let's imagine that you stick with that, and are nominated and elected anyway, which I think you would be. But now you are President and let's imagine that there is a little boy out in Denver, Colorado, named Johnny, and that his mother wakes him up on Sunday morning and says 'Get dressed, Johnny, it's time to go to church.' And little Johnny says 'Why should I go to church? The President of the United States doesn't go to any church. He believes in God, but *he* doesn't go to church. Why do I have to go if the President doesn't?' How will his mother answer that one, General? How will all the mothers answer all the little Johnnys and Janes who ask that question?"

Ike frowned, but said nothing.

"General, who knows better than you that the President is a symbol, not only a political symbol, but a symbol of the highest ideals of the American people?"

Ike shrugged, and replied, "But I won't join a church to get votes," he repeated.

"You and Mamie were married in a church, weren't you?" the Congresswoman persisted.

"No. We were married by an Army chaplain. Mamie is a Presbyterian."

"Well, there isn't any problem then," Clare Luce said. "There is a Presbyterian church here in Paris. Next Sunday why not go to church with Mamie? Of course, there may be reporters there. When you come out, they may ask if you are a member of the Presbyterian Church. So what if you say 'No, but I always go to church with my wife.'? There are millions of American men who go with their wives to church . . ."

Ike went to church with Mamie.

Several years later when Clare Luce was visiting the President at the White House he mentioned that he had voluntarily and happily joined the Presbyterian Church after he was elected.

In 1951 Clare went back to Hollywood to work for Howard Hughes on an original screenplay to be called *Pilate's Wife.* After several months of effort the subject was shelved. She then tried her hand at another play. This one, *Child of the Morning,* had a week's tryout performance in Springfield, Massachusetts, with Margaret O'Brien in a stellar role. It moved to Boston, where it closed two weeks later. Miss O'Brien was a hit, the play was a flop.

In January 1952 Clare returned to Hollywood at the request of RKO. She was there in March and made some of the presentations at the Academy Award dinner. *Variety* notes: "Clare Boothe Luce was so excited she called it 'Seven Days to the Moon' instead of 'Seven Days to Noon' and fluffed on John Huston's name."

In March there was another rumor that Mrs. Luce might reconsider her decision and run for the U.S. Senate. She said she would neither seek nor accept the nomination and went off to spend a month with her husband in Spain. But before leaving she told reporters that Ike was her favorite for the Republican nomination for President.

Clare's old friend Henry Cabot Lodge was masterminding the Eisenhower campaign. He was delighted when Clare was named a delegate to the convention from Connecticut. Senator Robert Taft of Ohio was the preconvention favorite.

The first objective of the Lodge-Eisenhower forces was to destroy Taft. Once that obstacle was removed, they thought they could persuade the convention to accept Ike. The Taft supporters were reminding the country that in 1948 Harry Truman had advocated the nomination of Eisenhower on the Democratic ticket.

Luce and his magazines were solidly behind General Eisenhower, and his wife did her bit to scuttle Bob Taft when she told a Connecticut meeting that the Ohio Senator was a "me-too candidate" for the Republican nomination . . . that he had "undergone a belated conversion to the theory of United States leadership in world affairs."

When the convention nominated Eisenhower and Nixon, Mrs. Luce told reporters it looked as though Harry Luce might for the first time in his life be able to vote for a winning Presidential candidate. Then she flew out to California to resume her duties at the movie studios.

United States Senator Brien McMahon of Connecticut, a Democrat, was first elected in 1944 and re-elected in 1950. He died on July 28, 1952. Under Connecticut law, Governor John Lodge had to make an interim appointment to fill the vacancy until the next general election, which would come in November.

Clare Luce had just about finished her Hollywood script.

She had committed herself in Chicago to campaign for Eisenhower. Why not campaign as an interim Senator? Certainly Governor John Lodge would agree that she should be in the Connecticut picture to help the Eisenhower ticket.

On the twenty-ninth of July Clare telephoned Governor Lodge. She didn't ask him to appoint her to the Senate. She said she was calling to ask his advice and to get some answers to a question or two. One, did he want to become the Republican candidate for the Senate in the general election himself? Two, if he wasn't interested in going to Washington, did he think it would be wise for her to consider entering the contest?

Lodge told her he had no ambition to be a member of the United States Senate. He intended to serve out his term as Governor. He thought it was an excellent idea for Clare to enter the race. He did repeat that stock phrase about how it would be necessary for him to remain neutral and let the party leaders have a voice in selecting the candidate.

That same day the New York *World Telegram* carried a story saying Lodge was interrupting his Virgin Islands vacation to return to Connecticut because of the death of McMahon, and that it was expected the Republican Governor would name former Representative Clare Boothe Luce to fill the vacancy.

Two weeks later Mrs. Luce was in Connecticut. One of the first persons she talked to was Congressman Al Morano, who had been elected to the House in 1950 and would be running again this year.

Morano was skeptical. He remembered how Lodge had remained aloof and failed to keep his promise in 1950. He told Clare he thought the Governor wanted the Senate seat himself. Because of McMahon's death there were two senatorial seats open in Connecticut. Morano believed that William A. Purtell, who had been the Republican nominee for Governor in 1950, would run against the incumbent Bill Benton. And Prescott Bush, who had been the Republican candidate to oppose McMahon in 1950, and who had been soundly beaten, would certainly want to try for the Senate again. He suggested that Lodge might be hoping for a convention deadlock between the forces of Purtell, Bush and Luce—in which event, he could offer himself as a compromise candidate.

Morano's construction of the situation was correct.

Governor Lodge announced that with Mrs. Luce and Prescott Bush both in the race he didn't want to appear to take sides by appointing either one of them to the McMahon vacancy and would instead name William Purtell.

Why did Lodge pick Purtell, the man who had campaigned against him in 1950, in preference to Mrs. Luce, who had started him on his political career? At the convention she withdrew her name and threw her strength to Bush. There was no deadlock. Both Purtell and Bush were elected in November.

Clare had given up her Hollywood writing to plunge into politics. She intended to stay. Instead of campaigning for herself, she went on a speaking tour for Ike. The Luce magazines gave the Republican candidate a tremendous boost.

Immediately after the election Luce left New York for the Orient on a three-week tour. A week later the President-elect asked Mrs. Luce to come see him at his Commodore Hotel headquarters.

In 1967 Clare described what happened.

Without any preliminaries at all, the President-elect said, "Clare, you must be on the team. What sort of job would interest you?"

The question wasn't unexpected. She countered with a question of her own. "What do you have in mind, Mr. President?"

"How about Secretary of Labor?"

Mrs. Luce told the General that she didn't believe she was qualified by experience for such a post, and suggested that he might be thinking of her as Secretary of Labor for three reasons: first, he wanted a woman in the Cabinet to fulfill a campaign pledge; second, because he wanted a Catholic in the Cabinet; and third, because the fact that Mrs. Perkins, a woman, had been Roosevelt's Secretary of Labor would make a woman in the post more acceptable to public opinion. But the truth of the matter was that Labor needed a man highly conversant with labor negotiations, business and industry.

Ike grinned and said, "I am relieved to hear you say that. I feel that way myself." In asking the question Ike may simply have been testing her judgment. Mrs. Luce suggested that he might consider her as a delegate to the United Nations. The President-elect countered this by suggesting that she consider an Embassy. "What about Rome?" he asked. Mrs. Luce replied, "I think it might be difficult for the Italians to accept a woman, and I don't want any job that would separate me too long from my husband. I would like it, but I would have to think it over, and talk it over with Harry first."

"You do that," Ike said.

11

Ambassador

In January 1953 Clare Boothe Luce was unquestionably one of the most controversial figures in American politics. No woman had ever been named America's chief diplomatic representative to a major foreign power. Postwar Italy was the weakest link in the chain of defense the West was being forced to build against its onetime ally, Russia.

The Italians had simultaneously renounced the Fascism of Mussolini and the rule of the Royal House of Savoy. But in the June 1946 referendum the margin of victory for those favoring a republic over a monarchy had been less than eight percent.

Alcide de Gasperi, leader of the Christian Democrat Party, had been installed as Premier, with United States support, at the end of the war. The first elections held in 1946 gave the Christian Democrats only thirty-five percent of the vote. The situation had improved in 1948 and De Gasperi's Catholic center party had won a clear majority of seats in the Chamber of Deputies. By 1952 the Communists on the one hand and the Monarchists on the other were threatening to move Italy either right or left. Eisenhower had chosen this moment to appoint a woman with no experience in diplomacy as the U.S. Ambassador.

Mrs. Luce told her husband that if taking Rome meant they would be separated for long periods of time, or if he had any reservations about her capacity for the job, she would refuse. Luce said she must not refuse. He had an office in Rome. He could, he said, run his magazines from that geographical position just as well as from New York. He promised to spend at least six months of every year in the Italian capital, and he was confident his wife could handle the assignment.

If any man in the United States outside the State Department truly understood the magnitude of the Italian problem at that moment, it was Henry Robinson Luce. The *Time* and *Life* correspondents in Italy had kept the home office and the boss appraised of the bitter internal struggle for control of the Government. Luce knew that Ambassador Ellsworth Bunker expected the De Gasperi Cabinet to fall in the 1953 spring elections, and that Bunker, who had already resigned, had made his plans to leave immediately after the elections, which were scheduled for April.

By American standards the machinery of the Italian Republic was cumbersome and unwieldy. The President was elected for a seven-year term; Senators for six years, members of the Chamber of Deputies for five. The ten splinter parties had won fifty-two percent of the popular vote in 1948.

Most Americans believed Italy was firmly on the side of Western powers because of its wartime switch from the Axis to the Allies. Beneath the surface the country had been teetering on the brink of accepting Communism. The De Gasperi Government had instituted land reforms which were very popular, but they—if elected—proposed to make changes in the election laws which would greatly favor the Christian Democrats. This proposed election law—*"la legge truffa"* (the swindle law)—outraged the Monarchists, Fascists, Communists and Socialists, who said the law, if passed, would deny Italy true representative government. Owing to De Gasperi's advocacy of *"la legge truffa,"* the Communist cause was on the ascendancy. If Italy went Communist, the entire North Atlantic Treaty Organization would be in jeopardy, and whoever served as American Ambassador at the time would be blamed for this strategic defeat.

Certainly Luce knew all this. Nevertheless, he encouraged his wife to accept the appointment because he had confidence in her ability to meet the challenge.

On January 4, 1953, the Boston *Post* printed a story saying that President Eisenhower had offered the Rome appointment to John Lodge of Connecticut. According to the *Post,* Governor Lodge had refused to leave his elective position and urged that Clare Boothe Luce be appointed Ambassador in his place.

Lodge had in fact himself sought the appointment and had been told it was promised to Clare Luce.

On February 7 the White House announced that former Congresswoman Luce would be nominated as the U.S. Ambassador to Italy, subject to the advice and consent of the Senate. The reaction in Italy was immediate and violent. Officially, the De Gasperi Government approved. But the Italian press was filled with expressions of displeasure and embarrassment. Unidentified governmental figures stated that the appointment of a woman Ambassador was an indication that Eisenhower regarded Italy as a third-rate power.

In the United States the opposition press charged that Mrs. Luce was being given a political pay-off. Certain Democratic members of Congress recalled the partisan remarks made by her in various campaigns, and said that these disqualified her as a diplomat.

The Luces had been leading members of the political group which had denied Senator Robert Taft of Ohio the Republican nomination in 1952, and probably the Presidency. Bob Taft had every reason to resent the Luces. Instead, he teamed up with Senator Homer Ferguson of Michigan to push approval of Mrs. Luce's nomination through the Senate Foreign Relations Committee.

Mrs. Luce's name was brought up before the full Senate on February 26, but action was postponed until Monday, March 2. Senator Olin D. Johnston of South Carolina explained his reasons for requesting the delay. There had been some fear that ardent Roman Catholic convert Luce might consider herself Minister to the Vatican as well as Ambassador to the Italian Government. This, Johnston said, had been dispelled by Mrs. Luce's own testimony before the Foreign Affairs Committee. However, the Senator was still concerned over the advisability of changing our representation to Italy before its next elections, which had just been postponed from April to May. He suggested it might be advisable to postpone Mrs. Luce's appointment until after the Italian votes had been counted. Mrs. Luce, who was at that time being briefed in the Department of State, wholly agreed. She had herself urged the Department of State to keep Mr. Bunker on until after the elections.

Mr. Bunker was queried as to his willingness to remain on through the elections, but he refused to do so, as his departure plans had been made and his household goods had already been shipped.

In the Senate colloquy which followed, Senator Alexander Wiley coyly suggested that there was some talk to support a belief that Mrs. Luce's actual nomination would be deferred. Ferguson of Michigan was drawn into the discussion. He said, "I have no personal knowledge as to when she will take office. I understand that is entirely up to the President of the United States."

Action was deferred and Mrs. Luce's name was placed at the bottom of the list of nominations on the executive calendar.

Much later in the same session Johnston carefully explained that his opposition was not motivated "by doubt as to the personal integrity and ability of the lady from Connecticut." What he wanted to do, he said, was to impress upon the mind of the President the serious situation existing in Italy, his personal opinion that Ellsworth Bunker was doing an admirable job, and how important it was for the United States to remain aloof. "We should not," he said, "indicate that we are in any way interested in the election which is about to take place."

The presiding officer called for the question: "Will the Senate advise and consent to the nomination of Mrs. Clare Boothe Luce to be Ambassador Extraordinary and Plenipotentiary of the United States of America to Italy?"

The nomination was confirmed without objection.

What Mrs. Luce was learning in her long briefing in the Department of State was anything but reassuring to the newly appointed and confirmed Ambassador.

At the end of World War II the free trade unions in Italy were encouraged by the American Allied Control Commission to cooperate with the Communists. This had resulted in Communist domination and control of most of the industrial workers.

The approximately forty-seven million Italian people were sharply divided economically and geographically. The average per capita income in the well-watered industrial North was almost double that of those who lived in the arid South. United States military and economic aid was necessary to keep the country afloat. Die-hard Fascists were re-emerging to argue that a military dictatorship was the only mechanism which could keep the country from going Communist.

The Trieste situation had not been resolved. Most authorities gloomily predicted that any attempt to achieve a permanent settlement of Trieste might explode into World War III. The dispute over possession of the Istrian Peninsula and the harbor of Trieste at the head of the Adriatic Sea had actually commenced when the Romans conquered the city one hundred and twenty-eight years before Christ. But from the early fourteenth century to 1914 the area had been under the rule of the House of Hapsburg as a part of the Austrian Empire. At the end of World War I the Treaty of St. Germain awarded this strategic seaport to Italy.

The Italian Government had commenced an immediate program of colonization and had attempted to Italianize the indigenous Slav population. Under Mussolini the use of the Slavic language was forbidden—even the names of the dead on tombstones were Italianized.

In the final months of World War II Marshal Tito had driven the occupying German armies out of Trieste. The area had been placed under the control of the combined British, American and Yugoslav commissions and had been divided into two zones.

Neither the land area nor the population was important enough to provoke a war. But Trieste had become an emotional symbol. Italian politicians pounded the table and demanded its return. Marshal Tito massaged the nationalistic emotions of his people, and answered *"Never."*

Four days after her fiftieth birthday Ambassador Luce sailed for Naples, accompanied by her husband and his sister Mrs. Maurice Moore.

She was looking forward to the ten days of shipboard isolation as an opportunity to concentrate on her study of the Italian language and to have some long, uninterrupted conversations with Harry.

Critics who were unaware of Ambassador Bunker's refusal to stay on through the election period suggested that Mrs. Luce's arrival in Rome before the elections took place was an expression of egotistic bravado. They pointed out that experienced diplomats rarely go to a new post without a supporting staff, obviously unaware that the Department of State had counseled her to make no changes in her Rome staff until she had her feet firmly on the ground.

On the day they sailed, Mr. Luce boasted to the friends who came to see them off that his wife was modestly proficient in the Italian language. Four years earlier, before there had been even a shadow of a suggestion that she might become the American Ambassador to Italy, Mrs. Luce had bought a Linguaphone course in the language. Now she set up the machine in her stateroom. By the time they arrived she was up to tourist, if not ambassadorial, Italian.

In the American foreign service, "political ambassadors" are generally regarded disdainfully by most career officers. Diplomat Robert Murphy, who successfully carried out the most delicate of missions for three American Presidents—Roosevelt, Truman and Eisenhower—says that "Clare became a career diplomat five minutes after she was appointed. She had," he says, "a fierce, unshakable determination which carried her to success in every mission assigned to her by the State Department."

The new Ambassador spent her last day at sea reviewing the instructions provided by the State Department. Since Ellsworth Bunker had left Rome on April 4, she would be met in Naples by Elbridge Durbrow, a fifty-year-old career officer who had entered foreign service in 1930 and was presently the Minister Counselor in the Rome Embassy. The note said Durbrow was a graduate of Yale, Class of '26, and had continued his studies at Stanford and notable foreign-service schools in Europe. Durbrow was considered a comer. The second-ranking staff member to greet her would be Joe Jacobs, the Economics Minister; Admiral Carney was the Naval Attaché, General James Christianson the Army's. John McKnight, a former newspaperman, was the Embassy's press-relations officer. She must at all costs, her instructions said, avoid saying anything or doing anything which might be interpreted as an indication of U.S. support of any one of the contending parties in the upcoming balloting.

When the *Andrea Doria* arrived in Naples' harbor, a launch brought out the official welcoming party from the Embassy. The moment the introductions were over, Durbrow insisted on seeing the new Ambassador privately. "It's unfortunate, your landing in Naples," he told her. This rather surprised the new Ambassador, since the State Department had felt that her arrival on the *Doria* would please the Italians, who were very proud of the new ship.

Durbrow says he explained that "the Mayor of Naples, Achille Lauro, is the leader of the Monarchist Party. Your coming is a great event. They have dismissed the schools, the streets and the dock will be jammed with people, Lauro will have his picture taken with you, and his partisans will impress the susceptible Italians with the suggestion that the new Administration favors re-establishing the House of Savoy."

"Well, I'm here," the Ambassador replied, "and I can't change where this ship docks. So what do you suggest, Mr. Durbrow?"

Durbrow says he told her "Until you officially present your credentials to the Premier and the President of the Republic, you are not in fact the American Ambassador. I can explain to the Mayor that it would embarrass your Government and his if we violated protocol. He must welcome you as a distinguished American citizen, of course. I will explain the situation to the reporters. That ought to take care of it."

It was a difficult beginning. There was a press conference attended by some two hundred Italian journalists, all shouting questions at the same time. She got through this, and with Durbrow's help somehow avoided having her picture taken with the Monarchist leader. But this diplomatic strategy didn't go unnoticed. The reporter for the New York *Journal-American* wrote:

Thousands of Neapolitans, most of them women, shouted and applauded the first woman envoy to Rome as she landed on the Italian ship *Andrea Doria*. Completely ignored in the bedlam were her husband, Henry Luce, the publisher, and Achille Lauro, Mayor of Naples. The husband of the playwright and former member of Congress smiled proudly at the reception given his wife. The Mayor looked crestfallen. Mrs. Luce read a prepared statement in Italian appealing for Italy's continued friendship and support of the American peace policy and pledging America's continued interest in Italy's future.

One thousand policemen guarded the dock area, but the crowds broke through anyway. The Luces and Mrs. Moore were nearly mobbed before they reached the official limousines. The Communist newspaper

L'Unità described the Ambassador as an "elderly lady," and said she spoke English with a Brooklyn accent.

Villa Taverna, the official residence provided by the U.S. Government for its Ambassador in Rome, is a sixteenth-century palace surrounded by seven acres of trees all protected by a high stone wall. The new Ambassador soon discovered that as a place in which to live, Taverna had many shortcomings.

The Ambassador's private quarters, on the second floor, consisted of a spacious study, or office, with one large adjoining bedroom. Mrs. Luce liked to work late at night and sleep late in the morning whenever possible. Her husband was a practitioner of that old adage "Early to bed and early to rise." Mrs. Luce gave the bedroom to her husband and turned the study into a study-bedroom for herself. Durbrow says that the Villa had been built at a time when there was great fear of earthquakes. The architects designed hollow walls and then suspended the second and third floors on heavy chains. The theory was that this would permit flexibility without collapse.

The laundry room was on the third floor over the office-study. There had recently been installed a new American electric washing machine which the maids put into use promptly at 7:00 each morning.

The Ambassador's decision to sleep in the study and give her husband the bedroom, combined with the new washing machine, set the scene for one of the most bizarre incidents ever to involve an American Ambassador in a foreign country. At the time of her arrival the only problem was the noise and vibration from the laundry which traveled down through the suspended floor-ceiling and made it difficult to sleep later than 7:00 A.M.

Durbrow admits that the staff of the Embassy resented her appointment almost as much as did the Italians. Mrs. Luce soon realized this.

But there was no way to make a frontal attack on the problem. She couldn't walk up to her subordinates and say, "Now, look here, I know you disapprove of me, but I'm going to stay and we'll have to work together, so let's talk it out."

The stately Palazzo Margherita is located at that point where the Via Veneto turns slightly to descend into the lower city. Erected in the last half of the nineteenth century from a design by the Roman architect Gaetano Koch, the place had been the home of the Queen Mother of the House of Savoy from 1900 to 1926. At the end of World War II the U.S. Government purchased the building to house the offices of the U.S. Ambassador. The American Consulate and the proliferating U.S. foreign agencies occupied a cluster of buildings immediately adjacent to the impressive Palazzo.

The morning after her arrival in Rome Ambassador Luce rose early. Her trunks had not been delivered. She dressed in a slightly rumpled, severely tailored dark-blue suit, a wide-collared silk shirtwaist, and ordered the car. Then she sipped one cup of coffee and nibbled a slice of toast. Mentally and physically she was eager to tackle the job. It was 8:15 in the morning. She hoped the staff would understand from her appearance and her early arrival that Clare Boothe Luce intended to be a working diplomat.

Only about three miles separate the Villa Taverna from the Palazzo Margherita, but in the early-morning traffic movement was slow and spasmodic. It was eighteen minutes before nine when the first American woman Ambassador arrived at the Palazzo.

There were two ways to reach the Ambassador's office on the second floor—by elevator from the entrance lobby on the right or by means of a magnificent semicircular staircase. She chose the stairs, pausing halfway up to savor the atmosphere and to enjoy the delighted surprise she could see on the faces of the clerks, guards and minor functionaries who quite obviously had not expected her to arrive so unceremoniously or so early.

The Queen Mother's dining room, at the corner of the building overlooking the Via Veneto, had been converted into the Ambassador's private office. It was a high-ceilinged, almost square space ornately decorated in gold and cream.

At 9:30 that morning there was a brief reception for the staff. According to Durbrow there were more than five hundred employees performing various tasks in the Embassy and twice that number stationed at various posts throughout Italy.

In his campaign for the Presidency, Eisenhower had been critical of what he called the extravagances and the inefficiencies of U.S. foreign service. It seemed to Mrs. Luce that first morning that if the situation in Rome was typical, Ike's comments were justified. But her assignment was to implement U.S. foreign policy, not to function as an efficiency expert or to take charge of housekeeping chores.

As Durbrow and Jacobs introduced the other members of the staff, Clare felt an undercurrent of that same hostility she thought she had detected upon her arrival in Naples. It occurred to her that perhaps the ambiguities of the moment were responsible. Until she officially presented her credentials to Premier de Gasperi and President Einaudi, she was, as Durbrow had suggested the day before, just a distinguished visitor. Perhaps she was a woman invading what heretofore had been strictly a masculine preserve. Whatever the reason, it seemed to Clare her first task was to gain the respect, if not the affection, of her staff. A good way to start would be to get better acquainted with her subordinates, and to give them a chance to appraise her. She invited the Chiefs of Mission—Durbrow, Jacobs, Tony Freeman, Ed Adams, Gerry Miller, the military attachés and the other senior officers—to join her for informal discussions at the Villa Taverna every Monday morning. "It will," she told them, "give us an opportunity to exchange ideas, examine our common problems, and reach a general agreement on any proposed course of action."

These Monday-morning meetings became the pattern for what is now standard operating procedure in the foreign service, authorized by a formal decree issued by Eisenhower some five years later and designated "Little Country Teams."

According to Elbridge Durbrow, Clare held the first one in her bed-sitting room, an atmosphere calculated to help establish the rapport she was seeking. "I want this to be," she explained, "something like the editorial conferences we held when I was in the publishing business. There must always be someone who has to make the final decision. But you have all been at this thing much longer than I have, and I hope you'll express your ideas and opinions without hesitation."

All the hours of briefing Mrs. Luce had received in Washington before her departure were, she discovered, immensely valuable. But they were all preliminary. Now that she was on the spot she was forced to separate the theoretical situations from the existing conditions. U.S. involvement in all phases of foreign affairs had mushroomed like an atomic cloud after World War II. When Clare arrived in Italy the United States had an Ambassador to UNESCO in Paris, an Ambassador to NATO, an Ambassador in charge of the Marshall Plan, dozens of different air missions, the virtually autonomous Central Intelligence Agency, plus the consulate staff, heads of trade missions, and so many other official and semiofficial envoys that it was literally impossible to know them all or to keep track of their many activities.

Many of her employees in the lower echelons had been in Rome since the Embassy was reopened under James Clement Dunn in 1946. Ellsworth Bunker had replaced Dunn in 1952, and now, only a year later, they were confronted with the necessity of accommodating themselves to a new boss.

Gradually the hostility, or perhaps it was only a natural diffidence which she had detected at first, lessened. As the result of the weekly meetings, she developed friendly relations with Jacobs and Freeman. She learned to respect Durbrow. His habit of launching into lengthy lectures on every subject discussed annoyed her at times. What the man needed, she thought, was a good editor, but you can't edit a verbal essay.

Luce, who might have offered many suggestions, adopted a policy of strict noninterference, and Clare was grateful. He spent his days at the Rome office of *Time,* or prowling the ancient ruins, or asking questions about Italian politics and economics of anyone who would pause long enough to answer.

At the time there was no way for Ambassador Luce to discover just how much the staff appreciated her approach and Harry's attitude. But many years later both Jacobs and Durbrow confirmed the correctness of her intuition. Jacobs good-humoredly admitted that when he had heard the news of Clare's appointment he decided to resign and take his retirement. "All my life I had been working for two women—my wife and my secretary. I said I'd be damned if I'd work for a woman boss. When Mrs. Luce arrived in Naples I came to scoff, but I stayed to praise."

Durbrow told her that at first she was thought of as a rich, reactionary Republican sent over by Eisenhower to prove that his campaign criticisms of the foreign service were correct. "We suspected you planned to furnish your husband with inside information for a series of scathing exposé stories in *Time* or *Life*. We all thought our heads were on the chopping block."

The further postponement of the Italian elections until June complicated Clare's problems. The United States favored a continuation of the De Gasperi Government, but the Christian Democrats were in deep trouble with the electorate. Mrs. Luce didn't take any overt action which might result in the charge of American interference. There was, she thought, one way she could make her presence felt in Italy, so she set out to visit every principal city and region from the island of Sicily to the northern industrial complex around Milan. Thirty days after her arrival a newspaper poll revealed that almost fifty percent of the Italians knew the name of Signora Luce, the American Ambassadress. Only two percent had known the name of Ellsworth Bunker. It wasn't much, but at least it was something.

During this period when she was fighting to find solid ground, Clare discovered that one of the reasons for the concern her coming had caused the staff was purely social. No one knew exactly what to do with Harry. There were no standard provisions for seating the Ambassador's husband at a formal affair. The hostesses in Rome, great on protocol, struggled with the simple problem of where to put Mr. Luce at the dinner table. This was finally solved when he was given the honorary rank of Minister. This title put him at the foot of the list, below all genuine Ministers, but ahead of all Chargés d'Affaires. Harry accepted the situation without protest, commenting gleefully that it was much better at the lower end of the table because the girls were always younger and more beautiful.

Ambassador Luce got along much better with the Italian officials —Foreign Minister Attilio Piccioni and Premier de Gasperi and President Einaudi—than she did with her own staff. This was because she did her homework. When it became necessary to discuss a problem, she knew as much or more about the situation than they did, and she voiced her opinions in the same frank manner which had inspired *The New Yorker* to dub her "The Candor Kid" in its January 4–11, 1941, issue.

At the end of May, Clare went to Milan to speak to the members of the American Chamber of Commerce for Italy. The Embassy staff believed that before this audience it would be safe to at least hint at the U.S. State Department's desire for a continuation of a moderate government in Rome. The speech was staff-prepared accordingly. In general it followed the tone of the remarks President Eisenhower had made to the American Society of Newspaper Publishers a few weeks earlier. But there was one unfortunate paragraph: "I am required in all honesty to say this, though it cannot happen, but if the Italian people should fall unhappy victims to the wiles of totalitarianism of the right or of the left, there would logically follow grave consequences."

In Genoa the next night, speaking to the Propeller Club—an association of businessmen engaged in transport—Ambassador Luce spelled out how much U.S. aid (almost $650 million for direct assistance and more than $300 million as a part of the offshore procurement program for NATO) had done for Italy.

The "hint" in the Milan speech didn't attract much attention in the Milan press. But when Mrs. Luce got back to Rome she discovered these earlier remarks, coupled with a recital of American aid in Genoa, were being interpreted as a thinly veiled American ultimatum: re-elect De Gasperi or else.

The elections were held on June 7 and 8. The Christian Democrat Party lost forty-five seats in the Chamber of Deputies and fifteen in the Senate. Some of De Gasperi's supporters blamed the American Ambassadress for his defeat.

Long before Mrs. Luce's arrival in Italy, the polls had shown that the De Gasperi Government was in serious trouble, owing to De Gasperi's insistence on changing the election laws. The Embassy staff itself felt that the belated U.S. "hint" may well have prevented the loss of even more seats. De Gasperi himself remarked somewhat acidly that he doubted that the new Ambassador's warning had changed a single Italian vote. In his view, he said, what had defeated him was the failure of the U.S. and British Governments to help Italy find a solution to the question of Trieste which would return it to the Italian flag.

Jacobs, Durbrow and Miller all agree that the election outcome was decided months before Mrs. Luce arrived, and Ambassador Bunker's reports to the Department would seem to bear this out. In any event, there was a good deal more criticism in the American papers, which picked up the Communist charge, than there was in Italy.

On July 16 De Gasperi, with the unenthusiastic support of two minor parties in the Chamber of Deputies, formed a new Cabinet.

Fourteen days later De Gasperi's shaky new Government was defeated in the Chamber, and Giuseppe Pella, whose policies were slightly more acceptable to the Republicans, the Liberals and the Monarchists, was named Premier. Three days later this new Italian Government issued a bellicose statement alleging Yugoslavia was preparing to go to war over Trieste. Pella ordered the Italian Army to move into position on the border of Zone A, an action which brought an immediate belligerent response from Marshal Tito.

Faced with the arrogance of Tito and the politically inspired truculence of Pella, there was little the American Embassy could do without again being charged with interference.

To make matters worse for the Ambassador, the morale of the Embassy staff was low. While Ambassador Bunker was still in Rome, Senator Joe McCarthy had sent his aides Roy Cohn and G. David Schine to Rome to investigate reported disloyal subversion in the foreign service. They had left behind them many a demoralized Embassy in Europe. The Rome Embassy was no exception. Now there descended on Mrs. Luce's Embassy an aggressive, suspicious investigator named Walter McCloud.

Fulton Freeman, a member of the Rome Embassy, had served in China as an assistant secretary during those years when the Department of State was accepting the line that Chou En-lai and Mao Tse-tung represented honest, agrarian reformers. When the Chinese Communists took control of that nation, Americans critical of Roosevelt and Truman charged that left-wing sympathizers in the American Diplomatic Corps had helped the Communists. McCarthy's investigators regarded every old China hand as either a dupe or a traitor. Their target in Rome had been Fulton "Tony" Freeman.

At that point, Ambassador Luce probably knew a great deal more about China than she did about Italy. She told McCloud that there were few American Congressmen who had spoken up more strongly in the cause of Free China than she had, or who had a more consistent record of warning against a Red take-over of that country.

Freeman was a Class #4 foreign-service officer living in Chungking in the middle of a war. He was working for an Ambassador whose policy (like hers in Rome) was set by the President and the State Department. He could not have refused to obey his superiors. Moreover, it was downright silly to think that a Class #4 officer could significantly change the policies of Washington, even had he wished to do so. No Class #4 officer in the field is at a policy-making level. The Luces had had many talks with Freeman about China. It was clear to both of them that Freeman was a very gifted and loyal foreign-service officer, and that any other view was nonsense. The new Ambassador said there was no one of her staff she thought was a better officer. McCloud returned to Washington, and on reviewing Freeman's record, came to the same happy conclusion.

Everyone in the Embassy knew why McCloud had come to Rome. Mrs. Luce's steady defense of her colleague helped to change, no doubt, the attitude of her staff.

The trouble over Trieste was still threatening the peace of Europe when Clare went to Luxembourg in mid-September to attend a conference called by John Foster Dulles. The gathering was the first of its kind, an innovation which Clare thought very promising. Most of the American Ambassadors in Europe were present. The purpose was to provide a forum where they could discuss their particular problems and bring their personal experience to bear on the difficulties in the rest of the European community.

It was the first time Mrs. Luce had an opportunity to meet and appraise the talents of her peers in the foreign service. She was greatly impressed by the practical approaches taken by James B. Conant, former president of Harvard, who was then U.S. Ambassador to West Germany, and by Ambassador Charles Bohlen, stationed in Moscow. But it was Llewellyn Thompson, then serving in Austria, who made the greatest impression on her.

When the meeting was over, Mr. Conant invited the lady Ambassador to travel on his private train to Berlin, where an Air Force plane would pick her up and take her to Rome. Ambassador "Chip" Bohlen accompanied them.

During the journey to Berlin, she learned a great deal about the problems of our emissaries in Moscow and Berlin, the two European hot spots. On the last night the three Ambassadors discussed the Italian problem. Chip Bohlen told her, "Look, Clare, don't try to solve the Trieste question. Territorial problems are the most difficult of all." Trieste, he predicted sadly, would not be solved short of war.

By the middle of November it began to look as if war could not be prevented. Then the tension eased momentarily when Tito agreed to an Italian proposal that both countries withdraw their troops from the border.

Mrs. Luce wanted to go home to New York for Christmas. Instead, she decided to stay in Rome. If Trieste remained quiet, perhaps she could leave in time to celebrate New Year's with the Luce family.

Everyone at the Embassy thought the mutual pullback was only the prelude to another period of testing. As the months passed, the Trieste question began to boil up again.

Robert Murphy, in his book *Diplomat Among Warriors,* says, "At the Chevy Chase golf course we had named Hole #8 *Trieste,* because it encompassed about the same amount of territory which the Yugoslavs and the Italians were arguing about."

Mrs. Luce and her staff did not agree with the general acceptance of the defeatist attitude that "Trieste couldn't be settled." The real problem, her staff told her, was to get the Trieste question put on the agenda of the National Security Council. The Department of State had been unable to get it there, partly because of many other pressing problems, partly, perhaps, because they did not think it could be solved anyway. There was one man in the whole world with enough power to alter that negative thinking: the President of the United States. Mrs. Luce knew that no President has time to plow through long letters from Ambassadors (neither do Secretaries of State). She decided to write the President a very short personal note. But how could she put the complex Trieste problem into a very few simple words? Suddenly she remembered the old saying: ". . . for want of a nail the shoe was lost; for want of a shoe the horse was lost; . . ." Across the top of the sheet she wrote:

DEAR MR. PRESIDENT:
FOR WANT OF A TWO-PENNY TOWN.

For the Want of a Two-Penny Town (called Trieste)
A Prime Minister was Lost (de Gasperi)
For the Want of a Prime Minister . . .
Italy was Lost . . .
For the Want of Italy, NATO was lost . . .
For the Want of Europe, America was lost . . .
And all for the Want of a Two-Penny Town (called Trieste)
   . . . (signed respectfully) CLARE LUCE

Then she attached a handwritten note saying, "Please, Mr. President, put Trieste on the Security Council agenda. Give our Embassy a chance."

When the United States Security Council met in Washington, D.C., in January 1954, Trieste was on the agenda. The President had responded favorably to Clare's plea.

Everyone understood that the hard-line position publicly stated by both the Italian and Yugoslav Governments was dictated by political considerations. The politicians, fearful of domestic criticism, were afraid of appearing to compromise.

Ambassador Luce proposed that the United States take the lead in promoting a secret conference in a neutral country, to be attended by representatives of Italy, Yugoslavia, the British Foreign Office and our own State Department.

The Embassy in Rome would attempt to secure the cooperation of the Italian Government, and our Ambassador in Belgrade would make a smililar approach to Tito. It was decided that Ambassador Llewellyn Thompson would represent the United States. The discussions would be held in London, and the big powers would try to find a formula with enough face-saving sweeteners to permit both disputing nations to claim a semblance of victory.

Both Eisenhower and Foster Dulles were immensely encouraged when the Governments of Italy and Yugoslavia agreed to the U.S. suggestion and accepted London as a proposed site for the secret negotiations. Italian Premier Pella named Manlio Brosio as his deputy. Tito sent Dr. Vladimir Velebit. The British Foreign Office was to be represented by Geoffrey W. Harrison.

One incident which occurred during her brief visit home in 1955 might have had far-reaching consequences. Before flying back to Rome, Clare attended an off-the-record dinner given by American and foreign correspondents in Washington, D.C. The newsmen asked questions about the Italian Government, the Communist influence and Trieste, with the understanding that nothing was to be written about the affair and none of the opinions expressed were to be attributed to Mrs. Luce.

Three days later, when some of her comments were printed in *The New York Times* and reported overseas, Clare gave a convincing demonstration of shocked amazement. According to the report, the American Ambassadress had deplored the growing influence of Communists in Italian labor unions and the Italian Government. She had criticized De Gasperi for his quick concession of defeat after the 1953 elections, alleging that Christian Democrats had been the victims of fraudulent ballots. In cold print the remarks attributed to Clare were startlingly undiplomatic. She stoutly maintained the report was a gross exaggeration.

Ambassador Luce was much too sophisticated to expect that every newspaper reporter at that dinner party would treat her remarks discreetly. Actually she wanted the Italian press to record her distress over the Communist domination of the industrial unions. Anticipating that some reporter would be unable to resist the temptation to break such a hot story, Clare had prudently refrained from mentioning anything about the Trieste situation which had actually brought her to Washington.

The influential left-wing newspaper *Europae* published what it described as a verbatim report of the speech. Indro Montanelli, a distinguished Italian journalist, wrote a letter of protest to the publisher of *Europae.* He carefully avoided any discussion of the propriety of what Mrs. Luce was alleged to have said, and devoted his letter to proving that every statement attributed to her was an accurate, precise desciption of the current situation in Italy.

Clare believed the results obtained were worth the risk she had taken. She realized Ike and Dulles might not agree. She might be asked to resign. But in that event she had cleared the air for her successor and forced the Italian politicians to put aside their preoccupation with petty jealousies to face the reality of the Communist strength.

As a result of the *Europae* article, the Soviet Ambassador, Bogomolov, inspired thirty-five left-wing Italian Senators to demand the recall of Ambassador Luce, charging that Clare had attempted to interfere illegally in the internal affairs of Italy.

Mrs. Luce was in Fontainebleau, France, attending a North Atlantic Treaty Organization conference when the Communist demand was made public. Her off-the-record remarks in Washington had been critical of the Italian situation, but nowhere had she done what the Soviet Ambassador was now doing—namely, to demand official Government action. Her only comment was that "the story printed in the Italian papers was unauthorized . . ." and that she had been misquoted.

In Washington, American columnist Roscoe Drummond, who was chief of the New York *Herald Tribune* Washington Bureau, and who had attended the off-the-record dinner, supported Mrs. Luce's statement. He said, "It was clearly understood at the time that the conversation was wholly personal, private and informal. Publication of any remarks attributed to Mrs. Luce could therefore only be the result of a malicious attempt to embarrass her and distort her views."

Senator Homer Ferguson of Michigan took the floor to read a letter from the Italian Ambassador, who wished to inform the Congress that the Italian Parliament had completely rejected the Communist demand. Foreign Minister Piccioni, he said, had declared Mrs. Luce not only *persona grata,* but *gratissima,* to the Italian Government.

Nevertheless, Clare was relieved when the scandalous Montesi affair took over the headlines. The body of Wilma Montesi had been found on the beach about fifteen miles southwest of Rome. The magazine *Attualità* stated that the woman's death was the result of a drug orgy and was due to criminal negligence on the part of persons having politically powerful friends.

By the end of March the affair had become a full-blown scandal, completely dominating the newspaper headlines. The Chief of the Ministry of Interior Police Department, Pavone, and Foreign Minister Piccioni were forced to resign.

The charge that Piero Piccioni, the deposed Foreign Minister's son, was involved in the death of the Montesi woman was never proved. But for the better part of a year rumors of sex parties and drug addictions added to the instability of the Government.

In London the secret negotiations over Trieste made good progress during the spring and early summer. But in August they bogged down. The representative of the Yugoslav Government, Vladimir Velebit, began to insist on more concessions than the Italian, British and U.S. representatives were prepared to grant.

In Rome Clare was almost ready to grant that Chip Bohlen had been right when an American, who refused to identify himself on the telephone, promised to give her some helpful information about Trieste if she would see him privately.

Clare realized the caller might be an impostor. She had learned that some people would go to any lengths to see the Ambassador. But there was an implication that her anonymous caller knew about the talks in London. If he did, he just might have information which would be helpful. She agreed to see him. They met at the Villa Taverna late one afternoon.

The man's appearance was reassuring, and when they were alone in the Ambassador's study he came directly to the point. "My name wouldn't mean anything to you and I don't want to be involved in this, but I have been doing some work for the CIA in Yugoslavia. Their man in London is giving our people trouble, and I know why."

If the caller knew this much, it might be worthwhile to listen to him. "Is there something you think I can do?"

"The problem, Mrs. Luce, is the crop failure. Tito needs wheat. If he doesn't get it, there will be a famine next winter."

"How does that relate to Trieste?"

"Surely, Mrs. Luce, you know how the mind of a dictator works—create a crisis and divert the public attention, and I think that's what he intends to do."

"If the United States gave him enough wheat to carry them through this winter, would that help?"

The man smiled. "You have anticipated my suggestion, Mrs. Luce. A half a million tons of wheat would relieve the present shortage and unfreeze the situation in London."

Clare thanked her caller. Then because she knew that most human action is based on self-interest, she asked what he wanted in return.

Again the man smiled. "Something you can do quite easily, without any embarrassment—introduce me to Stavros Niarchos, the Greek shipping magnate. I have a personal matter I want to discuss with him."

"I will if your information proves to be correct."

There was a certain undeniable logic in the mysterious stranger's explanation of the sudden turnabout in London. Mrs. Luce telephoned Joe Jacobs at the Embassy and asked him what he knew about the wheat crop in Yugoslavia. He confirmed what her caller had told her. Three days later she was on her way to Washington.

"Your informant may have given you the truth," John Foster Dulles told Clare, "but Tito could never afford to admit to us or anyone else that he would trade Trieste for a gift of wheat."

The Secretary said the delicacy of the situation would demand an emissary who could deal with the Communist dictator in absolute secrecy, someone whom Tito would trust never to reveal the details of the arrangement.

"Let's not give up. There must be someone we can send."

"Put yourself in the Marshal's place, Mrs. Luce. The rulers of a totalitarian country are just as sensitive to public opinion as we are in a democracy. Tito has domestic enemies and opposition at home. He would be destroyed if the news ever got out that he had traded Trieste for a gift of grain to cover up the failures of his own farm program.

"Believe me, Clare, it won't work unless we can find the right man."

Two nights later, at a dinner party hosted by correspondent Arthur Krock, Mrs. Luce found herself seated next to Bob Murphy, the veteran trouble shooter of the State Department who had carried on the secret negotiations between the U.S. Government and the Yugoslav patriots during World War II. The conversation turned to the problem of Trieste. Murphy casually mentioned his long-established, friendly relations with Tito.

"You're just the man we've been looking for," Clare said. "I have an appointment with President Eisenhower in the morning. We need someone who can carry out a very difficult confidential mission to Tito. Would you go?"

"I'll go anywhere the President wants to send me," Murphy replied.

Twelve hours later Secretary Murphy was on his way to the island of Brioni, off the Dalmatian coast, where Tito had constructed a sumptuous summer palace. Murphy carried a personal letter from President Eisenhower to the Yugoslav dictator.

The Trieste affair was settled in London on October 5. Zone A, including the city of Trieste, with an area of 85 square miles and a population of 300,000, was returned to Italy. Zone B, with some addition from Zone A, comprising a total of 200 square miles and a population of 74,000, was annexed to Yugoslavia. Twenty days later the military forces of the United States and Great Britain, which had occupied the contested territories since the end of World War II, were withdrawn.

In his personal memoirs, *Diplomat Among Warriors,* Murphy minimizes the importance of the 400,000 tons of wheat the United States sent to Belgrade three weeks after the settlement was reached.

Only five people in the world knew the truth—the President of the United States, Secretary Dulles, Bob Murphy, Marshal Tito, and the American Ambassadress to Rome, who had started it all. When Britain's Sir Anthony Eden surmised the truth and cynically suggested that Murphy had gone to Belgrade and bribed the Yugoslav Government with a gift of wheat, the American diplomat categorically denied the charge.

The American correspondents in Rome, including Henry Luce, were caught flat-footed by the announcement of the treaty and expressed their resentment to the American Ambassador. She denied having any knowledge of the negotiations or the terms of the settlement. But years later when a prestigious American university published what was described as an accurate report of the settlement of the Trieste crisis and ignored Mrs. Luce's major contribution she thought the authors had done her an injustice.

During the summer of 1954, concern over the strength of the Communists in the Italian union movement caused Mrs. Luce to re-examine the American offshore procurement program. Authorized by an act of Congress to rehabilitate the industrial capacity of our allies by purchasing matériel for NATO's defense needs from foreign suppliers, the program had become the main economic support for the factories and shipyards in Italy.

The unions had prospered as the result of this full employment, and most of the shop stewards and union officials were Communists.

It seemed to Clare that we were feeding our enemies, but no one in the State Department was willing to support any kind of action aimed at lessening the power of the Communist unions.

Once more Mrs. Luce flew home to confront Secretary Dulles and President Eisenhower. She was, she said, prepared to resign unless the American policy could be changed. What she wanted to do was to cancel the offshore orders awarded to any plant where the Communist unions were in control.

President Eisenhower was in favor of any action which would lessen the Communist influence. But he believed that what Mrs. Luce proposed might be regarded as a hostile act and react against us.

"That isn't true, Mr. President," Clare told him. "Look, Giuseppe has a job. Maria is happy because he brings home the pay check to buy the spaghetti. If Giuseppe loses that job because he belongs to a Communist union, Maria will tell him to quit the union and go back to work. If it is ever a choice between spaghetti and a union card, Giuseppe will choose the spaghetti. He votes Communist now only because it's the easy, convenient thing to do, not from any ideological convictions."

Eisenhower refused to be convinced. How did anyone know what Giuseppe would do? If the offshore contracts were canceled and wide unemployment resulted, the Communists would be certain to exploit the situation.

Clare recited the facts and figures she had gathered on the importance of our offshore contracts to Italian industry. She felt that Eisenhower was being timid and Dulles obstinate. She threatened to resign and tell the American people that the Eisenhower Administration was ignoring both the intent of Congress and the letter of the law by permitting the use of these funds to strengthen our enemies.

Ambassador Luce isn't sure whether it was the intensity of her response or the fact that Dulles knew that the language of the bill authorizing offshore procurement carried a specific prohibition against what she said was taking place. But both Eisenhower and Dulles agreed to give her a free hand, with the understanding that if things didn't work out, the responsibility would be on her shoulders.

Back in Italy Mrs. Luce quietly but firmly informed the managers of the various plants that she would be compelled to cancel their contracts unless something was done to lessen the Communist influence in the unions. At first no one took her seriously.

The Fiat complex was by all odds the backbone of the Italian economy, and Fiat was about to embark on the building of Italy's first jet warplane. Dr. Valletta, the president of Fiat, came to the Embassy with the manager of the proposed new aircraft plant. To cancel the aircraft order at this time would inflict irreparable harm on Italy's self-confidence, he said, and prevent her from ever being able to defend the country against an aggressor.

The Ambassador replied she would hate to see this happen for Italy's sake, for America's and for NATO's. But Congressional legislation in respect to offshore procurement funds left her with no other choice. Her Government had advised that the orders should be canceled.

As the days passed, the tension increased. Each time Dr. Valletta came to call on the American Ambassador he brought with him a new group of plant managers. Over and over again he assured the American Ambassadress that management deplored the situation but was helpless to do anything about it.

In early March of 1955 it was announced in the Italian press that Premier Mario Scelba would leave soon on an official visit to the United States. This announcement brought a delegation of Italian industrialists to the Palazzo Margherita. The question of the offshore contracts had not been settled. It would be unthinkable, Dr. Valletta argued, to cancel them now on the eve of Scelba's departure to pay a state visit to the President of the United States.

The American Ambassador and her Minister Counselor, Elbridge Durbrow, pointed out that it might be very difficult for Premier Scelba if his presence in America caused the Congress to focus its attention on the Communist situation in Italy. Mrs. Luce told her callers that she had on that morning canceled one contract amounting to a little more than $300,000. She said she intended to accompany the Italian Premier to the United States, and would "do everything in her power to help him explain why Italy, a Western power and a friend of the United States, continues to tolerate Communist control of the union workers whose wages are being paid with American dollars."

According to Durbrow, Dr. Valletta shrugged his shoulders in resignation, turned to his associates, and said apparently the American Government had made up its mind to act.

That night when Clare returned to the Villa Taverna she found three boxes of red roses, each with Dr. Valletta's card. She assumed the Italian industrial leader was trying to soften her up.

Shortly thereafter Premier Scelba flew to Washington for a state visit accompanied by Ambassador Luce, or as the Italians called her, "La Signora."

The head of the Italian parliament was in conference with John Foster Dulles when an aide brought in a cablegram. Scelba ripped open the envelope, read the contents to himself, then turned, beaming, to the American Secretary of State. "I am pleased to inform you," he said, "of the results of the recent elections in the Fiat factory in Turin. When this vote was last taken the Communists received seventy percent, the Saragat Socialists and Christian Democrats thirty percent. Today's results are quite different. Sixty-two percent of the union officers elected are members of the right-wing socialist or Christian Democratic parties and only thirty-eight percent are Communists or Socialists."

The American Secretary of State and the American Ambassadress to Italy congratulated Premier Scelba for what they said was truly a great move to strengthen democracy in Italy.

Six weeks later when Clare encountered Dr. Vittorio Valletta of

255

Fiat at a social gathering in Rome, she graciously thanked him for the roses. "The flowers were very beautiful," she said, "but even their fragrance was powerless to persuade me to alter my position."

"Ah, but Signora Luce," Valletta smiled, "you misunderstand. I sent you the flowers after our last meeting at the Embassy, not before. I wanted you to know that privately I approved the strong stand your Embassy had taken."

12

End of a Mission

From the day she arrived in Naples the Communists and the Socialists found fault with everything Ambassador Luce did or said, or sometimes did or did not do or say. But even these critics admitted she was extremely popular with the Italian people. They attributed this to the fact that she was a beautiful woman. Whenever she appeared in public she was dressed and groomed to emphasize her femininity. Durbrow and Jacobs agree that Clare's beauty was an asset, but they believe it was her instinctive sympathetic response to the troubles and needs of the Italian people which earned their affection.

When the floods engulfed Salerno, the Ambassador and members of her staff went immediately to the trouble zone. It was her appearance as much as the food and medicine the Embassy ordered to be distributed which cheered the people.

The day before she was scheduled to fly back to the United States on an American airline in 1954, the Italian overseas carrier had a disastrous crash. Mrs. Luce promptly canceled her space and rescheduled on Alitalia—a demonstration of confidence which reassured both the Italian people and the airline operators.

Baseball hero Joe DiMaggio came to Rome and paused to pay a courtesy call at the Palazzo Margherita. Clare introduced him to everyone in the building, then linking her arm in his, said, "Joe, let's go down to one of those little sidewalk cafés and have a cup of coffee."

By the time they were seated the Via Veneto was jammed with Italians eager to see "DiMag." Joe shook hundreds of hands, patted

many a youngster's backside, and it did Mrs. Luce no harm to be standing behind him, smiling and helping it all along.

After the first traditional Fourth of July party at the Villa Taverna,
open to the public, produced a mob of ten thousand sight-seers, "La
Signora" gave up sponsoring this kind of public function. Instead, she
entertained the whole Diplomatic Corps on the U.S. national birthday.

Durbrow says that Mrs. Luce worked long hours and expected her
staff to do likewise. There were at least three hundred state functions
each year which were a must for the Ambassadress—luncheons, dinners
and cocktail parties. At the Villa Mrs. Luce entertained with small
dinner parties. The guest list was not limited to the socially elite or the
politically powerful. When Durbrow or Jacobs or any of the Chiefs of
Mission spotted a newcomer who they thought might be on the way up,
they had "the boss's permission" to bring the new man or new woman
to the Villa. It was a privilege the staff deeply appreciated. At the same
time it made it possible for the Ambassadress to make early contacts with
emerging new leaders of the Republic.

To escape from this goldfish-bowl-always-be-on-your-guard social
atmosphere, Mrs. Luce would slip away to the apartments of American
friends to talk about her old enthusiasms—domestic politics, the theater
and art. She frequently found refuge at the Stan Swintons, where she
would sit on the floor, abandon her diplomatic inhibitions, and engage
in discussions with the AP bureau chief which ranged from sophisticated
humor to America's domestic difficulties to sports. Swinton says sometimes they would spend a whole afternoon discussing the future of
American culture. It was the kind of catharsis she needed.

Time staffers in Rome resented the fact that they were not given
any inside track by the Embassy. When they complained about this to
Luce he said, "We are never going to let it be claimed that because my
wife is the American Ambassador our magazines have a pipeline to news
denied other correspondents."

The publisher's attitude didn't help his wife in her relations with
the staff of *Time,* but it did make it easier for her to deal with the foreign
and American press corps in Rome.

Disgruntled Italian and American reporters frequently charged that
Ambassador Luce was not the most diplomatic of American representa-

tives, but not even her enemies in the press ever suggested that she lacked diligence. All the accounts of this period emphasize "La Signora's" single-minded devotion to American interests.

In late 1954 Mrs. Luce happened to read an article in the American magazine *Blue Book* quoting the U.S. Commissioner of Narcotics, Harry Jacob Anslinger. The piece was an exposé of the narcotics trade. Anslinger was quoted as saying that Italy was the source of supply for most of the cocaine and heroin brought into the United States. The article pointed out that there were no restrictions on narcotics in Italy. It said the Mafia encouraged the preparation of drugs for smuggling overseas as a sort of home industry.

Mrs. Luce asked Charles Siragusa, the American expert, if there was any truth in the article. He assured her the facts were essentially correct.

Some weeks later, at one of the ceremonial affairs with which the United States surrounded its acts of largesse, the Ambassador was present at the Palazzo Chigi to sign a document which provided for the distribution of free milk and dairy products to thousands of undernourished Italian babies.

As she picked up the pen to make this act of charity official, she was struck with the incongruity of the situation. The United States was sending help to Italian boys and girls while the Italians were exporting dope to American youth.

Italian Foreign Minister Segni caught Clare's mood. He asked why the American Ambassador appeared so depressed. Clare told him. She pointed out that the Italian Chamber of Deputies had consistently refused to approve the international covenants for narcotics control.

Segni appeared to be sincere when he expressed his astonishment. He claimed he had not known of the traffic. He agreed with Mrs. Luce. It would, he promised, be stopped.

Within thirty days the Italian Government officially signed the United Nations agreement. The torrent of illegal drugs from Italy to the United States dwindled to a trickle.

In every one of Mrs. Luce's various careers one quality emerges as paramount—zeal. Her explanation is that she has always worked hard at every task she has undertaken. But her friends think this is an understatement. A genuine commitment to the objective, almost to the exclusion of all other interests, has contributed to her success. It has also caused some difficulties.

Approaching the ambassadorial assignment, Mrs. Luce determined to avoid anything which might make her appear pretentious to Italian eyes—she clearly understood the envious animosity generated in the States by her wealth, her political position as a confidante of General Ike, and Harry's power as the emperor of *Time-Life*—consequently, when the Luces went to Rome, Clare took no personal staff with her. This was a mistake, and one which she quickly recognized. It was impossible to cope with all the complex problems of the Embassy and the Villa without help. Clare's cram-course Italian language was incomprehensible to the Italian staff at the Villa.

Luce decided that what his wife needed most of all was an efficient social secretary, fluent enough in Italian to relay her mistress's commands. An American girl with some experience on an embassy staff would be just right. His *Time* office in Rome came up with a possibility—Miss Letitia Baldridge, born in Omaha, graduate of Vassar, who had worked in the American Embassy in Paris as social secretary to Mrs. David Bruce, wife of the Ambassador.

Miss Baldridge had been in Rome job hunting shortly before the Luces arrived, and she had been a guest of Ambassador and Mrs. Ellsworth Bunker at the Villa Taverna.

Luce contacted Miss Baldridge by cable, checked her credentials with the State Department and hired her. Time Inc. paid the salary since there was no provision in the Ambassador's budget for such an assistant.

Tish, in Clare's words, proved to be a jewel—not only an excellent social secretary, but the two developed a friendship which still endures. Together they redid the cold, ancient hallways of the Villa. The Luces brought over their personal collection of great paintings from their country place at Ridgefield and the New York apartment and the canvases of Monet, Rouault, Delacroix, Renoir, Goya and a host of other distinguished artists gave the Villa new warmth and elegance.

Various critics have accused Mrs. Luce of exploiting her sex and her beauty. In her role as the American Ambassadress she used both these personal attributes with tremendous effect.

At formal dinners where all the other guests were men, Ambassadress Luce paid particular attention to her costume and her jewels. Miss Baldridge has commented that her boss played the scene like a great actress, and the Italians loved it.

On evenings when there were no ambassadorial demands the Luces played Scrabble, or Harry read aloud to his wife. In later years he was to look back on Rome as one of the happiest periods of his life. He was the concertmaster playing second fiddle and enjoying the star's performance.

Clare insists that her success was in large part due to Luce's prestige and influence. In preparation for meetings with representatives of the Italian Government she briefed herself by reading the vast flow of confidential news constantly coming to Harry from *Time-Life* correspondents throughout the world. She and her husband didn't always agree on the meaning of the news, and he didn't approve of some of the stern positions she took vis-à-vis the Communist influence in Italy, but her conclusions were tempered and tested in the crucible of lengthy discussions with her husband, who was certainly one of the best-informed men in the world.

Not all of the crises at the Villa were diplomatic. When the Ambassadress's miniature toy poodle died giving birth to two puppies, Mrs. Luce frantically appealed for a nursing mother. The response was more than she anticipated. The people brought everything from lactating cats and donkeys to dogs. According to Miss Baldridge, a mongrel mother bitch was selected, which Mrs. Luce named "Signora Snackbar" and then christened the two newborns "Romulus" and "Remus." The Italians took credit for solving an American crisis, and one newspaper told the story beneath the headline: *Once again Italian mother's milk proves to be the best.*

Henry Luce annoyed some of his Italian contacts just as he annoyed many Americans, Britons, Frenchmen and Chinese by constantly asking *why*. His question wasn't so much a challenge of a stated fact as it was evidence of his insatiable desire to know all the background supporting an assumed conclusion. Luce was determined to discover as much first-hand information about Italian politics and Italian Government as he could, and while his wife was busy with her ambassadorial duties he met and talked with a complete cross section of the Italian public. He used his journalistic talent to dig out all the subtleties of the Italian political climate, and Clare says her husband gave her an insight into the Italian mind and passion substantially larger than anything she acquired at the briefings with her official staff.

In her second year in Rome it appeared to those close to Clare that the job was overtaxing her strength. Her complexion was sallow, her appetite poor. She confessed to Dorothy Farmer that her hair was falling out at an alarming rate. Finally she consented to go to the American Naval Hospital for a checkup.

After some preliminary tests and a very thorough physical examination the doctor in charge advised Clare to return to the United States for a rest. He told her that her symptoms could be explained by anemia or chronic alcoholism or lead poisoning. The idea of lead poisoning seemed farfetched. She was not an alcoholic. (Clare can make one martini last through two hours of conversation.) Anemia seemed to be the answer.

The doctor asked Mrs. Luce to stop at the laboratory and leave one more urine specimen. He had tried to make a joke of that third alternative, metallic poisoning, but his patient's symptoms were too suggestive to be ignored. Realizing that if his suspicions were correct the American Ambassadress's life was in danger in Rome, he urged her to go home. He also knew that if the press discovered the nature of the inquiry he intended to make, it might cause an international scandal. The doctor labeled this final specimen with the name of John Paul Jones and sent it off to a commercial laboratory with the request that tests be made to determine the presence of arsenic.

After a week in New York City Clare began to regain her strength. Her appetite improved and she was beginning to think the entire episode had been a psychosomatic manifestation of her growing frustration over the job. Then she received a longhand letter from Durbrow informing her that the chemical analysis revealed the presence of arsenic in her urine, and urging her to consult a toxicological expert immediately. He also said the CIA would have to be informed, and asked Clare to do it promptly.

Clare did see a doctor. A second laboratory test confirmed the presence of arsenic. Two experts from the CIA in Washington came to New York to interview Clare and talk to Harry.

When one of the investigators asked Mrs. Luce privately if she and Harry were having difficulties, she lost her temper and told him the question was unforgivable.

The CIA man told her she had been ingesting small, less-than-lethal doses of arsenic for a long time. He said the poisoner had to be someone who was close to her, who had access to what she ate and what she drank, and that until the mystery was solved, it was common sense to suspect everyone in her household and everyone on the Embassy staff.

Clare understood the words but she couldn't accept the notion that anyone was deliberately trying to kill her by administering arsenic.

The State Department ordered her to stay in the United States until the mystery was solved, and dispatched a team of experts to Rome.

Durbrow and the CIA man, Gerry Miller, were the only two members of the Embassy staff who knew about the suspected poisoning. When the American agents arrived, Durbrow announced they were representing a firm of engineers and architects commissioned to prepare plans for remodeling and modernizing the old palace. He told the staff at the Villa Taverna that the Americans would spend a week or two observing the standard routines—the preparation and serving of food, how the stores were handled, the housekeeping, and every item concerned with the operation of the residence.

This "cover" gave the investigators a legitimate reason to poke around the kitchen, examine the pantry, and determine which of the servants had access to the food served in the main dining room. They were particularly anxious to find out who prepared and delivered the trays which were frequently sent up to Clare's study when she worked late at night.

The two laboratory reports indicated that the doses of arsenic had been extremely minute. Small doses of arsenic are difficult to detect, but the cumulative effect is fatal.

Gerry Miller had already assigned his agents to investigate the background of everyone who handled food at the Villa. He was particularly interested in the servants' political connections, and had developed up-to-date dossiers on all the Americans in Rome.

The next two weeks were pure agony for Durbrow. Clare's tenure in Rome had not been marked by tranquillity. If it developed that someone on the household staff had been trying to kill her, the scandal would most certainly affect American-Italian diplomatic relations. If the poisoner proved to be a Communist, the uneasy Cold War peace might be shattered. It gave him nightmares when he considered how the rival factions of Italy would exploit the situation if they even discovered that the investigation was taking place. With Mrs. Luce in the United States, it seemed to him there was little chance of solving the mystery. It would, he thought, be necessary to catch the poisoner in the act, and unless Miller's men could identify someone who had both the motive and opportunity, literally everyone at the Villa was a suspect.

Finally the investigators came to Durbrow. They wanted Mrs. Luce to return to Rome and give them an opportunity to watch everyone who prepared or handled her food.

Durbrow refused. He wasn't going to risk the Ambassadress's life as a decoy, even though the scheme might identify the poisoner. Any dramatic revelations would have too great an impact on U.S. foreign relations.

There apparently was no way around the impasse. How could they discover who was intentionally poisoning Clare if she wasn't there to be poisoned? Was there any way she could be accidentally receiving small amounts of arsenic? If so, why wasn't anyone else in the Villa exhibiting similar symptoms? The investigators focused their attention on the Palazzo Margherita and found nothing. Then they came back to the Villa and concentrated on Clare's living quarters.

One of the CIA men observed an accumulation of gray dust on the Linguaphone record exposed in Clare's bedroom. He put it down to sloppy housekeeping. Ten minutes later a maid appeared with rags and mops and began to clean. The agent asked her how often she dusted the room.

"Every morning" was the reply.

The agent asked her if she had dusted the Linguaphone record the day before.

"Si, Signore, and every day."

The windows were closed. The room was unoccupied. How could that much dust accumulate in twenty-four hours?

The next morning the agent came back ahead of the maid. There was a new accumulation of grayish-white dust on the black wax record. Pure arsenic is yellowish-white. The agent carefully brushed the dust into a clean envelope and sent it to a laboratory.

When the laboratory report came back the mystery was solved. The ceiling of Clare's bedroom was decorated with stucco roses, heavy with paint. When someone walked on the floor above, or when the American washing machine was set in motion, the vibration shook the ceiling on its suspended chain structure, and the arsenate of lead in the old paint on the roses precipitated into the room.

It was easy to understand why Mrs. Luce had felt better when she left the Villa Taverna on a vacation trip. But why, the agent asked, had not Ambassador Bunker or Ambassador Dunn suffered the same experience? The answer was simple. Dunn had used the room for a study. Bunker and his wife had slept in the bedroom which had been reassigned to Henry Luce. But Clare, with her penchant for working in bed, had been exposed to the poisonous environment as much as eight or ten hours every day she stayed in Rome.

The ceiling was repainted, the washing machine was moved, and Clare returned to Rome.

It wasn't until she gave President Eisenhower her resignation more than a year later that the public heard anything at all about the poison. Ike wanted Clare to stay on. She insisted it was time to leave and he demanded her reasons. She told him she had never quite regained her strength or vitality as a result of the arsenic episode. The President inadvertently leaked the story to a Texas correspondent.

Henry Luce was furious. He had kept the sensational item out of *Time* for more than a year. Now his magazine was being scooped by a Texas White House correspondent. The next week he published the entire story.

Some weeks later, when the Ambassadress was back in Rome, an

Italian Government official said to her, "Mrs. Luce, you said it was the paint from the ceiling which caused your poisoning, but of course everyone here believes it was the Communists. If only you had said it was the Communists, then the press would have maintained the paint was responsible."

Perhaps the best evidence of the effectiveness of Clare's opposition to the Communists in Italy is to be found in their reaction to her speeches and the policies she carried out.

Palmiro Togliatti, leader of the Communist Party in Italy, attempted to capitalize on the Italian superstition about blue eyes, and branded Clare a witch. In parliament he described Clare as a "carrier of misfortune," a phrase used in Italy to describe a possessor of the evil eye.

This charge prompted Dorothy Thompson to devote one full newspaper column to an attack on American Communists and a defense of Clare.

At the beginning of 1955 the State Department gave Clare two simultaneous assignments: one, persuade the Italians to sign the Status of Forces Treaty (an agreement establishing jurisdiction over American soldiers on foreign soil who were accused of crimes under the laws of the host country), and two, procure from the Italian Government an invitation to station U.S. troops in Italy.

At the time, the United States had only one division of atomic artillery in Europe. It was stationed in Austria, and treaty terms required its imminent removal. The Department of Defense wanted to keep this division of "Long Toms" available in southern or central Europe.

Giovanni Gronchi had been elected President of Italy in May of 1955. He and Mrs. Luce were not on the friendliest of terms. She thought of Gronchi as a pompous, bureaucratic, ex-military man, and she suspected him of being willing to cooperate with the domestic Communists.

The Russians were demanding that the United States remove all its atomic weaponry from Europe. There was, she thought, little likelihood that Gronchi would agree to shifting the offensive "Long Toms" from Austria to Italy, but she had to try anyway.

She made an appointment to discuss the matter with Foreign

Minister Segni, who said he would receive her at the Palazzo Chigi at 6:30 on a Thursday evening.

When Clare returned to the Villa Taverna about 3:30 on that day, hoping to spend the next two hours marshaling her arguments, she found unexpected company: three members of the military's top brass who had come to Rome on a secret mission. The Ambassador could not refuse to receive them.

At 5:30 she excused herself, went upstairs to change her clothes and freshen up, and ordered the car. Normally the trip from the Villa to the Chigi could be made in fifteen minutes, but not wanting to be late, she told the driver to be ready at 6:00 sharp. She wanted at least thirty minutes of undisturbed privacy to think about how it would be best to approach the Italian Foreign Minister.

As she entered the Embassy car she asked the driver if he knew where they were going.

It was the custom for the staff to instruct the chauffeur in advance of each mission, and when he responded "Si" she rolled up the glass window which separated the front seat from the rear of the car and turned her mind to the problem at hand.

Not until the Chrysler swung into the courtyard of the Caranoli (the presidential palace) did Clare discover where she was. Then it was too late to do anything about it. The smartly uniformed *carabinieri* were standing at attention. Count Piccioni, the ceremonial officer assigned to the President of the Republic, was coming down the steps to greet her.

Her visit, he said in extravagant diplomatic Italian, was unexpected, but of course she was welcome. Signor Lucioli had gone to inform President Gronchi of Clare's arrival.

What was there to do? Admit her mistake and perhaps provide the gossips with a juicy morsel? "I have come," she said, "on a matter of grave importance. Will the President see me for a moment?"

Count Piccioni assured her that President Gronchi would be delighted to entertain the American Ambassadress. She was ushered through the courtyard, into the elevator, and upstairs to the palace offices.

Gronchi kept her waiting almost twenty minutes. Clare realized she deserved it. An unannounced call on the President of the Republic was a serious breach of etiquette.

Gronchi's greeting was correct, formal and cold. What, he inquired, was the matter of grave importance which had brought the American representative unannounced to the Caranoli?

Clare told him she had come because she was greatly concerned for the defense of Italy.

President Gronchi appeared surprised.

Mrs. Luce explained that the Americans had pledged to protect the integrity of Italy, but U.S. forces were widely dispersed. An enemy, she said, following the classic route from the north, could occupy Milan and the industrial centers before our troops could react.

This approach excited the soldier in Gronchi, who assured the Ambassadress it would be relatively simple to defend the northern passes against an invader. He sent for a map and explained precisely how the defenders could be reployed.

Mrs. Luce agreed, then pointed out that Italy lacked any artillery. She said the U.S. division presently stationed in Austria must go home very soon.

Gronchi admitted it would be necessary to have big guns in the passes if his plan were to be successful. Then he asked why the American division was being transferred out of Europe.

"La Signora" explained that under the Austrian treaty the "Long Toms" were committed to leave Austrian soil within ninety days, unless of course, she added, they were invited to stay in some friendly country. Gronchi took the bait. "Would," he asked, "the United States consider relocating the division in Italy?"

Mrs. Luce admitted this was a possibility.

Gronchi asked her how it could be accomplished.

She told him that a formal invitation from the Foreign Minister of Italy to the American Embassy would be immediately forwarded to the Pentagon in Washington.

Gronchi thanked her for coming and promised his Government would act within twenty-four hours.

The division of "Long Toms" was redeployed to northern Italy.

In the atmosphere of resultant cooperative good will, the Italian Foreign Minister signed the Status of Forces Treaty. Telling about it later, Clare says that when she found herself at the Caranoli she had only one thought in mind—somehow she must convince Gronchi that her visit had a serious purpose. Knowing the President fancied himself an expert military strategist, she had opened the conversation without any real plan for proceeding.

When Ambassador Luce left Italy, the newspaper *Europae* published a list of her diplomatic blunders. The most serious, they said, was her unannounced call on President Gronchi shortly after he took office. What the reporters didn't know was the beneficial result of that chauffeur's misunderstanding.

In June of 1955 Clare and Harry went to the south of France to visit Sir Winston Churchill, and he encouraged Clare to try painting for relaxation. He told her painting was a "must therapy" for people in public life whose minds are continually occupied with difficult problems, and he gave her her first set of brushes, her first box of paints, and a copy of his pamphlet "Painting for a Pastime." It was the beginning of an artistic effort which she still pursues. Some of her work has been highly praised by the critics.

In later years, when Mrs. Luce was painting in Phoenix, her husband thought enough of her work to suggest a one-man show, and was furious when she would give a painting to a friend. This to Clare was praise from Allah. She recalled that Winston Churchill had given her husband a painting for his New York office. On a visit to the States, Churchill had called on Luce and had been pleased to see the picture hanging in Luce's private office. Harry told him it was a good picture but it would be improved if there were something in the foreground, and he thought a sheep would be proper.

The next day Churchill sent his secretary over to pick up the painting, and Luce, recalling his criticism, was afraid that he might have offended England's wartime Prime Minister now turned artist. But there was nothing to do but surrender the canvas. It was returned within a week with a sheep painted in the foreground.

When Clare resigned her post she assured President Eisenhower her decision was based entirely on a personal need for rest and relaxation. But this wasn't the only reason, and perhaps not the most important one.

In 1954 and 1955 Radio Free Europe had broadcast from a station in Munich encouraging the Hungarian patriots to resist the Russian occupation. John Foster Dulles had laid great stress on the principle of self-determination of all people. This, combined with his unfaltering opposition to Communism, created the impression that the United States would assist any oppressed European minority anxious to overthrow the Communist dictators.

The Hungarian revolt commenced on October 28, 1956, and escalated into a great tragedy. United States intelligence forces were caught napping. The State Department, apparently unprepared and timid about taking affirmative action, wrung its hands in despair while the Communist tanks slaughtered the helpless Hungarians.

On October 29 Clare went to Mass at the only Hungarian Catholic Church in Rome. When she returned to the Villa she found a very bewildered and distraught guest rapidly drinking himself into oblivion. He was an American CIA agent Mrs. Luce had met some years before who had been assigned to Hungary. He had been present when the revolution started. He believed, as most Hungarians believed, that once the will to resist was demonstrated, American material—small arms, bazookas and antitank guns—would be provided.

For the next four days Ambassadress Luce wasn't sure whether the man would go crazy, destroy himself, or just consume all the whiskey in Rome. She sent a frantic, coded cable to Washington, imploring that assistance be given to the Freedom Fighters. As the hours dragged on, she realized the United States had no intention of doing anything. She had bucked both Ike and Foster Dulles to carry on an aggressive anti-Communist policy in Rome. Now, here was an opportunity, she believed, to deal a telling blow against the expansion of world Communism, and she had to face the fact that the American Government, her Government, was choosing the coward's way out.

Her mission seemed pointless. Of what value to win an economic battle or lessen the influence of Italian Communists if the American Government refused to support its words with deeds?

When Clare's departure was announced in Rome, even the politicians she had opposed expressed regret. Only the Communist press cheered. The Italian Government gave a farewell luncheon, and Foreign Minister Gaetano Martino told his guests, "Ambassador Luce was responsible for bringing spiritual, political and economic unity to Italy." He said the new spirit of friendship existing between his country and the United States was the result of Clare's energy, passion and intelligence. Then he presented her with the Grand Cross of the Order of Merit of the Italian Republic.

Clare, in a simple turquoise-blue dress with a rose pinned at her left breast, stood up to respond. There were tears in her eyes. She looked, as Harry said afterward, "delicately tired and determinedly triumphant."

Elbridge Durbrow believes that the amazing achievements of Mrs. Luce as the United States diplomatic representative in Italy is attributable to her capacity for concentration and hard work. He says the State Department gave Ambassadress Luce thirteen difficult assignments and she successfully completed all of them. It is also true that in the most difficult moments Henry Luce was an invaluable asset. He not only had access to a great deal of factual information from *Time* staffers covering Europe, he was also a powerful, prestigious figure. The Italian politicians were undoubtedly influenced by their knowledge that (1) It would be useless to try to deceive Mrs. Luce about any major fact because her husband could tell her the truth; and (2) The voice of *Time* magazine enjoyed greater credibility throughout the world than did the official voice of the Italian Government.

Mrs. Luce is inclined to credit good luck and the entree that being married to Harry gave her with that select circle of powerful world politicians for her achievements as Ambassadress.

Embassy officers deny this. They say the force of Mrs. Luce's personality charmed the Italians, who might have been able to resist the strength of her diplomatic logic. Twelve years after Mrs. Luce left Rome a number of Embassy employees exhibited tenderness, affection and admiration for the lady who had been their boss. When this writer visited the Embassy in Rome in 1968, most of the functionaries from the reception clerks to the secretaries were eager to talk about "La Signora," and their descriptions of those years when the lady Ambassador presided at the Villa and the Palazzo suggest that Clare won the hearts of the Italian people. The beautiful American lady completely contradicted that popular image of the ugly American, who, according to some writers, is responsible for the loss of U.S. prestige overseas.

13

Brazil?

Mrs. Luce came home from Italy on December 27, 1956, with three new interests and no desire to continue in politics. Earlier in that Presidential year there had been speculation about a woman Vice-President. The press suggested Ike might want to choose between Clare Boothe Luce and Senator Margaret Chase Smith.

Diplomat Robert Murphy says that Mrs. Luce was hoping to be appointed Ambassador to Moscow, and had campaigned for the job with her friends in the State Department. The truth is that while Clare might have done an excellent job representing American interests in Russia, she knew that post must go to a career diplomat, fluent in the Russian language, one who had experience in dealing with Iron Curtain countries. Besides, she was exhausted. She didn't bother to deny the speculation in the press that she might be named Ambassador to Russia.

Her new interests were painting, as the result of Sir Winston Churchill's encouragement; mosaics, which she discovered in Italy; and scuba diving. She had managed to find a little time for painting in Rome. The Italian mosaics intrigued her. Always a strong swimmer, she found the idea of exploring the ocean's depths appealing.

When all the necessary debriefing had been accomplished, and the official papers were safely deposited in the United States diplomatic archives, she flew out to Phoenix, Arizona, for a period of rest at Elizabeth Arden's exclusive Maine Chance. She thought two or three weeks of supervised diet, regular hours, exercise and massage might be just what she needed.

At the end of the second week, bored with the cloistered feminine society of the Arden spa, she sent Harry a telegram urging him to join her. He could, she said, stay at the Arizona Biltmore, enjoy two or three days of golf and perhaps they might have a week of vacation together when her regimented rejuvenation was complete.

The winter climate of Phoenix was warm and dry. Clare enjoyed the bright sunshine, the desert colors and the relaxing atmosphere.

Luce did come to the Arizona Biltmore. When Clare joined him they took long twilight walks around the hotel's private golf course, which is surrounded by residences. The exercise, the quiet and the isolation combined to make Clare think she felt better than she had for many years.

Luce enjoyed this escape from the dual responsibility of running the magazines and being the consort of the lady Ambassador. Their nightly walks took them past a pink-stucco, tile-roofed Mediterranean villa facing the fifteenth green, which had been built by millionaire Tommy Manville. They thought it was a charming house. When Harry learned the place was for sale for $250,000 he suggested they buy it. He argued it would be easier to commute between Phoenix and Manhattan than it had been to travel between Connecticut and South Carolina because Phoenix had direct airline service to New York. He didn't want to retire but he would like to slow down.

The house was built around a courtyard, or loggia, with grass, a giant olive tree and flowers. There was a tremendous living room, a dining room big enough for any sit-down dinners they might want to give, a delightful glassed-in porch, and five bedrooms, each with a private bath—plus quarters for servants, garage and service area.

Luce pointed out that the space at the front entrance could be converted into an office for Clare if she wanted to write. He suggested they build a studio beyond the swimming pool where his wife could have the proper isolation for painting.

They closed the deal the next day and commissioned an architect to carry out the proposed changes. After three more days in the sun, they went home.

Mrs. Luce's inquiries about American mosaicists had produced the information that Louisa Jenkins, who lived on the Monterey peninsula in California, was one of the best. Clare flew out to the Big Sur country, met Miss Jenkins, and commissioned her to design and construct a mosaic for the chapel the Luces had given Stanford University as a memorial to Ann. Miss Jenkins, a hardy, no-nonsense kind of woman, said she would be delighted to submit some proposals and the two women became good friends.

When the weather got bad in New York, Clare flew to Bermuda to pursue her interest in scuba diving. She successfully descended to a depth of more then fifty feet, took numerous underwater pictures, and wrote a three-part article for *Sports Illustrated* to report her new experience. When next she saw Miss Jenkins, the lady mosaicist expressed great interest in scuba diving. The two women went to Florida to carry out the first part of a bargain—Clare was to teach Louisa how to dive; Louisa was to teach Clare how to make mosaics.

That first year home was a busy one. There were so many things to do, old friendships to renew, and new interests to satisfy that Mrs. Luce was able to compensate for being out of the public eye as Ambassador to Italy. She certainly hadn't retired in any accepted sense of that word.

In March the press carried an item that CBL was writing a new play to star the Gish sisters, Lillian and Dorothy. (She wasn't.) In April the University of Notre Dame named Mrs. Luce as the 1957 recipient of the Laetare medal, given to outstanding American Catholic laymen. On April 9 she was given the first annual Mary MacArthur memorial award for distinguished public service at a testimonial dinner at the Waldorf-Astoria Hotel in New York. On April 30 the United States Chamber of Commerce named Clare one of nine great living Americans. Others chosen were Cecil B. De Mille; Bobby Morrow, the Olympic track star; Colonel Frank K. Everest, who had just flown an experimental rocket plane nineteen hundred miles per hour; Victor Riesel; Secretary of the Treasury George Humphrey; Dr. William C. Menninger of Topeka, Kansas; artist Norman Rockwell; and J. J. Warren, a poultry-farm operator who had developed a champion hen.

In May she became the first woman speaker in the ninety-four years of New York's Union League Club history, Fordham University gave her an honorary Doctor of Letters degree, and Temple made her an honorary Doctor of Law.

The Luces spent Christmas 1957 in the remodeled, redecorated house on the Biltmore golf course in Phoenix. Mrs. Luce told reporters she intended to settle down in her new studio and do some serious painting. She also said she planned to write her memoirs.

Life at the Luce house settled into a relaxed routine. Clare frequently spent the mornings in her studio painting, where the sign on the door said: "Do not disturb except in the case of an authenticated atomic attack on New York City or Phoenix."

Harry played nine holes of golf or spent the time in his office between breakfast and lunch. Afternoons were for napping or swimming or shopping or visiting. Clare used her remarkable talent for selecting interesting people and recruited a coterie of the most interesting and diverse personalities on the Phoenix scene: Gene and Nina Pulliam, he the publisher of the Phoenix newspapers, with additional interests in Indiana; Judge and Mrs. Walter Tang, representing the Chinese community and Harry's early life interest; painters, artists, writers, and a very few of the social elite who were invited to the two or three big affairs the Luces gave each season. They accepted only a modest number of invitations to go out. What the Luces seemed to enjoy most were quiet dinners with one or two other couples. Servants were always a problem, and except for Arthur, their faithful chauffeur, messenger and handy man, the turnover was rapid. Luce paid little attention to his own creature comforts and was easily satisfied, but his wife, a perfectionist, alternately infatuated and infuriated the help.

Faithful retainer Dorothy Farmer refused to come to Arizona in the winters and Clare had to "put up with" a succession of Arizona secretaries.

Because the Luce household bills were all paid from a disbursing office in New York City, local tradespeople encountered annoying delays. Like many other very wealthy people the Luces never seemed to understand that if the extra gardener hired for some seasonal work didn't collect his money at the end of the week he and his family might go hungry.

When it suited her mood Clare was available for participation in local activities with the art and theater groups. When she chose to be aloof no one could reach her. Telephone calls were not returned. The Luces were admired and loved by some and passionately disliked by other Phoenicians.

There was a bridge group because Harry loved cards; an artist group because they were both interested in paintings and the theater; a society group representing the wealth and position of the community; and the avant-garde intellectuals Clare attracted.

In New York and Connecticut Clare had been the social hostess, making people who truly didn't interest her feel welcome in the Luce house. In Phoenix Harry took on these duties, and Clare reserved her attention for the people who stimulated one of her particular interests.

Luce's nephew, Tom Moore, commented on this reversal of roles, saying that Uncle Harry had seemed to mellow while Aunt Clare became more independent.

The mental competition which had been so apparent in the earlier years of their marriage was still visible. Both Luce and his wife enjoyed being center stage, but there was also a new tenderness.

It is difficult to reconcile the record of Clare's activities in 1958 with her self-proclaimed position of "seeking seclusion to paint and write." When this was pointed out to her she said that pressures were sometimes very difficult to resist.

In February the Luces entertained Vice-President Richard Nixon, his wife Pat, and Clare's old friend Speaker Joe Martin, who had come to Phoenix for a Republican rally.

On February 21, Henry Luce was hospitalized at St. Joseph's in Phoenix. The public was told he had pneumonia, but the doctors told Clare her husband had suffered a slight heart attack. They predicted a complete recovery.

When Harry came back to the Biltmore house after ten days in the hospital, he promised his wife he would plan to take things a little easier. But he didn't regard the episode as serious and he didn't want anyone, particularly his associates on *Time,* to know the truth about his illness.

In March Mrs. Luce was the guest of honor at the Screen Producers Guild dinner in Hollywood. In Hedda Hopper's report of that affair she is quoted as saying she was engaged in finishing a book which would be an anthology of all her plays, including the unpublished screen script of her story *Pilate's Wife*.

In April 1958 an off-Broadway group called The Black Friars' Guild presented a production of her last play, *Child of the Morning*. John McClain in the New York *Journal-American* called it a straggling and pretentious effort. Whitney Bolton, in the New York *Telegraph*, described it as an absorbing play.

In May The Lambs club gave playwright Clare Boothe Luce an award for her devotion to the theater. Harry had apparently completely recovered from his episode in Phoenix, and that summer the Luces went to Nassau, where Clare continued her scuba diving. She accepted speaking engagements before numerous Republican clubs, worked on her mosaics, and was quoted in an interview in the *Catholic Transcript* as saying, "The pleasure of helping youthful fingers cement common pebbles and bright tile squares together brings an inner satisfaction unlike any produced in our multifarious public careers." The article explained that Clare was teaching four sons and daughters of the Luce household employees to make mosaics.

In October 1958 President Eisenhower appointed Ambassador Luce his personal representative to attend the funeral of Pope Pius XII. She flew to Italy with John Foster Dulles and John A. McCone.

Mrs. Luce spent ten days in Rome, returned to New York on October 25, and five days later the President named her his representative to attend the coronation of Pope John XXIII. She flew back to Rome and this time Harry went with her.

On November 12 the Luces came to Phoenix to open the Biltmore Estates house and a week later Clare went to Dallas to receive the highest award of the National Society for Crippled Children and Adults.

On January 14, 1959, columnist Elsa Maxwell quoted Clare as saying, "I don't want to be in public life anymore. I wish to remain out of the circulatory stream of political adventure. I want to write books, read books, write plays and play bridge." That same week Henry Luce had an interview with John Foster Dulles, who inquired about Mrs.

Luce's health. Henry told him that it had not been better in years. Dulles then inquired if Mrs. Luce would welcome another ambassadorial post. Harry's response was "You'll have to ask her."

Mrs. Luce was then almost fifty-six years old. Despite the exhaustion she suffered in Rome, her tour as Ambassador had been a rewarding and satisfying experience. She had been involved as a participant in the making of history. The painting and the mosaics provided an outlet for her artistic talent, scuba diving was fun, but for more than a quarter of a century she had marched beside and matched wits with the movers and the shakers of the world. Henry Luce himself welcomed the idea of a new appointment for his wife. He, too, had enjoyed Rome, where he had been able to relax and shed some of the burdens of Time Inc. And Luce was very curious about the political and economic situations in South America—an area he had never visited.

Even after her plays were smash hits on Broadway and earned prodigious sums at the box office Clare Luce never regarded herself as a great playwright. She thinks she was a good editor and a good foreign correspondent and the record bears this out. But her service in Rome convinced her that she had a talent for diplomacy. She had been successful where the men who preceded her had failed. Durbrow, Jacobs and Bob Murphy all explained Clare's achievements by saying she worked at the job. In 1959 Clare Boothe Luce was anxious to go back to work.

On February 20, 1959, the White House leaked the news that Clare was being considered for appointment as Ambassador to Brazil. Two days later the Government of President Juscelino Kubitschek revealed it would be happy to receive Mrs. Clare Boothe Luce as the Ambassador from the United States. The announcement was in response to an inquiry from the U.S. State Department.

On February 26 the White House announced that Clare Boothe Luce would be reassigned as Ambassador to Brazil and that her name was being sent to the Senate for confirmation.

In Phoenix, Clare told reporters she would be delighted to serve her country in any capacity. When the impending appointment was announced in Brazil, students in that country and in Bolivia rióted in the streets to express their resentment against *Time* magazine. Harry's publication had printed a wisecrack about Bolivia, suggesting that the only solution to that country's problems would be to divide it in parts and apportion it to its neighbors.

Former President Harry Truman commented gleefully, "What a nice thing it is to have Mrs. Clare Boothe Luce in the grease in Bolivia. He [Mr. Luce] spent a lot of time trying to put me in the grease but never succeeded." And columnist Drew Pearson suggested that perhaps Mrs. Luce could not serve effectively in the new post because of the *Time* story.

In the Senate Clare's old friend J. William Fulbright announced he had "no present plans to question Mrs. Luce's qualifications." But Oregon's Democratic Senator Wayne Morse, a member of the Foreign Relations Committee, told reporters that he intended to oppose Clare's appointment. Morse asked the Senate to delay consideration until the former Ambassador could be questioned extensively by the Foreign Relations Committee.

The reporters described this as a most unusual action. They implied that Morse was acting out of spite, and that Ambassadors who have served their country well are not required to undergo any further examination by a Senate committee when reassigned to a new position. The truth is that there is no standard procedure. The Senate, since it must confirm the appointment of Ambassadors, has a right to interest itself in the attitude of anyone who is being named to a new post.

In Phoenix, Mrs. Luce wasn't at all disturbed when informed of the Morse statement. She knew that *Time* magazine had been extremely critical of the Oregon Senator when he switched his allegiance from the Republican Party, which had elected him in 1952, to the Democratic Party, and helped organize the Senate against President Eisenhower. But she didn't think Morse had enough influence to be anything more than an annoyance.

On April 7 Clare flew to Washington. Senator Morse announced he couldn't think of voting for the former Ambassador to Italy unless she documented and proved the charges made by her against Democratic Presidents Franklin Roosevelt and Harry Truman during her House service. Morse had been one of F.D.R.'s appointees to the National War Labor Board, he had served in the Senate with Truman, but when he first ran for the Senate in 1944 he had been extremely critical of F.D.R.'s conduct of the war. Morse had campaigned for Ike in 1952, and then in a fit of what most politicians thought was personal peevishness had changed parties after the 1954 election. The Senate had been evenly divided between Republicans and Democrats and it was generally believed Morse had made the switch in a trade for a committee post which the Republicans had denied him.

When Mrs. Luce appeared before the committee the Oregon labor-oriented Democrat really went digging into the past. He quoted Clare's campaign speeches in 1944 and 1948, her statements in the House, and particularly her charge that President Roosevelt was the only American who ever lied us into a war.

Clare refused to back up. She admitted the language might have been a little inflamed but it was campaign oratory. She cited historians Charles Beard, Robert Sherwood and Henry Stimson, the former Secretary of War, in support of her contention that Roosevelt had indeed not dealt candidly with his constituents.

Morse charged that Clare's speech in Milan, Italy, had been willful interference in Italian politics. He implied that she might have business holdings in Brazil and be seeking a commercial advantage. He charged Ike was making a pay-off because Harry's magazines and Harry's money had supported the Republican victory in 1952 and 1956. (The Luces contributed $60,000 to Ike's second campaign.)

The pot continued to boil, and because the Oregon Senator was also attacking *Time* magazine, Harry Luce was put on the defensive. He didn't want Clare to go to Brazil and said so publicly.

As the days passed and the Oregon Senator's statements became more and more intemperate, Clare began to wonder if he might not destroy the possibility of her becoming an effective representative of the United States in Brazil.

When J. William Fulbright joined the chorus, making a statement to the effect that the new Ambassador should display temperateness and good taste, and that he believed Clare was unqualified to be Ambassador to Brazil on these grounds, the Republicans came to her defense.

Senators Alexander Wiley of Wisconsin and Barry Goldwater of Arizona took Fulbright to task. Tempers flared on the floor of the Senate. Finally the Foreign Relations Committee voted sixteen to one approving Clare's appointment. The one dissenter was Wayne Morse.

Majority Leader Lyndon Johnson agreed to put off the vote of the full Senate at the request of the liberal Joe Clark of Pennsylvania, who had been enlisted by Morse. Clark said, "There is nothing in her record to indicate to me that Mrs. Luce is qualified to be a diplomat. The role for which I believe she is well qualified is that of a political hatchet man. She does very well at making inflammatory, demagogic political speeches. She and her husband contribute heavily to the Republican coffers, and for this she is being rewarded with an Ambassadorship." *

On April 28 Allen Drury, writing in *The New York Times,* said:

Senator Wayne Morse and five other Democratic liberals today forced a delay until tomorrow on the final vote on the nomination of Mrs. Clare Boothe Luce to be Ambassador to Brazil. Morse said, "Mrs. Luce should be judged by two standards—is she honest? Is she reliable? I am satisfied that Mrs. Luce does not meet either criteria."

On April 28 the Senate voted seventy-nine to eleven to approve Clare's appointment. The vote demonstrated two things: Clare's standing with an overwhelming majority of the members of the Senate and their contempt of the demagogic Wayne Morse. But the long harangues, the headlines echoing the vindictive charges, had convinced Mrs. Luce that she could not become an effective Ambassador. Moreover, Harry was greatly disturbed over the prospect of her going, and becoming a permanent target for the fulminations of the Senator from Oregon.

Clare says it never occurred to Harry to use the pages of *Time* and *Life* to destroy Morse, whose inconsistent voting record and close association with Dave Beck's Teamsters Union made him extremely vulnerable.

On Wednesday, April 29, Harry issued a statement in the defense of his wife, saying:

For twenty-five years in the course of her public life my wife has taken not

* Clark and Morse were both defeated in the 1968 elections.

only the criticism provoked by her own views and actions, but also many punches which were intended for me or for the publications of which I am editor-in-chief. The attack of Senator Wayne Morse is perhaps the most vitriolic example of this.

He concluded by saying he had asked his wife to resign the appointment after the Senate confirmation.

On April 30 the Chicago *Tribune* revealed that Senator Morse had telephoned Clare's personal physician to inquire about her mental health and to ask whether or not she had recently been under the care of a psychiatrist. (She had not.) Most of his colleagues in the Senate called the action despicable and reminded Morse, a lawyer and onetime Dean of the University of Oregon Law School, that he had attempted to violate the privileged communication between physician and patient.

Ohio's Democratic Senator Stephen Young read into the record a poem originally written about the daughter of Lord Asquith, onetime British Prime Minister, titled "The Woman with a Serpent's Tongue." It began:

> "She is not old, she is not young . . .
> The woman with a serpent's tongue . . .
> The haggard cheek, the hungering eye . . .
> The poisoned words that wildly fly . . .
> The famished face, the fevered hand . . .
> Who sleights the worthiest of the land . . .
> Sneers at the just, condemns the brave . . .
> Blackens goodness in its grave . . .
> In truthful numbers be she sung . . .
> The woman with the serpent's tongue."

Senator Young didn't say the poem was a description of Clare, but the implication was plain.

Mrs. Luce telephoned Stan Swinton, her friend from earlier days in Rome, who was then with the Associated Press in New York City, and told him she wanted to make a statement.

Swinton was glad to have the scoop. "Just say this, Stan," Clare said. "I am grateful for the overwhelming vote of confirmation in the

Senate. We must now wait until the dust settles. My difficulties of course go some years back and began when Senator Wayne Morse was kicked in the head by a horse."

Swinton copied the message and then said, "Clare, you don't want to say that. You won. This will just start things all over again. You know how clannish the U.S. Senate is—Morse can make lots of trouble."

"Stan," Clare said gently, "do you really think that if I publish this statement, the question of my appointment to Brazil will be re-opened on the Senate floor?"

"That's what I'm trying to tell you, Clare."

"Thank you. That's what I'm hoping for. If the question is re-opened, the Senate may get around to discussing the situation in Brazil, which, in my mind, has been completely ignored."

The opposition, led by Morse, with support from Fulbright, had not only failed to bring up the current internal situation in Brazil, they had carefully avoided any reference to what was probably the best evidence of all so far as Mrs. Luce's qualifications were concerned.

In May of 1953, as a beginning Ambassador, Mrs. Luce had published an evaluation of our foreign service in the *Foreign Service Journal.* She aligned herself strongly on the side of the professional career diplomat, deplored the fact that because some ambassadorial posts are so expensive they are denied the career men, and pointed out that even political appointees should be chosen for their ability rather than rewarded for past domestic political support, and should be judged on their performance.

In the October 1957 issue of *Foreign Affairs,* an American Quarterly Review, Mrs. Luce discussed again this question of whether the United States should be represented overseas by professionals or by amateurs. In that piece she gave full praise to Senator Fulbright, whom she hailed as a "real diplomat." In a succeeding paragraph she wrote:

Where does the conclusion that amateur diplomacy is the American method leave the ambassadorial question? Closed? Not at all. It simply puts it into proper perspective. It consequently permits us to raise the ambassadorial issue in realistic terms; namely, who should represent Americans abroad: the professional, the amateur, or the best qualified man who can be found?

Obviously the latter, and just as obviously the reasonable presumption must be that the professional is most likely to be that man.

Later on in the same piece Mrs. Luce urged an increase in diplomatic allowances to permit career men to serve in such admittedly expensive posts as London, Paris, Bonn, etc., and concluded her discussion saying, "Diplomacy is a pragmatic art. 'By their fruits ye shall know them.' "

Had the issue before the Senate committee been confined to an examination of Mrs. Luce's performance in Italy, any opposition to her reappointment would have appeared to be irrational.

The Associated Press carried the statement Mrs. Luce had given Stan Swinton, and the next day she offered her resignation to Dwight Eisenhower. She told the President:

Regretfully I am submitting my resignation as Ambassador to Brazil. I do so not for professional reasons, but because I am persuaded after much reflection that it is no longer possible for me to accomplish the mission which you have entrusted to me. It is a mission of supreme importance to Americans. As I wrote you on February 28 when accepting it, I remember so well the first time you talked to me after the 1952 election. You spoke with deep urgency of your desire to further the consolidation and expansion of firm and prosperous accords with all the Latin American nations. And I wrote "Brazil is indeed a mighty land whose fortunes we hope will be evermore happily and fruitfully linked with our own" . . .

She continued:

The vote of my confirmation in the Senate committee of sixteen to one and on the Senate floor of 79 to 11 was indeed an example of bipartisan support on foreign policy, but unhappily, in spite of the best efforts of 79 Senators, the climate of good will was poisoned by thousands of words of extraordinarily ugly charges against my person and of distrust of the mission I was to undertake. These charges were inescapably printed around the world.

Mr. President, I am aware and appreciate that as you said, both Brazilian and our public have overwhelmingly discounted the furious, and

I think foolish, attacks made against me. Yet it would be imprudent of me, and no true service to you, to ignore the fact that the broadcasting of these mean charges has planted the seeds of hostile suspicion. All through the course of my mission these seeds could be watered carefully, either by their author for unknowable motive or by any political element with the clear motive of discrediting America by the simple device of disparaging an American Ambassador. And so—most easily—there could be denied any chance of attainment of fruitful accords between those countries.

Even this cautious consideration, Mr. President, might be surmounted were it not for the fact that the American author of these charges happens, by reasons of seniority, to be the chairman of the Senate subcommittee on affairs of the American Republics, to which my mission would be obliged to look for support. Common sense indicates that the good will and support which the rest of the Senate has given will not be forthcoming from the subcommittee chairman. A continuing harassment of my mission with a view to making his own charges stick is the natural course the chairman would follow. And the sad fact is not that I, but Brazilian-American policy, would be the victim.

It therefore seems indisputable that in this time of grave economic difficulties in Brazil the best interests of that country, as well as of the United States, will be served by your selection of another plenipotentiary.

Again I regret with all my heart that I will not have the opportunity to be of this service to you, to our country and to inter-American relations.

Reluctantly, President Eisenhower accepted Clare's resignation. He realized that she had correctly evaluated the vengeful character of Wayne Morse, and just as correctly appraised what the disastrous effect of that opposition would be on any efforts to improve relations with Brazil if Clare Boothe Luce were the American representative.

On May 1 the White House announced it had accepted Mrs. Luce's resignation and would nominate someone else for the post in South America. Ike named John M. Cabot, a highly regarded career diplomat, to the position Clare had resigned.

Subsequent events justified Clare's decision. Relations between Brazil and America deteriorated, and Cabot held the post for only a little over a year. Brazil was a hopeless assignment. Eisenhower was nearing the end of his term of authority, and the Brazilians regarded

Cabot as an interim appointee who would certainly be replaced by a new Administration.

Even though she resigned, Clare had the genuine assurance that both John Foster Dulles and the President of the United States had expressed their confidence in her. The Senate vote in her favor had been overwhelming, and the national press, which had rarely been on her side, interpreted the opposition of Wayne Morse as an intemperate and deplorable display of personal feelings.

The Luces spent most of the summer of 1959 in New York and at Ridgefield. In September Clare signed a new contract with *McCall's* to write a monthly article under the title "Without Portfolio." The magazine agreed to pay her $3,000 for each piece and Harry commented that *McCall's* was getting a bargain.

In October Luce left for a world tour to cover all the *Time-Life* offices. Clare went with him as far as Honolulu. Then she came back to Phoenix, reassured by Harry's promise that he would make arrangements to shed the major burden of his responsibilities to *Time*. They would, he told her, do just what they wanted to do in the way of speeches, public appearances and social engagements.

14

"I had reached my depth..."

The last eight years of Clare's life with Harry were by far the happiest ones. There was a tranquillity in their relationship based upon a genuine mutual respect and the careful observation of each other's independence —a visible, polite affection unruffled by any deep passion.

Clare no longer had a great desire to achieve anything. She was willing to do only those things which interested or entertained her. She had given up skin diving because, in her own words, "I'd done it . . . I had reached my depth. If I went deeper, I felt I would perish, and there was no point in doing the same thing over and over again."

She stuck with her painting. Her subjects were mostly still lifes, although she did one rather remarkable portrait which she said was of her father. The resemblance to Harry Luce was unmistakable. And she painted a picture of Harry which was such a good likeness he challenged her, contending that he didn't have the dewlap she put on the canvas. Then when he looked in the mirror he confessed that he had never really noticed it before.

Clare took no part in the 1960 Presidential campaign. Her long friendship with Joe Kennedy and her genuine fondness for his son Jack resulted in a strict neutrality. *Time* and *Life* were very kind to the Senator from Massachusetts. In January of 1961 the Luces went to the Inaugural Ball as guests of the new President.

One columnist observed that these two prominent die-hard Republicans stuck out like sore thumbs in the jubilant Democratic gathering.

Mr. and Mrs. Henry Luce were newsworthy wherever they went, and when she chose to be a public figure Clare continued to exhibit her talent for being controversial. On January 15 she told the Dallas, Texas, *News* that President-elect Kennedy's Cabinet choices had been superb, that had she been the President she would have chosen both Dean Rusk and Arthur Goldberg. Commenting on an erroneous newspaper report, she recalled that she had once told a reporter, "My hobbies are Siamese cats, needle point and shooting." The paper dropped a comma, scrambled the words, and it came out "needle point and shooting cats." She said the mail was about even after that. Many people said she was terribly cruel, but a man from Waterbury wrote in and said not many people had the courage to admit it, but he too shot cats, had done it for years, and warned her not to shoot them from the windows because the bullets ricocheted.

After the Kennedy inaugural Mrs. Luce is quoted as having said that had Richard Nixon chosen a Jewish running mate, either Senator Barry Goldwater of Arizona or Senator Jacob Javits of New York, it would have helped eliminate the religious bigotry that issued from that campaign.

In April of 1961 Clare was hospitalized in Phoenix for pneumonia, and Leonard Lyons in "The Lyons Den" reported that "a columnist once printed a series of erroneous reports that Henry and CBL were being divorced, and that Luce then would marry Lady Jean Campbell, granddaughter of Lord Beaverbrook." Mrs. Luce, in dismissing the rumor, said, "I would marry Lord Beaverbrook and become my husband's grandmother."

Clare refuses to discuss the alleged talk of divorce beyond saying that all happily married couples have their moments of uncertainty, that by the time the Lyons quip was printed the incident was ancient history. And certainly from 1961 until the day of his death Henry Luce appeared devoted to his wife.

Clare gave speeches on such vexing problems as the population explosion. She said an alternative was "population annihilation." Of American foreign policy, she said the U.S. had lost the diplomatic advantages once provided by its armed might; and she attacked the television industry "as an instrument for the wholesale debasement of the

public taste and moral fiber." Writing in *McCall's* magazine, Clare conceded that in the course of a week there were a very few good programs
on television—a few stunningly good. "However," she said, "they are
dribbled and dabbed among a flood of shoddy, corny, stupid, vulgar,
obscene and just plain silly ones. Television programming will not improve," she said, "until the television audience itself asks and accepts
answers to the question of who is to be held accountable for what appears on the wave lengths—the government, the broadcasting companies
the sponsors, the advertisers, the authors or the public."

The networks ignored her charges, but it was pointed out that Time
Inc. owned and operated television stations in key markets.

In January 1962 Clare's *McCall's* article created a new furor when
she said that Jackie Kennedy's choice of Paris gowns was no help to
the U.S. fashion world. Clare wrote that Mrs. Kennedy must ask herself: "Not what do these clothes do for me, but what do these clothes I
wear do for the United States?"

When the article appeared, reporters contacted Clare, who was
visiting Louisa Jenkins at the Big Sur in California. She commented, "I
think Mrs. Kennedy would look gorgeous in a gunnysack and they
would have to stand on their heads in front of a Coney Island mirror to
get criticism of Mrs. Kennedy out of what I wrote." But the controversy
raged in the press for weeks.

In June of 1962 the *Hollywood Reporter* announced that Clare's
play *Love Is a Verb* would be produced by Richard Charlton on Broadway. But that plan was never brought to fruition.

In the fall of 1962 Clare wrote a series of articles for the *Chicago
American* on Cuba and America's relationship with that nation. She
asked, "Why has the Cuban alliance with Communism been allowed to
grow into a major menace in the Western Hemisphere? Why is the
President so calm now when two years ago he expressed alarm over a
much less perilous situation in Cuba?"

In January of 1963, speaking to the World Affairs Council in Los
Angeles, Clare charged that U.S. foreign policy has followed a line of
peaceful coexistence and asserted that this policy against the use of
force as an anti-Communist political or diplomatic weapon, even when
it would be prudent and cheap to do so, has had the support of the

American people for many years. She said that while the American people want to stop Communism they don't want any Americans to get hurt in the process. She named only three men in her lifetime who had possessed the kind of courage to move in and stop Communism: Winston Churchill, Harry S. Truman and Charles de Gaulle. She predicted that "unless the seventeen-year-old foreign policies of this nation are changed, at the end of another seventeen years the only parts of the world that will be non-Communist will be those nations who are under the U.S. nuclear umbrella or one of their own."

Speaking to the students at the University of Utah, she asked her audience, "Is there something wrong with our ideas, something wrong with our riches? Have we been dishonest, lacked courage or not been faithful in pursuit of our valid foreign policy goals to prevent Russian domination of the world?" In all these things, she explained, the U.S. measures up. "Where then," she asked, "is our error? We have had as a nation a false morality about force. We have not understood as a people the diplomatic or political uses of force."

Clare spoke in opposition to the space race and said the money being spent to explore outer space would be better spent exploring inner space. She called Project Apollo a "Moon Doggel that at best would take man to the moonlit gate of the limitless mansion of the universe." Clare said that her scientific friends could predict no near-term benefits from exploring the moon, and we had more pressing problems: "Elevating the condition of the Negroes, foreign aid, and other advances that could be made in science, particularly the study of oceanography."

When the Russians sent a female cosmonaut to orbit the earth, Clare pouted, saying, "The Russians have shown that they know how to get ahead of us by letting women assume an equal share of society." The old feminist convictions surfaced rhetorically.

In 1963 Clare got back into politics by agreeing to serve on the National Republican Citizens Committee Critical Issues Council, headed by Dr. Milton S. Eisenhower, brother of the former President.

In March of 1960 the New York *World-Telegram* reported that Mrs. Luce had "gone to Arizona to finish her autobiography, a project which she has never started." In 1965 Clare made it quite clear that although the idea of writing an autobiography intrigued her, she felt she would not be free to say in the first person all of the intimate things concerning Harry, her brother David, her mother, her first husband, her daughter Ann, and her true feelings about the Catholic Church, which should be said. She suggested she might write such a volume but it would be preserved for posthumous publication. And it was out of that conversation and many others that this project was commenced.

When Barry Goldwater became the Republican candidate for President in 1964, Clare addressed the convention and joined the Goldwater team. She served as co-chairman of citizens for the Republican nominee, but the old fire was gone. No one asked her to make television speeches. They were, she concluded, interested only in her name. Mrs. Luce recalls one incident in that 1964 effort with a certain amount of rancor. She was invited to attend the Goldwater appearance and television broadcast scheduled from Milwaukee, Wisconsin. Local Republicans had made vast preparations to originate a live, nationwide presentation of the Senator, erecting a pyramid for the camera in the middle of the ballroom, which required that some tables had to be placed in a second room where the diners would see a television monitor but not the Senator. Clare was at the head table as Co-chairman of Citizens for Goldwater-Miller. A minute or two before the broadcast was scheduled to commence she was summoned to the broadcasting booth, which she says was up two flights of very steep stairs. When she arrived she was told that Denison Kitchel, Goldwater's manager, had decided not to broadcast the Senator's speech live from Milwaukee and would substitute instead a tape which had been used earlier. Clare's assignment was to introduce the tape. She didn't have the foggiest notion of what the tape was all about; she was out of breath and suddenly on camera.

Goldwater staffers in Washington concluded when they watched the introduction that Mrs. Luce was drunk because she was uncertain of herself and her introduction was almost out of context.*

Time and *Life* supported Lyndon Johnson in 1964, but this had no effect on the Luces' personal relationship. They entertained Lyndon be-

---

* Kitchel was opposed to permitting the Senator to make a live television appearance for some reasons never clearly explained.

fore he departed for Los Angeles when he was seeking his party's nomination in 1960. During the talk at table Lyndon assured them he would never, never, never accept the Vice-Presidency. A week after he had taken the second spot with Jack Kennedy, the Luces again saw Lyndon in New York, and when Mrs. Luce asked him what had made him change his mind, he said somewhat prophetically, "At least I'm only one heart beat away from the job I really want."

In 1966 Harry Luce withdrew from any active part of the management of the magazines. He chose Hedley Donovan to be his successor, but it was a busy retirement. Harry's mind still wanted answers to questions. He studied the magazines before and after they were printed. He constantly fired off telegrams demanding to know why this and why that. He kept his secretary in New York busy and piled extra work on a succession of secretaries who were employed by Clare in Phoenix.

Luce never really retired. He was interested in everything and everyone. When LSD came into the news, he, Clare and Clare's friend Gerald Heard took two "trips" under the guidance of Dr. Sidney Cohen, who was a house guest in Phoenix at the time. Harry insisted that under the influence of the drug he could hear music—something which he said his tone-deaf ears had never truly appreciated before. Clare recalled that all the colors of the day became more vivid. She was able to separate them in her mind. Neither one had any bad experience. Harry was still questioning the critics of LSD after the drug came into disrepute.

During those years the Luces had two circles of acquaintances in Phoenix—one included all the patrons of the arts, the editorial writers and executives of the Phoenix newspapers, the social group and the winter colony. Clare entertained these people at large and sumptuous cocktail parties, having as many as one hundred and fifty guests in one evening. She and Harry enjoyed bridge and for this pastime a special set of credentials was required. No one who was not an excellent bridge player was ever invited a second time. The parties Clare appeared to enjoy most were intimate dinners to which she rarely invited more than two or three other couples. On these occasions there was serious conversation, usually with Harry Luce holding court in the front room and his wife challenging the minds of her other guests in the *lanai.*

At some of these parties Clare made no effort to conceal the fact that Harry's long dissertations bored her. Sometimes she would go into the bedroom and come out with needlework. At other times she would invite one or two of the guests in whom she was truly interested to visit her studio. This was considered a rare privilege.

The Phoenix Little Theatre group revived Clare's play *The Women*, and Barry Goldwater's sister-in-law played the lead role of Crystal. The production was a tremendous success and both of the Luces appeared to enjoy this entrance into community activities. But most of their time was spent following purely personal activities. Harry became involved in raising funds for the national Presbyterian Church. Clare wrote her monthly articles for *McCall's*, accepted a very few speaking engagements, and worked hard at her painting. During her years in Phoenix she had a succession of small dogs and Oriental birds. The dogs died or were sent off for one reason or another, but the bird, or birds, were brought out on every occasion to perch on Clare's shoulder, flit about her face, and frequently leave their droppings on Harry's suit, Clare's exotic costumes, or the hand of an unwary guest.

Being in Clare's studio was something like a scene from *You Can't Take It With You*. She could concentrate on her painting while ordering Arthur to bring a refreshment. Her pet myna bird sang "The Stars and Stripes Forever."

On Wednesday, March 1, 1967, the Luces flew to San Francisco where Clare was scheduled to speak to the Commonwealth Club on Thursday. Harry wanted to prowl the Haight-Ashbury district to see if he could discover for himself why the hippies were choosing their particular way of rebelling against society. He had great confidence in the youth of America. He was both offended and fascinated by what he thought was the meaningless cult of the flower children. They returned to Phoenix Friday night and on Saturday Harry played his usual nine holes of golf on the course just behind the house. Sunday morning he sent his breakfast tray back to the kitchen untouched.

"No, I'm not sick . . . there's nothing wrong with me," he told Clare gruffly. "The food was all right. I just didn't feel like eating it."

At noon Clare telephoned their family physician, Dr. Hayes Caldwell. She told the doctor that Harry didn't want him to come out but she did.

On his first house call the doctor could find nothing grossly wrong with his patient. Luce's pulse was steady and strong, blood pressure normal, no fever. The doctor thought Harry would be much better in a day, but on Monday he wasn't better. He hadn't eaten anything. There had been no change in blood pressure or pulse, no elevation of the body temperature, but Caldwell ordered an ambulance and sent Harry to St. Joseph's Hospital where it would be possible to make a more thorough examination. His wife went with him. She wanted to stay with him Monday night, but Harry insisted she go alone to a long-planned dinner party. She left the gathering early to call Harry at ten o'clock. He was, he said, feeling much better and would obviously be home in a day or so . . . the trouble with doctors being that when they didn't know what was wrong with you, or if anything at all was wrong with you, they invariably send you to a hospital. He was quite comfortable, nothing to worry about.

At 3:15 A.M. Tuesday morning Henry Robinson Luce died of an acute coronary thrombosis. It had never occurred to Clare that she might outlive her husband. They had never discussed death or what to do. She had no real understanding of her husband's complicated financial situation.

Tex and Beth Moore flew out from New York City in Nelson Rockefeller's private airplane. Henry Luce III came from London where he had been serving as chief of the *Time* bureau. When the family gathered it was young Hank who revealed that he and his father had discussed arrangements and that his father wanted to be buried in the cemetery at Mepkin because he knew that's where his wife would want to go eventually.

Henry Luce was buried in the private plot near Moncks Corner, South Carolina. A Protestant minister read the services while the monks sang their chants in the chapel. On the hilltop there are two great oak trees, their roots and trunks separated. As they climb into the sky their branches intermingle to become one mass of foliage. Tom Moore sees in these trees a symbolic representation of Clare's life and her marriage to Harry. "Two human beings," he says, "fiercely independent, strong, eager to reach into the sky, individualistic . . . but in the heights of achievement inseparable."

After memorial services in the Madison Avenue Presbyterian Church in New York City, the family gathered in the Moores' apartment. The presence of the young—the children and the grandchildren —comforted the older generation. To the youngsters, death was an incident, meaningless at the moment, a date for the future. Gradually Clare appeared to realize that had Harry been there he would have called for an end to the gloom. She thought of the sermon Dr. Read had delivered. If it had been submitted to Henry Luce, editor in chief of *Time,* she thought he might have scratched on the copy, "Just a little overdone, don't you think?"

Tom Moore says all the young people gathered around Clare's chair. She asked them questions and gradually the conversation was of hope and the future and optimism and contending, living ideas. Tom says that he and the Jesuit theologian John Courtney Murray were amazed at his aunt's capacity to bring everyone around her into a participation of the vital aspects of living.

Luce left all of his personal possessions to his wife, or perhaps it would be more accurate to say that he didn't leave any of his personal possessions to anyone else. He made no provision for giving a watch or set of cuff links or any small memento to either one of his sons. The estate, amounting to well over $100 million worth of Time Inc. stock and other investments, had been carefully parceled out beforehand. His widow received a lifetime income from $30 million of Time Inc. stock, producing a before-tax return of about $500,000 a year.

Gradually the full extent of her dependency and her loneliness dawned on Clare.

Now it was up to her to manage the apartment and decide whether she should spend the money to replace the air-conditioning system or sell the condominium. She ultimately sold it and moved into an apartment in the Sherry-Netherland, where the hotel would provide maid service.

There were other decisions to be made. What about the Phoenix house and the house in Hawaii that she and Harry had been planning for more than two years? When she discovered how rich Harry had really been, it seemed ludicrous to her that he had opposed new drapes for the Phoenix house and insisted on keeping a ten-year-old Chrysler car.

It had been more than thirty years since Clare had had to worry about money or debts or management of household accounts. Harry had provided whatever was needed. But now her after-tax income would be less than $150,000 annually, and she suddenly felt very poor. The apartment in New York City cost $35,000 a year to maintain. Her staff —her secretary in New York and one in Phoenix, the maids, the cooks, her chauffeur . . . the total was staggering. And Clare, who has given away $2 or $3 million in her lifetime, felt as poor as in those forgotten days before her mother married Dr. Austin. Of course it was relative and in time her attitude has changed.

She was particularly disappointed that Harry had made no provision for the servants, especially for Arthur, who had been with them for seventeen years. She first thought of giving the Phoenix house to the state of Arizona for a governor's mansion and taking advantage of the tax credit. In the end, however, she sold it. But she did give her books, a collection of art posters, and a host of things of value to the Arizona State University at Tempe. She modified the plans for the Hawaiian house and decided to complete it.

And when she moved back into the Sherry-Netherland Hotel her life had come full circle. She was back in the same building where she lived when Harry Luce came to call to tell her that she was the woman he intended to marry.

Index